Here I am
LaoWei

Here I am LaoWei

这里我是老卫

China is A Different Place.
Eyes Wide Open in ShenZhen.

For my family (including, for the time being, two grandchildren), my friends and my staff. Especially for those people around me who take part in my work and my observations in China and who want to learn more than what I have occasionally told them.
And for those who do not always want to hear or read the same stuff about China.

Based on the 2nd, slightly revised and updated German edition
© 2011 Bernhard Wessling
1st edition 2010 (German)
Translation by Andreas Möhn
Set, cover design, manufacturing and publishing:
Books on Demand GmbH, Norderstedt
ISBN 978-3-8448-7273-6

Content

What purpose this book does not serve yet is meant for (Preface) 7

Some characters, some places, pronunciation guide and some "thank you" 9

That's how it started 12

ChangChun 13

Negotiating a joint venture 14

'What if they all decide to move into the city?' 15

To China with Chancellor Schröder and Tycoons 16

My fear of ShenZhen 19

Chinese dimensions 20

The first steps 22

The young city of ShenZhen 23

Life in ShenZhen 29

Our driver 43

Football in ShenZhen 45

Gan Bei 56

Exhibitions 59

How do I best establish a company in China? 62

Nature in the juggernaut city 66

Minor entrepreneurs 88

The staff 104

LangLang and me inaugurate a new concert hall 108

I am trying to learn Chinese 113

In hospital 117

Stock market hype, top and flop 124

Noise 126

Toothache 128

The "China capital of crime" 130

Serial suicide at Foxconn 133

The 2008 Olympics 140

Encounters in the botanical garden 150

Getting and raising children with joy and sorrow 159

Odd: a World Cup with 33 teams 167

The Chinese New Year 172

LaoWei does not only play football 189

Appendix 211

   What happened "after the deadline"? . . . 211

   Conflicting findings in books on China 212

What purpose this book does not serve yet is meant for (Preface)

This book is not a travel guide and no instruction set for how to behave in China as a tourist or a business(wo)man, it does not contain any tips on how to avoid pitfalls, and no hints about how to live as a foreigner in China.

It is a description of those observations as I could make in China during my now almost six years working there. Because some of these observations contradict some of the advice, tips, rules, instructions and manuals for China, this book has been first developing in my head, then in my camera and finally on my laptop.

This book is not a counterargument to the manifold Chinese books that you can buy. Some I have read that present themselves as tourist guides, as guides to discover China, or as indispensable reference works, without which you cannot do in China any work or business successfully, without which you cannot avoid those pitfalls as are lurking everywhere. Even if some of my observations may contradict some statements about China made in other books, I will not object to these books. Contradictory statements about China may be (but not necessarily!) correct.

China is huge, China is very diverse. What you will find in BeiJing with its many government officials and foreigners, or in ShangHai (上海), the economic centre with a high proportion of foreigners, and what may be representative or normal there may be very different from what you will find in the boom-town of ShenZhen, the fourth-largest city in southern China. This is a modern, new city, virtually without history, consisting of 99 % immigrants and relatively few foreigners. I have been living there for almost six years. From there, I'm travelling on business inside and outside China.

China and the Chinese are much more varied and unique and different from each other than for example the Americans. The cultural diversity is more comparable to Europe. There are much less cultural and linguistic differences between Texas and Alaska, between Kansas and New England, than between central ShangHai and peripheral ShangHai, let alone between ShangHai, ShenZhen and ChongQing (重庆). You don't have to understand it, but you should simply take note, that you wouldn't generalise everything. Wait a moment, I am sorry – readers and other authors may generalise and try to understand as they like, it is just me who doesn't want to generalise but simply to describe my personal observations during my time in China, when I had to do (at work and in the free time) almost exclusively with rather normal average Chinese.

And I would also not like teaching the Chinese about what I believe to be their weaknesses, nor how we think they should reform their government and better organise their society. Because I do not know how the Chinese could improve either, I do not even know how we could improve our society in Germany (although I think I know quite well what is going wrong with us), how can I, as an outsider, give advice to the Chinese? The other authors seem to think different.

There is no country in the world that you would get to know and really understand as a foreigner on holiday or on business trips. I bet you cannot even understand France when viewed from Germany (and the French are our neighbours) just by one or a few voyages.

Can even Northern Germans really completely understand inhabitants of the Ruhr area, Bavaria or the Rhineland?

How much more difficult we find understanding the incredibly diverse and sophisticated, but not uniform Chinese culture. As a foreigner (probably not even as a Chinese) you cannot grasp China "as such" by observing the situation in BeiJing or ShangHai where most of the foreigners in China live and where the authors of the Chinese books that I know spent some time.

Even from ShenZhen you cannot grasp it. Perhaps no one can understand China comprehensively, but only partially. China is too large, too diverse and of much more varied structure than we Europeans might think. In my opinion, this cannot be described in a single book. The attempt of doing so would require more than a human life (and China would be then again different).

I do not try and do not claim to describe and explain "China". I also do not claim to know more than the writers of other China books nor want to correct them. I only intend to describe some of my observations, and I am committed to reproducing them correctly and authentic.

I cannot guarantee that they are typical, only that they have taken place more or less as told here. In any case, my stories describe some facets of Chinese life, not: Chinese life as such.

I am describing a little bit of life in China as it occurs every day, in diverse and different form from what you may have thought, and even after reading this book there will be new observations everywhere and ever again that will be different from what we expect them to be (and different from what I would expect and describe).

This book is conceived of as a complement to other books on China. Although it was not my intention, it may happen that some reader may get practical hints out of this book. In any case, I would like to help setting apart, expanding and enriching our understanding of China.

Some characters, some places, pronunciation guide and some "thank you"

It is common practice in China to refer to a person not only by family name but also by position or function or by a characteristic quality, this habit I have adopted here. Therefore, the characters in this book are called, for example, "Mayor Song" or "Engineer Su" although in Chinese the proper word order is: "Song CunZhang", or "CunZhang" for short, and "Su GongChengShi", usually "Su Gong" for short.

I also think it was a pity if the reader should pronounce in mind those names as the way the Chinese phonetic system PinYin might suggest. Professor Xu is not referred to as "Ksoo" but -- if you follow Wikipedia's definition, entry "PinYin" - in a way – about like "chü", the "ch" being a sound that you make with the lips spread and the tip of your tongue curled downwards and stuck to the back of teeth when you say the vowel. The "ü" is equivalent to the sound in German "üben" or French "lune". To get this sound, say "ee" with rounded lips. PinYin has very clear rules on distinguishing "u" or "ee" from "ü". In PinYin, you write "ü", some phonetic systems replace it by "v".

Name	Who is it?	How is it pronounced?
LaoWei (老卫)	this is me	Lăo: emphasis from high to low and back Wèi: emphasis from high to low stress, the vowels in „wei" are like those in "bay"
WeiSiLin (卫斯林)	my full name	SiLin: Initial voiceless "s", the "i" is very low back in the throat; lin = "linn"
SunLi (孙黎)	my first staff	SunLi: sounds almost like „Sue-Ann-Lee", just that there is no hiatus at the "-" but a gliding vowel.
Engineer Chu (褚)	her husband	Chu: "choo" (note: in PinYin, „u" is sometimes „ü", for example, with Professor Xu)
HaoKang (昊康)	her son	How kang (I will spare the reader from that „hao" is actually emphasised with the 3rd voice, i. e. hǎo)
Professor Xu (许教授)	Professor of the Chinese Academy of Sciences, almost my joint venture partner	See above
Wang (王)	Craftsman	„W" as in "where, why, water", „a" as in "calm"
LuLu (璐璐)	his wife	"Loo-loo", with a very short "oo"
Song (宋) Da Song	Former farmer	"Song" Da like "dah"; the Older Song
Xiao Song Song DeLian (宋德廉)	his son, chief physician	Little Song, the "x", as mentioned above for Xu: a crossover between soft „sh" and „s" His full name, the "d" is followed by a very short vowel like that in "turn", lian may be either "Lee-ahn" or "Lee-Ann" (but with a short "ee")

Name	Who is it?	How is it pronounced?
Engineer Su (苏)	Formerly an engineer, now bird photographer	"Soo"
ShiTou, „Stones" (石头)	Football player	The „i" is very much in the back of the throat
YeDan (叶郸)	Early pensioner, painter, professor	"Yeh-dahn" with a short "a"
Fang ShiFu (方师傅)	Drivers who used to be racer	"Fang": "a" like in "calm", but short; "Shi" see above for my friend "Stones", "Fu" = "foo" or "phoo"
BaiJiu (白酒)	Not a person but a shot, literally „white wine", but this is misleading	Bai as "ba-ee" jiu: "j" as in „James", then „ee-ouw", all together: „jee-ouw"
Si Hai Gong Yuan (四海公园)	A favourite park	„Si" as above, "hai" like "hi", then "gong" as written, "yuan" has this darn ü-sound while "-an" is just like the first name, "Ann"
Lian Hua Shan Gong Yuan (莲花山公园)	Another favourite park	Lian = "Lee-Ann"
Xia Sha Cun (下沙村)	„Village" in ShenZhen	Xia roughly like "chee-ah", cun = "coo-Ann" (no hiatus, just glide from the "oo" to the "a": "ooa"!)
Fu Tian (福田)	District of ShenZhen	Fu = "phoo"; Tian = "Tea-Ann"
ShenZhen (深圳)	The main location of events in this book	Shen = the way it looks, zh = a voiced sh, as in French "journal"
BeiJing (北京)	Capital of China, occasionally mentioned	"Bei" like "bay", Jing = the way it looks

All persons who are mentioned in this book have been given a different name by me than those they have got in reality. Also I have slightly altered some events in terms of time, place, storyline, or characters, in order to make recognising anyone more difficult and to protect the privacy of individuals.

I want to thank the translator Andreas Möhn (and the translation reviewer Nardina Alongi) who – as far as I can tell – did a very good job in transferring the style of my original German book into (British) English and their patience in the discussions with me.

Two persons who are playing an active role in this book, SunLi and ZhangMiao (you will get to know them later) have reviewed this English translation of the original second German edition, and have checked it for accuracy whereever I as a foreigner could have misinterpreted something. A third person (who does not play a role in this book), a Chinese business partner, also reviewed the English manuscript.

I am very grateful to all three of them for their suggestions, hints and the active debates with me. As a result, this English version is slightly different from the German original (which neither of the three was able to review), not drastically different, only in a few details which I can confirm with some modest degree of satisfaction.

Moreover I am grateful that SunLi and Zhang-Miao not only had allowed me to include some personal details already for the German version (while they did not know what I would write about), but finally after reading the English version approved and released with some smile.

That's how it started

There was no way how to go on like that. From China only bad news were sent. Once a transaction failed, another time, a customer had trouble with some facility, persistent shortcomings in quality, persistent complaints by customers, and then, suddenly, out of the blue there came a note from our Taiwanese distributor: 'The day after tomorrow, the process line for our customer 长浩 ChangHao will be installed. Who will be there? What do you mean: impossible? Do you not want to have any new customers?' What line? Who is ChangHao at all? We don't know that company. Why don't we know anything?

My Vice-Director for Sales – as well as our Sales Manager – kept flying once every three months to China, spending five to eight days driving around with our distributor and then returning with the same old hat: 'Our concepts are not fitting for China, we have to adapt to local conditions there, our distributor knows better than us about that.' And this, in an epoch when production is massively getting relocated from Europe and the USA, preferably to China.

I was fed up. The customers refuse following our process requirements the way we had developed them, and then they complain about inferior quality? Production lines are installed that we do not know about nor could design in cooperation with the customer, and then our processes are supposed to operate in them? None of our proposals, appropriate for Europe, already established in Korea, are right for China? Chinese customers do not accept them? I refused to believe that.

Some time ago I had already once confronted our Board of Advisers with the problems that I had with our Vice-Director. I had indicated then that I would suggest to fire him. That was what I did in the end. And two weeks later I returned to China. Four years I had not been there.

ChangChun

I wake up. My room is dark. Where am I? I grope for the window, a thick and heavy curtain blocks the daylight. I move it aside and have a look. Ah, some US-American city. Uh? Why the USA? When did I fly there? And which city is this after all? … Slowly I get more awake and remember: In fact I had taken a plane from BeiJing to ChangChun (长春), hadn't I? That is a city to the far North of China, and the North is poor, and China is an underdeveloped country. Right, BeiJing is the capital, there they open the shop windows for foreigners like me and make everything as proper and modernistic as possible – but they don't do that in ChangChun?

I wonder about my mental condition, perhaps for some fractions of a second, but it feels like an endless time. At last I note that there are Chinese characters down below, outside, and yes, now I remember to have arrived at ChangChun airport, yesterday evening I checked in at the hotel, and now the information sheets on the desk confirm that I am here indeed. However, this looks more like Philadelphia …

I am preparing a joint venture with a subsidiary of the Chinese Academy of Sciences. I have known Professor Xu (许教授) for years: He is young, highly intelligent, funny, open, dynamic, and quite ugly, showing protruding teeth.

We drive to his factory at the outskirts of ChangChun. Every ten kilometres my local time shifts back another 20 years: Here, ChangChun slowly turns the way I might have imagined it if I had had enough imagination. Horses and donkeys pulling carts with all sorts of charges. Heaps of coal in the street being shovelled on other carts, in addition to heaps of kale – ah no, this is Chinese cabbage, getting loaded on yet other carts.

One weekend, at my request we drive to the border with Inner Mongolia. I want to observe cranes. At the end of the 300 km drive we are back in the year 1398: no electricity, no water, the huts are roofed with corn leaves, the lake has fallen almost dry, before the huts peasant women are threshing grain by hand, with flails. Every 50 km I felt we drove about 100 years backwards in time. The donkeys are running free. Dogs roam. Children are naked. It is touch dry. I am getting thirsty just from the view of the drought.

Only one thing reminds me of the modern era, in which I live: My mobile always finds a full-power signal. This day, I will observe seven different species of cranes – and the way of life centuries before my time.

Negotiating a joint venture

We exchange contract drafts. Professor Xu and I agree that we want to found and manage a joint venture in ChangChun, intending to become supplied with intermediate products from Germany plus the required knowledge for further manufacturing steps and applications. But the provincial government disagrees. They want us not to provide intermediates into which our intellectual property has been dispersed to be used but not pirated; instead they prefer that we would grant the joint venture a license to produce the intermediates themselves.

I refuse. The government of the Jilin Province (吉林) invites me to negotiate.

For the third time I take a plane to ChangChun, this time in mid-winter, it is minus 25° C outside. I don't let myself be fooled again in the morning, I know after all where I am. After a day of fruitless negotiations the vice-governor invites us to dinner. We meet at a large round table, looking to me as if it had been sized to five metres across. There are about 20 people, Professor Xu is absent, I am alone with at least 19 government officials.

All of them are friendly, they smile at me, the first toast is applied in halting English. The most varied dishes are served. Every five minutes one of the other diners approaches me with a kind invitation to empty with him the shot glass: ‚Gan Bei!' BaiJiu is poured into my glass, that is a clear Chinese liquor, high-percentage, highly dangerous. As an addition, Chinese red and white wines are served like a dog's dinner. (BaiJiu tastes better, but is more hazardous.)

Everyone wants to drink with me, and every time I have to empty the glass. How nice is everyone!

I am very friendly and my glass is always empty, my mouth is often full. Sometimes my glass is not empty from drinking, but the large plant in that pot behind me – if I remember properly, it was a bamboo – is still drunk for days after. According to informed sources it had to be taken to the plant hospital in emergency at night. At the end of the evening everyone is boozy except me. I drank the least of all.

No contract closed. The intellectual property will remain in Germany. Professor Xu understands and respects my decision, the provincial governor has had something else in mind.

'What if they all decide to move into the city?'

Professor Xu is from a very poor family. He grew up in the wetlands and channel networks far beyond the 'water towns' around ShangHai. Meat never got on the table there, with a few exceptions: If he managed to catch a mouse or a rat, then he grilled it on a stick over an open fire, still no meat on the table, but at least in the stomach.

Back when I visited him in ChangChun, his father was still a self-sustaining peasant who grew himself all that he needed for living. His income, as far as money was concerned, was equal to about ten Euros. Per year. Everything that he and his wife were eating and drinking they produced themselves.

Because of his exceptional talent and performance, Little Xu very early received a scholarship. He was not even 30 when he got an appointment as Professor of Chemistry at the Academy of Sciences.

A few years later he finally succeeded in convincing his parents to visit him. He picked them up in his native village, together they drove to the airport and flew from there to ChangChun. ShangHai and ChangChun were cities of a kind that his father and his mother had never seen before. For them, it was unthinkable, in terms of money, ever to travel there.

The second evening they went to a restaurant for dinner. The son invited his parents, along with his wife and their little baby. Father and mother were not shown the menu table, the son ordered the dishes.

When the bill was brought, the father heard the amount that was to be paid. Right at the table he started crying bitterly and could not stop. His son had at that one evening spent four or five times as much of money as he had available for a whole year.

This story moved me very much, and it reminded me of the trip to the border with Inner Mongolia. On the way to there, country and villages had looked increasingly poorer. You have to understand that in China, not just anyone who wants to may move to a city and find a job there. I asked Professor Xu: 'What if suddenly, at the very same day, all those poor maize and cabbage farmers within a radius of 50 km would decide to move into the city?' – 'Well, then we get a problem.'

To China with Chancellor Schröder and Tycoons

11 September 2001. I am driving a rental car in Wisconsin from the crane reserve Necedah National Wildlife Refuge to the nearest larger town that features a FedEx station. Some equipment supplied for the whooping crane release program I need to send back to Germany for repair. This has nothing to do with my chemical and commercial work, I am a hobby crane explorer and engaged in the program for saving the North American whooping cranes.

The ‚National Public Radio' station which I always attend to in the car when in US, because of its more profound news and analyses and because of the classical music, tells that a plane has crashed into one tower of the World Trade Center, there is fire, there is chaos. In the next village I drive to the roadside, find a phone booth and call my financial advisers.

While I am at the phone, that second plane crashes into the other tower. Every reader knows what followed. But back then I did not know how to continue: financing the company was tough to impossible, our capital reserves (stocks and other financial assets) kept melting away as the famous snow in the sun.

Even while I was in the wetlands of Wisconsin, far from all events, waiting for the opportunity to fly back to Germany, a letter from the Federal Chancellery descends on my unguarded desk in my German office. Well, it was certainly sent automatically, without taking the current situation into consideration: Chancellor Schröder invites me to accompany him in November on his next trip to China. Me? Now?

Yes, I had written to the Chancellor at some point. I had described the situation in Chang-Chun (without mentioning the unfortunate bamboo), but I did not expect any response to that. I had merely desired to tell someone in that governmental space station where everyone fantasizes about all those fantastic opportunities in trading with China how the common person fares who wants to launch an insignificant joint venture and is tried to be made drunk (in vain) by the provincial governor. And now I was expected to travel with all the top politicians and Tycoons to China?

I put the invitation aside. Do I have the money, the relaxedness and the time to go on such a trip, right in the turmoil of world history and business financing?

Of course, in the end I go. Curiosity and adventurer's soul triumph over sober reasoning. Maybe I can even learn something?

In November 2001, I am sitting in the second governmental plane. In the first one there is Schröder with various journalists and politicians, the second is occupied by Müller, the Minister of Economy, and a 50-member business delegation comprising 49 Tycoons of rank and fame, and one no-man – me.

Then I am standing with the leaders of German industry on the red carpet in the Great Hall of the People while Schröder is welcomed by the Prime Minister, Zhu RongJi, with all honours of protocol as you know it from TV. It looks nice, but of course it is just diplomatic entertainment.

The following dinner at the giant restaurant of the Great Hall of the People is another remarkable event. I present to Prime Minister Zhu RongJi and Chancellor Schröder a CD containing self-recorded photos and audio files of cranes from all over the world. The calls of cranes that migrate across all national boundaries shall be my icon of international understanding.

The next day, I meet again Professor Xu who delivers some other proposals suggested by the provincial government. But these as well do not convince me, we obtain no result. The joint venture plan has failed.

Several events, visits and official meetings are scheduled in BeiJing and ShangHai. We, the Tycoons and little me, ride with a bus. Sometimes I am sitting next to Heinrich von Pierer (of Siemens), sometimes to Jürgen Weber (then the chief executive of Lufthansa), and we also talk about cranes. Ron Sommer (Deutsche Telekom's Board Director at that time) is very relaxed, like everyone else on the bus, much more relaxed than you may imagine when watching the TV coverage. But the "Bahnchef" (as he is called in German media), the Railway Boss, Mr. Mehdorn, the CEO of Deutsche Bahn, is the generic comedian. He keeps entertaining us with small performances of stage quality. I am involved in the talks as if I had always been one of them and yet another key member of German big business.

Just by the way I learn a lot from the other fellow travellers about China through discussing my problems with the provincial government of Jilin. The Volkswagen sales director informs me that – after several clues, strange observations and systematic own investigation – they discovered one day a ghost factory where some Chinese cloned original VW parts.

The main shareholder and CEO of a large high-technology company tells me of the chief assistant and a manager who were related to each other and had secretly built up a trading company that bought valuable resources from his company for far less than the normal price, claiming these raw materials were dirty and not compliant to specifications. The family-owned trading ring then relabelled them, so that they were now clean and pure and valuable, and sold them at the best price somewhere in China.

The police did not initially want to pursue the case. Then the German director was threatened to be arrested and expelled, then for some time his business license was revoked. Meanwhile the official stamp (without which no company can legally do business in China) suddenly was possessed by that manager who had set up the trading company together with the chief assistant. Only by threatening to inform the Minister of Economy (whom the main shareholder personally knew) this affair was finally settled and the sale of company values ended.

My company (if I would ever have one in China) would never have such importance that a threat to inform the Minister of Economy might leave any impression in a similar situation.

Another delegation member tells me that they had lost a whole subsidiary because the Chinese manager one day went with the company stamp to the authorities and rewrote everything in his own name. Although it was later be proven in lengthy court proceedings that this was effectively the theft of an entire company, the only benefit was some financial compensation, but the subsidiary was gone.

All this does not give me much hope, but rather my fears grow out of hand. If I ever had the courage to set up a company in China (which I would actually do once but did not know on this trip), I will have to take care not to drown in a mud of corruption and family clique – and especially keep an eye on the stamp! But how?

In ShangHai, we have important appointments: The first is to celebrate the construction of the first support pillar of the magnetic levitation train system Maglev. I am impressed to see how the Chinese manage this project and even placed a factory for concrete pillars just there, only for constructing the Maglev, which will be dismantled again after completion.

Also there is a German-Chinese joint venture which has built a trade show exhibition hall that is now being officially opened in our presence. Then we help more vigorously at the opening of the first OBI store (a "do-it-yourself" tools and consumables market) in China. In the evening I am accidentally sitting next to Manfred Maus, the founder of OBI, and he tells me and all our neighbours at the table how he was doing market research (with an interpreter) in China to find out what the Chinese are expecting. He went to young families in new housing areas and asked them himself. This leaves a great impression with me.

But something he must have done wrong, because when OBI had already 13 markets in China (including that first one to whose opening we attended), in April 2005 they completely pulled back from the country. The year before, the chief executive of OBI Asia had departed on his own ways, together with the core of management, and also the most important trade and joint venture partner, Haier, had withdrawn.

From today's perspective, two of the most important economic projects that we supported during this journey, the magnetic levitation train and OBI, have thus failed. For whatever reason – the Germans had drawn the short straw. And what kind of reports I collected on the bus trips was anything but motivating.

With a background like this, a few years later I am suddenly back to China – permanently.

My fear of ShenZhen

I am not fond of cities. I am even less fond of big cities. They lock me in: the crowds, the tall buildings, the narrow streets. You can not even see a hundred metres afar. I am dedicated to nature, the sea, wide roaming views, trees, waves, birds.

I yearn for opportunities to look far out into the land, at least once a day, at least at the weekend.

A city of some tens or hundreds of thousands of inhabitants may attract me perhaps if there are a few good book-stores, even more if there is a well-stocked map store, and at times I must have the chance to attend a concert of classical music. Only for such purposes I go ‚downtown'. Wandering around, shopping, a few days vacation there, ‚flying to New York over the weekend', how awful! A city of more than one million inhabitants I perceive as a hideous threat.

When I was wound up in China, it was unavoidable that I would set up my base in GuangDong, a province in southern China. The majority of our clients is located there, and from there I would also be able to visit East China, Korea, Taiwan, Japan and Singapore. At first I was planning to live in a small town on the outskirts of GuangZhou. At the weekends it was wonderful – hills, forests, rivers, birds, I could go for a walk and wonderfully relax.

But for the daily business, it was simply the wrong choice. The traffic connection was unbearable, and I also did not want to be permanently reliant on an interpreter, nor dwell during the working week in constantly changing hotels. So I decided to look for an apartment in ShenZhen.

ShenZhen is medium-sized by Chinese standards. Which means that officially it has seven or eight million people, in fact, according to some sources, 12 to 15 million. If I previously felt uncomfortable with cities of more than 50,000 inhabitants and threatened by one million of them, how should I ever get acquainted with more than ten million residents?

Chinese dimensions

Trying to imagine dimensions in China is a hard thing to do, at least for an average German. Even the ‚medium-sized' city of ShenZhen is a behemoth, extending across 100 km (east to west) by 10 km (south to north) at the narrowest point and by 40 km at the widest, in its west. Millions of people dwell and work in an area that is similar to the shape of a sausage which someone has beaten flat on one side.

I am from the Rhein-Ruhr-Area, which is the largest conurbation in Germany and the fifth largest in Europe. About five million people are living there, compared with ShenZhen that is about a third of its people, in an area more than twice as large as ShenZhen's.

Driving north or south from the town of Herne, the approximate centre of the Rhein-Ruhr-Area, you will leave the cityscape latest after 30 km and arrive in the less populated countryside of the Münsterland or the Sauerland (both are admittedly still more densely populated than the Tibetan Highlands), whatever direction you may have taken.

But if you drive two, three or four hours by car from ShenZhen to the north (and a little later to the west), you pass through other such behemoths – provided you do not stay in one of the inevitable traffic jams. First, there is DongGuan, about as large as ShenZhen but with one third more residents, next, GuangZhou, the provincial capital, deeply rooted in history, three times as large as ShenZhen and twice as populated.

To the south of ShenZhen no major sparsely populated areas can be found, either. Within sight of the sea there is already HongKong.

Well, far in the North of the behemoths DongGuan and GuangZhou there are vast agricultural areas. Known are the large banana plantations, there you get a very delicious variety (shorter but thicker as we know it). To the south, in the delta of the Pearl River, vegetables are grown and there is a lot of aquaculture. Somehow they have to feed those dozens of millions of people.

So, ShenZhen and DongGuan together cover roughly the surface of the Rhein-Ruhr-Area but feature more than six times as many inhabitants. Add GuangZhou, and on an area that is less than three times as large as the Rhein-Ruhr-Area there will live as many people as in half of Germany. And we have not yet considered ZhongShan and ZhuHai, again with millions of inhabitants each.

And all of these residents are competing with each other every day, in every respect. Much more than we may believe, observing from our outside position, China is a boiling kettle of competition, of people moving on with tremendous speed like drops of water on a hot plate that try to find a cooler place the first, so as not to evaporate the first.

That is why everyone wants to be the first to arrive where everyone wants to go, whether at the bank counter or at the other end of the city or in its centre. The same rules formally apply to road traffic as in Germany or the U.S. or England, in reality some... else. The honking is so overwhelming sometimes and in certain places that one day I said: 'They are practising for the Big South China Honk Festival, I suppose?' – 'What festival?', our driver asked, confused, because he had never heard of this competition – no wonder, for I had made it up just then.

If the semaphore switches from red to green, no one knows what will happen: Anybody may set off quite comfortably, but it may also happen that someone spurts ahead from the rear, brakes away to the left and turns left into the side road in front of everybody else. If the semaphore is wired that way that at the same time it will show green light to the opposite lane, then those in the real rush will try to bend left before the approaching traffic, even if that means to slow down for a few dull pedestrians, because you cannot disregard flattening twenty people on the road: It costs too much speed.

Strangely enough, no one complains about that. There is honking everywhere, at every opportunity, but during such actions, no one does – unless the meddlesome fellow suddenly stops in the middle of the track. But if he rashly draws through and spurts ahead, this is acknowledged as advantage in competition. You might have been faster, too!

Excellence in competition, even in traffic, is generally acknowledged in China. Those common German wisenheimers do not seem to exist in China: No one will overtake another car that was reeving in front him, honk, curse or even drive pathetically slow before him to 'punish' him.

The first steps

I get the all-inclusive package: HongKong airport pickup, plus a small detour to impress me, then we drive across the border to ShenZhen, to 'Mainland China'. While in the beginning I feel comfortable and protected because our distributor takes so much care of me, a little suspicion shows up: The more I enjoy the care-taking, the more I will get dependent on it. However, I do not at this time know how things will further develop.

We arrive in ShenZhen and fetch SunLi, a lady who has applied to us: She wants to work for us.

The first interview is a bit tenacious. She is very reserved but her English is good and her understanding of the market is as well. It occurs to me that she does not just say what I want to hear: She does not give me easy answers, but rather uncomfortable ones. She tells me that she was already interviewed by two managers of our company. I pretend to know about that though in fact I don't, and I explain that I would like to picture this myself.

She is a Master in a specialised field of engineering. Her studies she completed at a top-level university in BeiJing, and then she worked for four years at one of our customers. She is married to an electronics engineer and will probably want to have a child at some time, at least within the next few years, because of the biological clock that otherwise will run out. That does not concern me now, who knows what will happen till then, it will somehow work out.

After the interview I do not make any promise, I'll tell her later my decision on whether or not I will take her. Only our distributor is slightly annoyed: Why do we need our own employees in China? Is he himself not our best translator and assistant for any kind of trouble? Why do I book hotels independently, that is: why do I let my own staff do it and not our distributor? But appointments with customers will be arranged only via the distributor, won't they? – No, I will arrange appointments as I see fit, about that I am leaving no doubt. I will myself visit customers as appropriate, and sometimes without the distributor's company.

This is what I will learn about back in Germany: The sales director, now laid off, and his sales manager were adamantly opposed to hiring the young lady whom I interviewed. They considered her weak ('in this business women cannot prevail') and they were uncomfortable with her non-standard replies. It seems she had a too independent mind and (despite her reserved attitude) self-confidence for these two guys. On the other hand, her appearance (and the way she was dressed) did not leave a lasting impression, and certainly not that of a modern manager. That, however, seemed to be the most important factor for my former vice-director.

Strange that the two guys had not told me anything about their former interview. I hired the young lady.

The young city of ShenZhen

SunLi (孙黎) and Chu (褚)

1996 – the 18-year-old SunLi is on the way to one of the most prestigious universities in BeiJing to begin her studies there. The train needs 33 hours to take her from home to her destination which is 1,500 kilometres away. During the seven years that she studies in BeiJing, the travel time gradually shortens from 33 to 27 hours, then to 22, and finally to 13; today it will be even less, and in a few years high-speed trains will serve this route, too, and shorten the trip to between five and six hours. Arriving in BeiJing, she moves into a student residence, where her father had already lived 25 years ago, he was then of course in the men's wing, not with the female students. Very little has changed since then, China is still not out of stagnation, the policy of opening has just begun. Nobody knows what will be the results.

There is a single phone down in the entrance hall, a harridan who runs the house makes sure that no young men sneak into the women's wing, the young female students are dwelling six by six in one room each, they sleep in three bunk beds. There is little space. Washing and showering must be registered, hot water is not all the time available. At 11 p.m., the light is switched off.

A few years later she has completed her Bachelor and begins a Master's study. This time, she lives with three other female students for years in one room for four. With almost all of these former room-mates she will keep contact even as a professional. With some male students, too, friendships have developed that will last for decades.

Sun and Chu, the engineers, have known each other since middle school days. They are studying in different cities, working hard and determined, both had no time (or no eye?) for any serious love affair. When they later meet again, the two get closer and after certain considerations, discussions and musings agree to get married. Both have neither a home nor a job. Engineer Sun does not write applications, she visits some job-fairs at her university.

An electronics company in ShenZhen recruits her, she gets a four-year contract although her education is much different from what this job requires. First, she moves alone to ShenZhen to get acquainted with her new profession from scratch. At the same time her husband is looking for a job, after several months he also moves to ShenZhen because he finds a job with HuaWei (华为), a then largely unknown emerging company that is providing hardware and software for telecommunications networks. Today it is ranked second or third in the world.

The telecommunications company HuaWei is a prime example of the dramatic changes that the former fishing village of ShenZhen has witnessed within the recent 30 years. In 1979 a decision was made to establish in ShenZhen one of the four special economic zones of the Pearl River Delta in the province of GuangDong (or Canton). Deng XiaoPing thus intended to reform China's economy, which later proved to be successful. August 26, 1980, Deng XiaoPing opened this first economic zone in ShenZhen, this is now considered the birthday of this city. While I am writing this book ShenZhen celebrates its 30th birthday, and Deng XiaoPing would now be 106 years old.

Out of a 'village' of about 30,000 inhabitants (along with a few neighbouring villages perhaps 100,000 inhabitants), who all lived mainly on fishing there, developed within this extremely short time a megalopolis of about 15 million inhabitants. Many millions of today's residents are not registered, that is why they are not counted officially. Yet they live here.

Within the first decades, factories of cheap goods such as clothing, shoes and toys moved from nearby HongKong, which they considered too narrow and too expensive, to ShenZhen. Soon, however, the cheap production relocated on to DongGuan and further inland while in ShenZhen, electronics industry sprouted.

With modern high-tech companies ShenZhen attracts the best trained, ardent and ambitious young people. They want to work with HuaWei (华为), ZTE (中兴, ZhongXing), Tencent, IBM, HonHai (鸿海, Foxconn), the automobile manufacturer BYD, in software companies and dynamic start-ups, as well in the financial industry and in the vast logistics area at the port which has become the fourth-largest in the world, as well in the building construction industry and in numerous service companies that advertise, print, customise, consult, sell – or as lawyers, accountants, management consultants, all of which are in demand by the industry.

And on the eve of the 30th anniversary of the birth of ShenZhen, the automobile company ChangAn, based in ChongQing, announced to build a car factory in ShenZhen.

The HuaWei company is now feared everywhere in the world, but even within, let alone outside of China it is little known that the founder, who leads the company with strictest rule, owes only 1.42% of the (non-tradable) shares. The remaining more than 98% belong exclusively to the now 60,000 employees. They are organised in a holding company. There are no other shareholders, or mutual funds, pension funds, VC investors, nor state institutions or banks.

Anyone leaving HuaWei sells back his shares to the holding at the prevailing daily rate.

Of course, ShenZhen is not a city of 90% academics. The booming economy also attracts the less educated, ordinary workers, by far not only migrant workers but also skilled workers or trainees, artisans and minor entrepreneurs running restaurants, car, bicycle and scooter shops, hiring in turn young people who co-operate, cook, serve, sew, supply and dispose. All kinds of shops spring forth, grow if they meet a demand or shut down if not accepted.

Together with employees of public administration, physicians, nurses, kindergarten and school teachers (both male and female) and the surrounding barbers, beauty parlours, massage parlours and whatever else it takes in a big city (and what it does not take, such as charlatans, fortune tellers and hand-line viewers) – all of them are the reason why ShenZhen is now economically the fourth-largest city of China.

On arrival in ShenZhen the young couple, Chu and SunLi, contributes to the average age of ShenZhen's population dropping below 30 years. As both of them a few years later exceed 30, they conceive a son named HaoKang who, together with millions of other babies and toddlers of young families in ShenZhen, further lowers the average age. Allegedly it is annually decreasing, now to 27. If you happen to walk through the streets and parks, you will take my word for granted.

The young parents, Chu and Sun, together with millions of others, are also the driving force of the construction boom. During their first year of profession they buy an apartment. A few years later, they purchase a second, larger one, but do not inhabit it (nor rent it out). Here or into the first apartment the grandparents are supposed to move in and take care of their future child. The two do not want to see their baby (which they are planning for) raised for many years by his or her grandparents in the home city. They do not think like many other young Chinese parents who want their children to be – as is traditional – not only with the grandparents, but also far away in another city.

Both apartments are almost immediately paid in big portion from the savings of the three families – Chu and Sun and their parents each – the last 'rates' each just a few months after purchase. Engineer Chu earns well at HuaWei. But he must also work exceptionally much.

SunLi is also working hard. First she must learn about the complicated manufacturing processes of her first company, monitoring for many hours into the night the test production of new products for the customers. Later, when she becomes the first employee of that German company which intends to use ShenZhen as its base for technically looking after its customers in China, the task gets even more intense. Her mother often says that her foreign boss was certainly quite o. k. but a little exploitative, for he demanded far too much from her, would she not better leave and find a more peaceful job? But as her husband works at least as much and she sees the progress of the work, and also because she thinks that not her foreign boss was asking this but the customers did, the hard work prevails for the time being, day after day.

» **A painter takes her baby on her back at work in the artists' 'village' of DaFenCun**

» **In the Four Lakes Park a little boy is eagerly running after soap bubbles incessantly produced by a 10-year-old boy; the little one is just impressed with the bubbles and wants to follow them, not destroy them.**

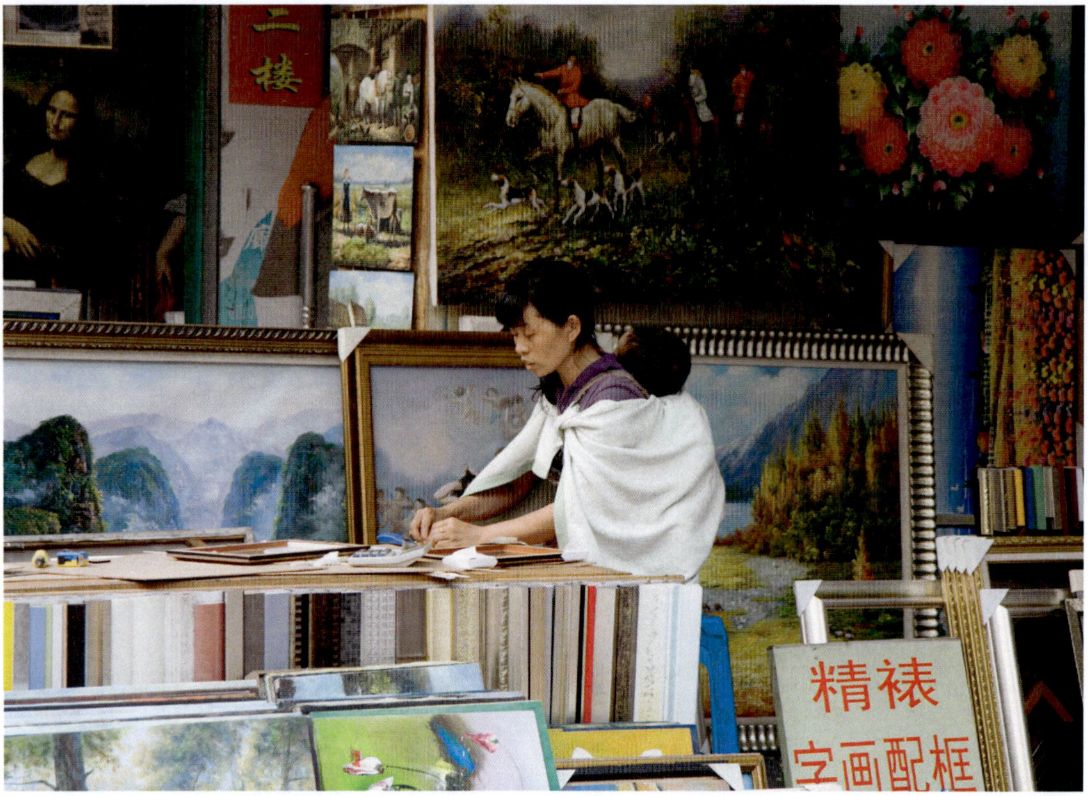
二
楼
精裱
字画配框

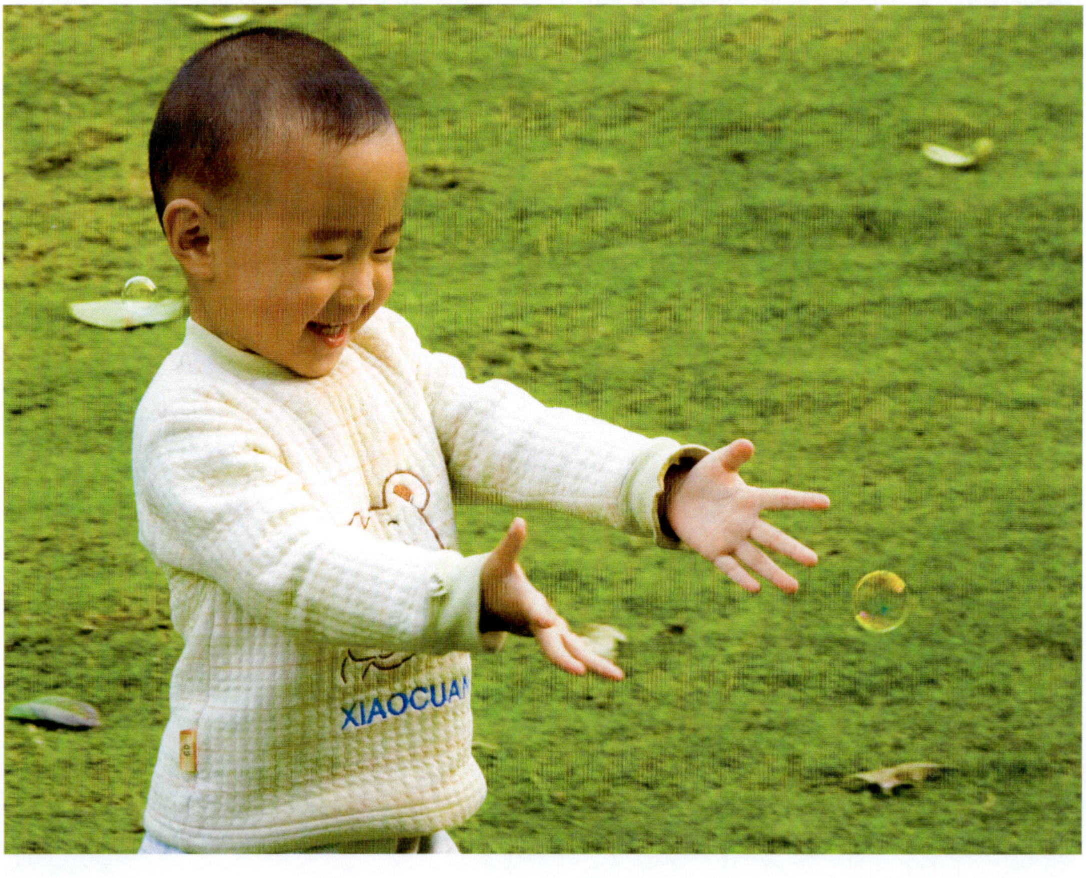
XIAOCUAN

» By late afternoon, a boy rides on his two-wheel rollerblade (only one wheel in front and back, you must be able to balance very well, momentum you gain by a sideways movement of the rear half of this vehicle, between the rear and the front half there is a joint), lost in thought and completely in balance with himself.

» The girls return from school, they go home for lunch, they already practice how they will later, as adults, also constantly chatter about everything.

» The adolescent girl considers herself most beautiful and documents it – for lack of a suitable partner – herself

Life in ShenZhen

Craftsman Wang

Craftsman Wang lived for ten years in ShenZhen. He comes from a small town in the interior but was afraid not to be able to provide his child with the future he was hoping for. His parents and the parents of his wife died early, nothing will hold him back there. With his wife 'LuLu' (璐璐, Pretty Gem of Jade) and the baby he moves to ShenZhen. First, he has a full-time job as a factory worker, his wife takes care of the child. When he comes home, she goes to work in a large sewing company nearby. She works every night, he works during the day, so that the child is always supervised and observed.

A few years later they feel that they cannot go on like that. They live separate lifes, they are tired, they are overworked. So they decide to open a workshop. Craftsman Wang can fix anything, he is also doing this in the factory, he never waits for the internal workshop; so in a side street he opens up a bicycle and moped repair shop. Here it is always busy, for all sorts of small shops, craftsmen and restaurants – if one may call those small food stalls restaurants – , are located on the ground floor of the houses and opened from early morning until midnight, or longer if needed.

In the evening, LuLu offers in the street hot meals, snacks, and meat skewers. Now they are together all day, working and living on the street, sleeping in a small room in the back of the shop, virtually in the office. There, they also make the accounts, if one wants to call it that. In the workshop there is a TV-set that runs all day. Xiao LuLu (Little LuLu), their daughter, goes to school now.

At noon she comes home for dinner with a handful of friends. mother LuLu is cooking, they eat on small plastic stools on the street. Next door and along the whole street it looks all the same. Children are washed, bathed, fed, they get their hair cut outside, the older children do homework in the afternoon in the "office" of the workshops or in the front, in the shop room. The clothes hang on the shop doors or on the street in the branches of the trees.

The children are playing together outside the store or at the computers, the adults are loudly chatting – if no customers happen to be there – out of one store and into the other, and if the car traffic was not so noisy they would try that across the street, too. This way, if someone wants to talk to his opposite neighbour, he or she has to cross the street in person.

The neighbours are running all kinds of shops, there is a barber shop where I am occasionally having my hair cut. All the hairdressers there are men, most of which appear to be or are openly gay (one of them asked me once for my phone number ...), while women and girls are responsible only for hair washing and scalp massage, which belongs to hair care in China and is a blessing. A few hundred metres away, six hairdressers are standing at the street junction on the pavement, here the hair cut does cost only a fraction of the price in the shop that in my view is already very low, anyway. Whether painting shop, pharmacy, metallurgy ('five metals'), bedding, lamps or laptop repair – in the street you will find everything you need! LuLu's competition offers delicious 'baozi', a kind of steamed, filled bun. The baozi are available with various meat or vegetable fillings or with soup which you better suck out before eating the entire bun lest it might splash onto trousers or shirt.

In the parallel road shoes (and other leather goods) are getting repaired in the street, there are at least a dozen shoemakers, some have a small shop, others mobile devices on the street, again others are working behind a fence, a woman in front is recruiting customers. Near my apartment I have my private cobbler for my persistently needed backpack repairs, also this a small roadside shop. Not far away is tailoring.

At evenings and on Sundays when fewer customers ask for service they sit together, play cards, drink tea or beer, on special days at times baijiu, but rarely the good MaoTai liquor, which is usually too expensive. Like that is the street at which Craftsman Wang set up his workshop: a small village in the megalopolis.

"Mayor" Song

"Mayor" Song is a former farmer and has never been a mayor, even not a "village mayor", but in his old village, he was the most respected farmer and the village people always called him "village mayor Song" or in short: "village mayor", whoever else was the real village mayor. Nowadays he is an investor. Being 75 years, he has come a long way in ShenZhen. In his 'village' of XiaShaCun (Village under the Sand), now a part of ShenZhen, he is one of many acknowledged and respected old men. In 1979, when the special economic zone was established in ShenZhen, he grew vegetables on a good piece of land he had inherited from his parents. They were one of the few farmer families in this fishing village, and his family was the most respected one, and especially he himself got highly respected by the villagers because of his friendly character and his willingness to help anybody and everybody.

Quickly the city overgrew the territory of the 'village' of XiaShaCun, and "mayor" Song sold his land. With the money, he built one of the first large apartment buildings in XiaShaCun and lives of the rental income of other houses that he built later. Long since he does not care himself any more about the administration. Why should he listen in his age to the complaints of tenants that there are drips, that the light does not work, that the door is stuck? The spring chickens he has hired know better.

"Mayor" Song, as he is nevertheless still respectfully called (and most probably most of the younger people who address him like this, believe he has been the former village mayor which certainly is not true), loves his white (and often not quite white) undershirts, he has only one single 'real' shirt which he wears when they meet Sunday for dinner. Otherwise he does not need it. If it is cooler in winter, he puts on a somewhat aged leather jacket whose surface knows to tell a narrative of labour and food, this jacket he loves. That he cannot close it any more because his belly bends a little too far outward does not matter. "Mayor" Song has no car and does not need it, all he needs is within walking distance. What he cannot find in XiaShaCun, he finds in walking distance to the neighbouring village of ShangShaCun (Village above the Sand).

During the day he takes care of his business, meaning that he will have a breakfast in a small restaurant at the corner of the road, then he walks around in the village, talking with anyone and everyone, keeps his finger on the pulse and ponders whether he should demolish and replace that house or rather renew it. And maybe he should link those little apartments into larger units to be bought by the spring chickens who are running around everywhere, conceiving countless kids, then he would get rid of his concerns as a landlord. He might just try this with one of his four houses. One disadvantage is that the houses are so close together, the streets are occasionally just two metres wide and the houses grow six or eight stories high! Do young families want to buy property there? On the other hand, they move in here like mad, copulate and conceive, drive cars so big that others should be ashamed of them – why would they not buy homes here? There is an ever active life here in the streets and alleys, he and all the other people around like it that way.

So, consider that well, he has to discuss it in detail with his friends, some of them have similar concerns and also burden themselves with such considerations. The wife of "mayor" Song has no such worries. She meets all day long with her friends, there is much to chat about. Early in the morning at half past six she rises to join a qi-gong team, after all they want to hail the day in sportive manner, inhale and exhale properly and not get rusty. She is not at all the eldest in the group.

On weekends they meet with a private choir to sing in the park. It's so nice to sing all these old songs! And before and after you can share the news with all your friends and acquaintances: the children fall in love and apart and again in love and into marriage, they beget themselves children, move to another city, set up a business and the grandchildren are in school (one's grandchildren are always the best). The fountain of discussion and exchange is inexhaustible.

In the afternoon (and evening), "mayor" Song is playing cards with a few friends, it may occupy him for many hours. Most often they are found at the same place, but sometimes he goes to the park nearby where he meets some very witty players whom he reluctantly confronts because he will usually lose, yet sometimes it does itch him to go.

Ultimately, it does not matter if he loses, at least not with regard to money. He is spending very little anyway, so sometimes he may invest a few hundred yuan in gambling.

His fortune he will inherit to his son, Xiao Song. Xiao Song is not much of 'xiao' any more, that is 'small', but in his profession he has already been for a long time 'lao', an 'ager', being 48 years of age he is no longer that young, either. He is the head physician at the largest hospital in ShenZhen and chief of several medical divisions. There he is respectfully called Lao Song, or sometimes Dr. Song, which he refuses every time with a smile. He is, after all, a simple farmer's son, at least in his memory. At the medical and scientific centre of the BeiJing University he has once studied, it is the prime medical school in his country. Although he received offers from abroad, he has remained in China and returned to his native town where he helped to modernise the huge central polyclinic in ShenZhen. All this did not detract from his humble attitude.

If he arrives in his 'native village' XiaShaCun after about an hour drive – he does that about once a month – he is then happy just to be Xiao Song again. His father is proud of him, his mother even more (and after the visit there is even more gossip to tell to her friends). Surely they are exploiting him, too, 'but only very rarely, only very occasionally, actually almost never,' for her son is after all such a respected physician and may advance matters faster than if they went just so to the nearby polyclinical centre. He likes to meet old friends from school, plays mah-jong (in Chinese: má-jiàng) for hours, it relaxes him and he is good at it.

Several times the amount that his father might occasionally lose at cards the son is earning within a single weekend at home. First tea is drunk, later in the evening they switch to beer and finally to MaoTai that is easily affordable in XiaShaCun. Xiao Song does not ignore any of his old friends, whenever he feels that he could help, he does it. His friends do not exploit him, they know he will support them if they need him.

But they help him as well: One of them in purchasing a car at lower rates, the other in the supply of furniture (which he makes himself in his workshop for a good price), the third sometimes with very fresh food from his shop, the fourth of them in commissioning a place in kindergarten for his daughter, later in finding a good site where to study. It's a give and take, none among the friends would like to take advantage of the other, it's embarrassing for everyone to discover they have taken more than they had given.

Engineer Su (苏工)

Engineer Su is now a meditative old man. 30 years ago, he came to ShenZhen as an untrained construction worker, determined to make his fortune. His wife he had left in his village in SiChuan (四川) for she did not want to join him, they had no children. Now he is 72 years of age and a vigorous, agile pensioner.

After having worked a few years on many of the countless construction sites in the emerging modern ShenZhen, he felt it was too much for him. He wants to proceed, to learn, and he is retrained in evening classes to become an engineer. First, he works at a cheap producer of shoes, but he does not enjoy the pressure of work and the remuneration.

He winds up in a company that builds wastewater treatment facilities, where he gains know-how, develops solutions, discovers that he is creative and rises in the hierarchy. His salary increases year by year, his new lifemate who has worked in a restaurant finally leaves her work, for they do not need two incomes any more.

Now he's been retired for almost ten years and enjoys his life in ShenZhen. He is a member of an urban bird photography association that some pensioners have founded, his lifemate is member of a private orchestra. Both of them are out every day of the week, unless it's raining terribly which, I must confess, occurs often in summer. No wonder that ShenZhen records an annual rainfall of nearly 2,000 mm, while Hamburg with no more than 750 mm of rain per year might just appear as rather arid.

Photographing birds is a passion that Engineer Su has grown late into, just before he retired. He started to take pictures with analogue reflex cameras, but when a few years later digital reflex cameras were introduced to the market he always bought the currently best and newest types. In his closet he keeps seven cameras and at least a dozen lenses. 'What should I spend my money for, if not for such an interesting hobby?' Engineer Su asks. 'There are no children and no grandchildren, my lifemate does not need any money for her hobby, as she has an instrument that she will never replace with a new one.'

If he does not photograph, he edits the digital images gained during past excursions and publishes them in the forum of the association where they are discussed.

Both of them meet every day with like-minded people. They have much to tell in the evening when they go to dinner together and find some friends from the neighbourhood there. Once and again, former colleagues from waste-water treatment ask engineer Su for advice, sometimes he can help, if only by a simple obvious question that did not come into his ex-colleagues' mind, but often he must decline: 'Very often I'm outside, my thoughts do no longer revolve around the precipitation and filtration of waste-water, but the shade and luminance of my images. And whether I will succeed in capturing that bird that I missed yesterday on an image tomorrow.'

Sometimes he accompanies his lifemate into one of the parks where she performs on a Saturday or Sunday afternoon. The orchestra just arrives there, chairs and speakers are brought along, they start to play, and the park visitors gather by and by, listen, applaud, go away, come again, just as they please. Engineer Su knows neither how to sing nor how to play an instrument, but he likes to attend at times. His lifemate cannot photograph, and many thousands of photos of all the time the same one bird make her feel tired, but sometimes she even considers one or another of his photos quite nice.

» Craftsman Wang repairs an electric scooter, a boy from the neighbourhood looks with interest, criticism and competence.

» The laundry is dried on the street.

» The neighbour's daughter is fed on the street.

» LuLu sells hot snacks in the evening.

» "Mayor" Song , lost in thought, walking through the small park.

» His wife has already moved her body early in the morning.

» The streets in XiaShaCun are narrow, but everyone likes it there.

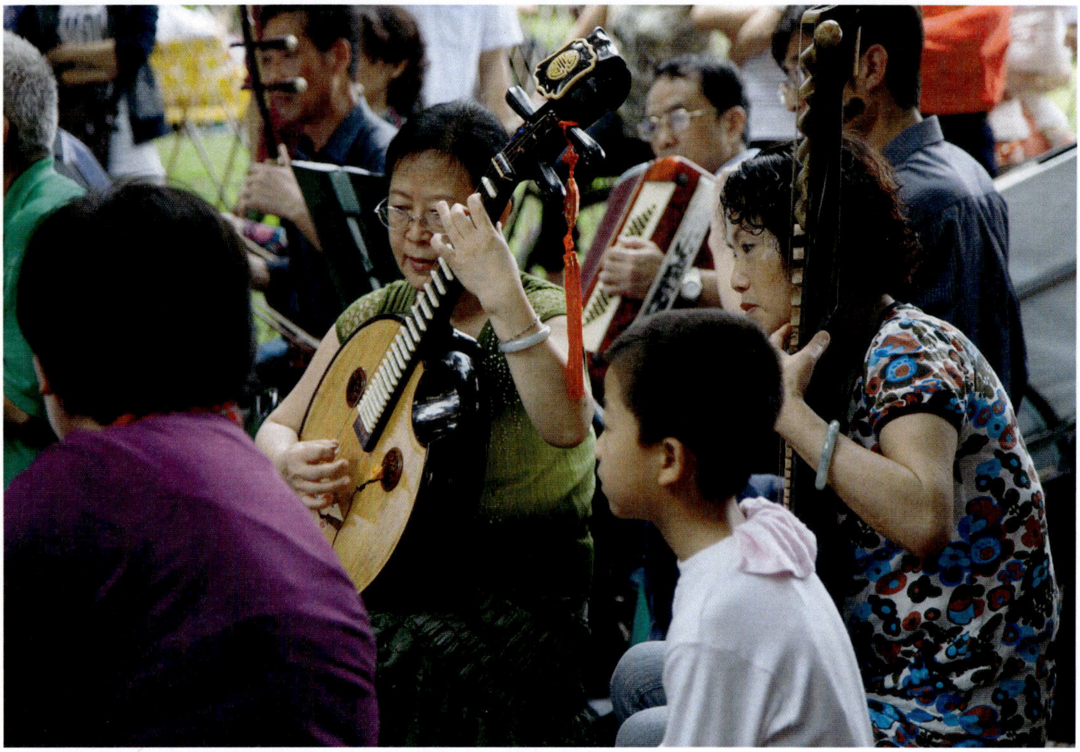

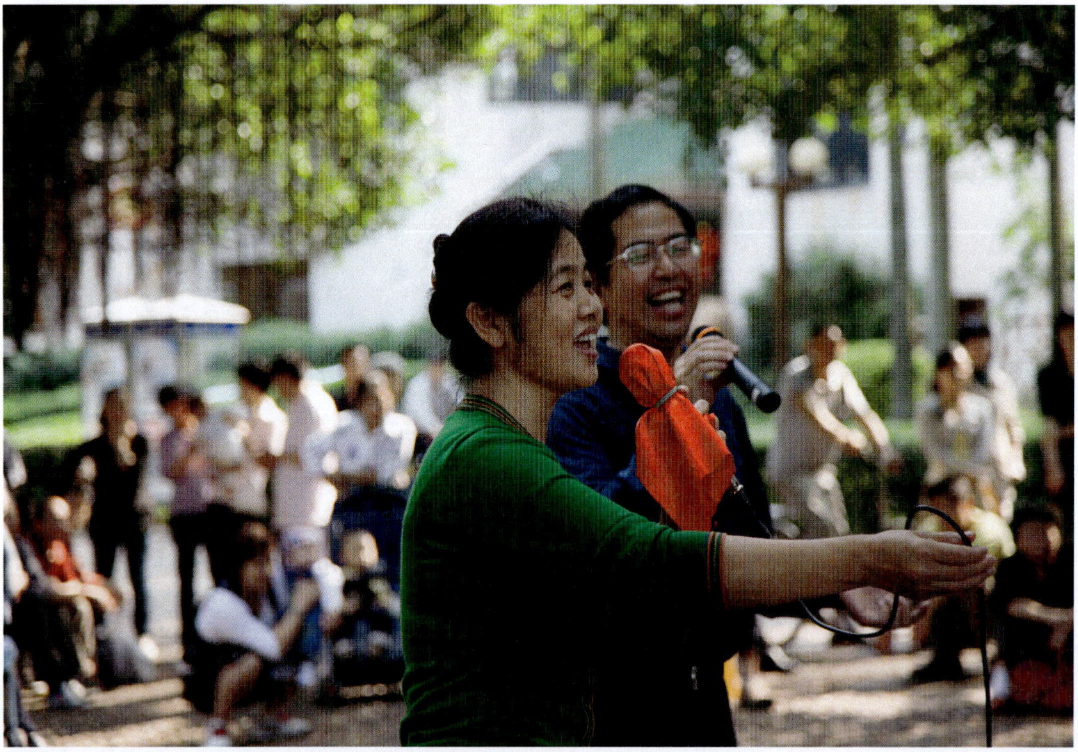

39

» Many music lovers have joined small or large orchestras and choirs which often perform in various parks, including engineer Su's lifemate who plays in such an orchestra.

» Without a set-up shop you sell on the go.

» The external observer will never find out what is sold here. The picture reflects the development of China – a combination of modern audio products and symbols of recent history.

» On the market people carefully select and never without careful consideration and discussion.

» Everything is prepared for the evening rush to the roadside restaurant.

» Anyone who finds the time will play cards; that can happen everywhere, in parks, on the street, in shops.

Our driver

Every few weeks, I take the plane from China to Germany, work there for two or three weeks at the headquarters of the company, guide everyone 'back on track', motivate them, listen to their concerns and ideas, discuss projects, do that tedious administrative work, and then I return by plane to China. Sometime in the early months of this way of working and travelling when SunLi accompanied me to the ferry, the worst case happens. Just before I check in, there is a sizzling flash in my mind: My laptop is still lying on the living room table! This means disaster for my working schedule of the next two weeks.

Quickly we make up our minds: I will tell at the ticket check, above at passport control and on the pier at the ferry that there is something to be replenished. SunLi will as quickly as possible try to take a taxi to my apartment and retrieve the laptop. I give her the key, she knows where the apartment is because she has helped me to find and rent it.

Outside, in front of the ferry terminal, there are regular taxis – the drivers refuse the drive, in particular they do not want to wait in front of the house until she gets down again. Precious minutes elapse. But there are also other fellows hanging around, white card drivers who offer passengers to take them to their destination off the clock. Only the third driver asked is willing to drive the ten minutes distance, wait outside the house, and return SunLi with the laptop to the ferry terminal.

These and other details I find out later by telephone, in the meantime I am discussing with the ferry personnel and the passport inspectors, for if SunLi is able to retrieve the laptop she has to pass the first ticket check but has no ticket, then she has to get upstairs to passport control and handle me the laptop 'across the border', but in-between the ferry must not leave, for it is the last one for today, otherwise I would miss my plane. All of this has to be accounted for.

Speaking with the tongues of angels, at that time without any word of Chinese, I at last persuade them all: the ferry will be waiting for the laptop, the ticket check will allow SunLi to pass, passport control will allow that I get the laptop handed over.

At the same time in SheKou (蛇口), that suburb of ShenZhen which accommodates the ferry terminal, an obviously insane driver rushes with 80 or 100 kilometres per hour in wavy lines, overtaking all the other cars even on the opposite lane, along the roads, across red semaphores. He tries to comfort SunLi, who is close to breakdown, telling her: 'Don't worry, I was a racer once.' Does that really comfort?

In less than twenty minutes SunLi is back, hands me the laptop across the border, the passport control officers smile, they have helped with their flexible approach (and they all like to help), the ferry departs less than ten minutes late, the passengers did not even notice. If later the ferry is late at times I send an SMS to SunLi, telling: 'Once again someone has forgotten his laptop!' For a while, this is our running gag.

Ever since the racer has been our driver on all client appointments in GuangDong, he demands a fair price, he is incredibly flexible and has, I think, a GPS wired in the brain, for he finds every way without GPS or map, sometimes he asks locals if we cannot find the road to our customers in the maze of industrial areas, but never he has lost his way. He is a genius, and he became our friend and is helping us wherever he may. The first few years we call him simply The Racer, although he has practised the sport only at a very young age. Later, when still a young man, he was a forklift driver for many years (for containers, i. e. very large forklifts, matter of fact he was a helmsman of container bridges) and lorry driver. He is still proud of that and tells of his outstanding abilities. A 40-ton lorry he can drive backwards to the loading point at a single sweep, as a container lorry driver he was able to place his container right under the container crane at once and not only after several attempts of going back and forth. He also took part in competitions for lorry drivers and has collected awards. All of this I learn after my Chinese has improved in later years.

Occasionally I visit his family. He has a 20-year-old daughter with his first wife from whom he is divorced, and a two and a half year old son with his second wife. I like to talk to his son. He does not use so many different Chinese words, and he understands me … Fang ShiFu (方师傅, Master Fang), as we call him, is now working just for us (or for me, on my private expeditions) and appears to have sufficient reserves; even if he does not drive us a whole week because I am for example in East China or Japan or Korea, it does not matter to him.

He has reserves and other revenue: His former boss for whom he had worked as a driver was once offering a very risky and difficult task, and our driver came forward. A customer who had not paid for a long time, was not to be moved by friendly means to pay at least a part of the supplies, was now to be persuaded in a 'somewhat less friendly' manner, because the boss did not want to get involved with the courts. A lot of money was in the game, very much now. Fang Shifu was free to choose the means, but he was expected to return with the money, at least a significant part of it. The boss had every confidence in him, he knew him from work in previous years to be absolutely reliable. Fang Shifu accomplished the mission flawlessly, the customer suddenly enjoyed to pay for whatever reason, his boss was very grateful and very generous: He entrusted him with two apartments, that Fang ShiFu is now renting. This revenue is sufficient to support his anyway modest way of living.

» **Evening return**

Football in ShenZhen

I am a football aficionado. Whenever possible I want to play football. Despite my not exactly outstanding size I enjoy being the goalkeeper, and I am not bad at it. And despite my advanced age I still show very rapid reactions, especially on the line and in the five-metre box. I am fairly agile and fast, I only cannot jump high.

After having rented an apartment in ShenZhen I want to be active in sports again at weekends, and not just walking and hiking. I want to play football again. I notice that there are many football pitches, but where are the clubs, how do I approach them (without knowledge of the Chinese language)? Sure, there are foreigners' associations and internet forums for foreigners where you may find football teams, too, but I want to play with Chinese, I do not want to lock off myself with other foreigners. Will I find teams of the same age somewhere?

In my German football club I am the goalie of the oldest senior team. But I am also able to compete with much younger players in company-facilitated football, especially in the fast indoor football.

I buy my first goalie equipment: shoes, shin pads, gloves, trousers, shirt, knee pads, elbow pads. Equipped like that I'm going one Sunday afternoon to a football pitch near my apartment, across from SiHai GongYuan, a park that would later become my second favourite one. I perceive at once that the teams playing there are no professionals but ‚leisure players'. No problem, that will make it easier for me.

But they are young, some of them are younger than my sons, which is making things less easy. I watch the match, I need a plan. It grows fruits while I observe one of the goalkeepers. He is totally incapable! The other one is o. k., but what about the one on the right side of the pitch? It seems that he never kept a goal before. This poor fellow looks rather unhappy! Is he hurt? Did he have to be the goalie because they had no better one?

I am standing behind the goal and go on watching. I warm up. I realise that there is no coach, no one who calls instructions from the outside. This is a self-organising match. After the next goal was scored against the poor chap I indicate to him with arms, legs and head: ‚Get off the pitch for a while, I will keep the goal for you.' He smiles kindly, no: he does so happy and relieved; I must focus, for there already the next attack approaches, the opponent's strikers are amazed: a new goalkeeper? And one who now saves every shot!

"My" defence and the other team-mates are surprised and delighted. I do not remember the result, especially since I cannot recall at which score I "had been" put in. No matter: It was fun! Unfortunately I did not know how to go on, something was wrong with the phone number that I gave to the team captain, I received no information about the next match at next weekend. This team I lost as quickly as I found it.

I had to use these tactics two more times, then – the third time – it worked out: one player – they called him Stones, his Chinese first name was ShiTou (石头) – spoke a reasonable English, we exchanged phone numbers, he said: 'Next Sunday at 2 p. m. there will be a match in WanXia, I will send you the address in Chinese, which you will show to a taxi driver who may drive you there.'

Next Sunday it turns out that the team in which I have recently put myself in is not the one in which I will be playing on Sundays from now on. Stones had been just a guest player there, it was pure coincidence (and persistence) that I met him, and now I have found a team, "Lao Niu" (老牛), the Old Bulls. Except that I am by far the oldest bull, on average, the other bulls are as old as my sons, then about 25, now about 30 years, the oldest other one on the team is 12 years younger than I am, the youngest just reckons 23.

We discover that while scatting along in the evening of the first Sunday match. From now on – till today it has been going on like that for more than five years – we will be playing every Sunday (if I'm in China) and then almost always go for dinner together. Here I learn to know China, at least a portion of today's modern China: emerging, ardent and well-paid young men, only a few of them married, no one has any children, they all have girlfriends who accompany us sometimes to the match and dinner, and they are working for a large part in the high-tech industry.

Not only the players of this team arrive together or alone with their car at the pitch (the 'pitch' on which we are playing most of the time is a larger site with lately nine individual pitches), no, all the players in general do arrive by car. There are the small cars, there are also larger and luxury cars, vans and SUVs. The footballers in ShenZhen are not poor unskilled labourers but self-employed or well-salaried specialists with an income above average, many of them are working in the electronics industry. I am the only one who comes regularly by bike, the only one among about 500 players who are every Saturday and every Sunday on the site.

At some occasion, someone pointed out: '30 years ago, everyone in Germany wanted to travel by car, in China everyone took the bicycle, today the Germans go again by bicycle, all the Chinese want to travel by car.' Splendid insight!

Over the years, I watch my team-mates getting married and having children. Their children are about as old as my first grandson (in the meantime, my grandson even got a little sister). Our football team is invited to many a wedding. In China I have visited during the last years more weddings than during my whole life in Germany. A wedding may be a smaller party for 80 guests or a larger one for 300 or 400. It may be the actual wedding party, or (if this took place in the home-town of the young man or his wife) a "lesser" later celebration with only 50 or 80 friends and neighbours and colleagues. Every time one or two round tables are reserved for our team, every wedding is a happy uncomplicated get-together, sometimes with a programme, sometimes without. For example, our centre forward LaoZhang who is himself running a small restaurant chain likes to perform with a friend as a music duo. Each wedding is a children's party, because all the guests take their children along if they have any, then they romp around the room. LaoWei is always an exotic exhibit, presented to parents and in-laws by the football player and his bride whom I usually know already from the pitch or dinner.

I'm the grandpa on the pitch – and at the weddings, being of the same age as the parents of the marrying players, but they need me, they do so urgently. This team has had for years no real goalie, they have lost many matches because they conceded more goals than they scored, and it is well known that this is not quite sufficient to win a match, not when doing the maths properly.

By and by I notice that goalies are real short supply, so my active attempt to enter the football player market in ShenZhen has actually revealed a market niche to be exploited. After the match, money is collected, everyone will pay about 50 RMB, so about 600 to 1000 RMB will get together, depending on how much the pitch plus costs for a referee will cost per match. The groundkeeper comes along, brings water and collects the money. During the first few weeks and months I am dismissed friendly if I want to give my contribution. I agree not to pay, thinking this is just some way of kindness to the poor old lonely foreigner.

No, later I discover: in this system of football in ShenZhen, goalkeepers pay not at all, none of them. Each team wants to attract a good goalkeeper who is lured by the fact that he does not have to pay. If there is no regular goalkeeper, one of the players has to keep the goal and this is compensated by him being exempt from the fee.

For the Lao Niu a new age has dawned: At last they are winning matches, because I am – except for high balls straight under the bar or into the right or left upper corner – a rather good goalkeeper and, surprisingly, I am getting even better still.

Since only two players are able to speak English to some extent, they demand from me at dinner Sunday night: 'You will have to learn Chinese! We will teach you!' What they do teach me, of course, are words and phrases of young men that I am only getting told while the girlfriends (and wifes) are absent … I forget them again immediately, anyway. But I am now motivated to learn Chinese.

Some of the players are true experts in football, real artists at the ball, some are gifted, have good talents, some are, well, willing to play.

ShiTou inspires me to play in his second team too, they are playing on Wednesday evenings at 8:30 p. m. under lights on an artificial pitch in MeiLin (梅林, "Plum Tree Forest"), a district in the West of ShenZhen that is remote from my apartment about 45 minutes by taxi. The artificial turf is top quality of a kind I have never seen before.

While warming up, I note: This is a different team. Their shots are so accurate and hard that it is unbelievable. When the match starts, I'm completely astonished. Passes almost always end up with the team-mate they want to pass to, those guys know how to play diagonal passes all across the pitch, and the ball arrives at the foot of the other player and does not dodge off there somewhere else.

The opponent has the same quality, here I am playing with two teams at the highest level, in Germany that would be at least fourth, maybe third division! In such teams I have never been allowed to play before, what luck, what opportunity! Again, I prove myself to some extent, these new friends accept me, not out of pity but because I show good reactions at the box. Keeping the penalty box under control is hard (also due to my lack of size) or 'has room for improvement', but I even do improve over time.

With this team I am playing for a few months, but they have a regular goalkeeper who is also quite good, and I have a big problem: Playing every Wednesday is stressful for me. Either my return flight from ShangHai is late, or I'm still stuck in a traffic jam on the motorway back from GuangZhou, and when I arrive at my apartment (without dinner), I still have to drive almost one more hour to MeiLin. Often I come too late or not at all or just one minute before the opening whistle.

I tell this to the other players, and with a heavy heart I cease to play on Wednesdays. Yet, even today I am sometimes called to the phone: 'Can you play by chance next Wednesday? Our goalkeeper is absent.' Whenever possible I disengage from everything else and go playing, it is a pleasure with this great team!

Yet I want to play twice a week, how can I arrange that? I ask around a lot and have a look, and finally it turns out that one of my Sunday team-mates, WangQiang (王强), is captain of another team that is playing on Saturdays. They call their team 'Tian Long' (天龙), Sky Dragons – and they have just lost their goalkeeper, for he has moved away. That fits so nicely, ever since I am also playing on Saturdays.

It is amazing to see how football works in ShenZhen. While at first I thought 'Well, that kind of grassroots football that we have in Germany does not exist here, there are only a few recreational players whom I found by accident', it turns out: That's real popular sport here in ShenZhen!

There are reportedly over 2,500 teams of this kind, and I believe this number to the letter. Everywhere there are pitches. For two or three years we have now been mostly playing on a site that now has nine of them. Many of such properties belong either to construction companies who plan to build real estate there at some time, or to the city of ShenZhen. Till then, these companies lease the sites to some 'football pitch management company' or individuals that establish pitches, take care and rent them. The managers of such pitches also arrange matches if some team does not find an opponent for the next weekend or the one after the next.

Fu JiaoChen (傅佼晨) is the manager of those nine football pitches on which we play almost every Saturday and Sunday. He lives with his wife and young son in very simple containers on the site, he also has his office there, and from there he manages the pitch assignment and ensures that all teams will have their opponents and the pitches are booked out. In all, he wants to have at least three matches a day during the week (under floodlights), and at the weekend altogether 48 matches (starting at 2 p. m.).

Several assistants he has hired, not to mention a host of ten referees – no match on his site may begin without a referee, and the ref must be paid by the teams as well. Other volunteers are cleaning up, bring water to the teams, collect the empty plastic bottles of water (there are no bottles of beer, no beer to be drunk on the site), repair the goal nets and ball nets at the sides of the area, mow the lawn in summer and water it in winter, during longer periods of dryness.

Groundkeeper Fu is a master in the art of living. He is not overworked, not at all. After lunch he begins his tea ceremony, he has the best teas, and he knows how to prepare them. And he has a professionally decorated tea table. Every few weeks, the German grandpa-goalie is even earlier than usual on the site, and then he is invited and they talk over the tea as much as his Chinese may grant them. Gradually there come the referees, they all get their tea before the opening.

Sometimes groundkeeper Fu plays himself, and sometimes all the referees together plus a few additional players are gathered into a team, and they also play against us at times. Don't be deceived, all those referees are excellent football players, unlike in Germany where we keep saying: 'He who does not know how to play football will be the referee.'

Groundkeeper Fu patiently introduces his son to the mysteries of football. There are no children teams, except at the primary schools. But his main job is to provide all teams with matching opponents and keep best pitches in prime condition – which pays for his living, at least for as long as the property will not be cultivated. What will happen to our football playing if buildings should once be raised on this or other sites, I do not know.

We only play once a year against the same team, there are plenty of others.

Somehow our organisers always manage to find opponents of about the same quality. One of the team is responsible for operating it, another for finance, a third one for the formation. We rarely play against grossly inferior teams, rarely as well against hopelessly superior ones, but often against some who are slightly superior but against which we can make a difference.

Only once we have been playing against my former 'Wednesday team', we lost 12-0, and only thanks to the outstanding German goalkeeper of Lao Niu an even worse disaster had been avoided, for the others might easily have scored 30-0. Of course the match was annoying for me, the opposing goalie (my ex-colleague) got absolutely nothing to do while I did not get to breathe, attack on attack was surging against my goal. In the end I could be proud of having kept more than I conceded, but my team-mates were sorry for me, my friends of Wednesdays, however, said that now for once I had been really busy and very good at it …

The matches often take place in a technically very good level and are very fair. Although we are playing with referees, players often indicate themselves if some move had been a foul, they stop the ball and put it down for a free kick even before the whistle was heard. But watch out if someone feels wronged by the referee or in his opinion was badly fouled on purpose – within seconds screaming may turn into a wrangle between four players, a few seconds later there is a brawl between ten of them, and the referee tries in vain to stop it by whistling. Just as quickly the emotions may cool down again, but sometimes it can also lead to the match being abandoned.

Often the goalkeeper makes the difference: If I'm in really good shape (I am not always), I am able to keep two or three shots that I would classify myself in retrospect as 'unstoppable', and my team-mates will claim later: 'I had seen that shot already in the goal, how did you ever block it?' Yes, sometimes I succeed in surprisingly good automatic reactions. I like matches in which the opponent dominates the match and often shows up before my goal. Then out of a few counter-attacks we just have to shoot one more goal than our opponent and win 3-2, although at least two of our goals had been simple shots and might have been kept, but the other goalie let them pass in a very unlucky manner because often he is no real goalie at all.

Well, like that it is, but a win is a win, and after those matches when he had been inferior in skills and yet scored three out of four attempts while the opponents scored two out of 20 (three of them being 100% bets), our dinner together is a veritable celebration. And LaoWei – this is my Chinese name which I had received after a few months in China on another occasion, more about that later – is then the hero of the day.

It is not always like that. Some times LaoWei has to face criticism, even on the pitch: 'Why don't you pick up the ball and have some calm enter the match? Don't pass that on at once!' Now try to understand that in mid-action – in Chinese! Or: 'The 2-2 draw you ought to have prevented, you were standing too far off the goal.' Certainly, sometimes the criticism is justified, but then again, not every time, because the pitch players commit many more errors than I do, just that my errors almost always mean a score or at least a very dangerous situation. And also – although very rarely, maybe twice a year – I may commit a very silly mistake when underestimating a simple stoppable shot and it slips right through while I am falling down. Then I would prefer to crawl under the grass and avoid the other players during half-time, so embarrassed I am …

The player on the pitch may miss the ball, but the goalkeeper has to keep it in any case, even if it dodges around on uneven ground. Especially in the early years we had sometimes very serious discussions. "TianLong" (天龙) I had to remember that we would sometimes like to win, too, that I do not always want to concede more goals than the opposing goalkeeper, and that I expect my advance mates to run and fight. They would rather just play nicely. We have changed that.

"LaoNiu" (老牛) I had to inform that criticising me on the pitch is not helpful even where it is legitimate. Criticism on the pitch just makes me feel less sure of myself, I cannot digest it at once, anyway I understand only half of it, answer only a quarter of it, it makes me angry and I may miss the next shot, that is no benefit for anyone.

Sometimes – very rarely – I reach for the very last resort, if I perceive the criticism as inappropriate I reply: 'Oh, you know what, you may accept another, better goalkeeper, there are plenty of them. Incidentally, I have an offer from TaiYangQiu (太阳球, loosely translated: Sunshine Football), they do not only offer me that I do not have to pay, but they even are going to pay me 100 RMB in addition for each match!'

Then, the debate quickly disintegrates into roars of laughter.

» This poor fellow had never before been goalkeeping, they have not found another sucker, soon he will be replaced by me.

» One of our best players during the shot on goal.

» Our outside left passes a cross.

» Before a tournament, the mutual welcome is perfect in form. LaoWei in the yellow goalkeeper dress. This one and the following two photos were taken by a photographer of the opposing team (playing in white) and sent to LaoWei after a discussion among fellow sportsmen.

» Now it is up to the goalie, for his own defender (blue shirt) is too late, the ball is on the way ..

» ... but LaoWei blocks it off successfully.

» The centre forward of our Tian Long team gets married, LaoWei is present, too (the one with a T-shirt showing his grandson on the front and a large '1' (= goalkeeper) on the back with the name 'Grandpa YeYe'). Our centre forward has found a very beautiful, very young wife.

» At the wedding ceremony the children recollect gold and silver scraps of paper that were shot out of a paper cannon, and they recharge the paper cannon tubes

» We toast to our centre forward, and wish him all the best.

» Children are watching one of the young couple's friend painting good wishes for them in beautiful chinese characters.

55

Gan Bei

And then, more often than not, ‚gan bei' (干杯) is proclaimed, which literally means ‚dry glass', ‚gan' meaning ‚dry' and ‚bei' referring to the glass.

At our first dinner together, when I was still a newcomer in the team, I was introduced and ‚checked'. Gan Bei was successively carried out with each individual, we introduced ourselves to each other. But the beer glasses are small, getting them dry is not a real problem, just two sips and it is done.

Both teams respect if I or anyone else should say: ‚No more, I've had enough.' Sometimes a compromise is found: ‚Okay, yi ban' (一半, half a glass!). I have never seen any of the players really drunk, not even at the fourth anniversary of the founding of the Lao Niu team. Not even if bai-jiu is served. They respect that I'll have one glass and no more.

Only once a few friends and I advanced too far: For some reason, four players thought that after dinner we ought to visit yet another place near their residential area. There is a ‚Seven Eleven', a shop which officially opens from seven o'clock in the morning until eleven o'clock in the night. I can confirm that (at least then) it was open at least until half past two in the night, for we were constantly able to buy more QingDao beer there (also known as TsingTao).

I really do not know how much I had drunk that night, but judging by the fact that we were still able to kick the ball around on the forecourt, and judging by the further fact that in the middle of the night I could still properly tell the taxi driver the Chinese name of my housing estate, I suppose I was not completely drunk. Pretty well drunk, yes, I admit that much.

It was huge fun. The customers noticed nothing the next day.

In 2005, more than six years ago, the Lao Niu team has found together in a very large settlement, WeiLan HaiAn (蔚蓝海岸). Some 20,000 people are living there in large high-rise buildings combined into four quarter settlements, each of them being centred around a park. That's more people than in the small town outside of Hamburg where I live in Germany, probably being concentrated on 5% of the area.

In this settlement there are five football teams, sometimes we play against one or another of them. LaoNiu is #4, that is not his performance level but his place in the order of founding and joining the team. Meanwhile, however, only about half of the players still originate from the settlement because one or the other player has moved away (but keeps playing with us) or ceases to play for any other reason, not to mention newbies like me joining from outside.

Tian Long has been created by aid of the Internet forum ‚ShenZhen Sports.' Here too, the team suffers over the years some fluctuation, but it is amazing to see how stable the teams are in general (even the opponents!). In the last two years, Tian Long has become almost half Korean: There's a fairly sizeable national minority of Korean ethnicity in China; they are all born there, have grown up and gone to school there. They have Chinese ID cards, speak Chinese and practice some profession here.

Among themselves they speak Korean. It started with one Korean who lives and works in China, and he has gradually added more of his Korea-Chinese friends to the team. All of them are very strong players, the best one is a young man who had even been playing a few years ago in the Chinese national youth team, but there – according to his own words, as far as I understand his Chinese correctly, for he does not speak English – he could not prevail because they would have ultimately only true Han Chinese in the team.

He has also played with the professionals in ShenZhen, but the professional league is not popular in China. It was tainted by corruption and therefore is of no concern to the active football players in China, especially in ShenZhen. None of my fellow players would watch for once a weekend match of the ShenZhen Football Club ...

Our Koreans (like many of my friends and I, too) do not only play with us in TianLong only but also in another team, in this case a purely Korean one. We have already played at least against four different Korean teams, even against those where some of our friends participate in. These teams are playing in a way that is completely different from any Chinese team, the Koreans run and fight for 90 minutes, their match strategy mimics that of the Korean national team – run, run, run, fight, never give up.

With the Koreans, our TianLong team got ever better and our Saturday night dinners more colourful and funnier.

No longer am I the exotic guest at the common dinner. While during the first few times the discussions almost exclusively revolved around me (work, family, home, views of China, eating habits and the like), this changed very soon, and everyone is now talking loud and fast and everybody at the same time about the latest current topics. LaoWei is of no particular concern any more, he is sitting at the table and able to participate in the conversation (if he can do or when he finds someone to help interpret), and my presence has quickly become common acceptance.

Both Saturdays and Sundays, we eat only Chinese. Saturday we change the restaurant frequently, it may be SiChuan, ShangHai, BeiJing or other Chinese kitchen, on Sundays we are almost always in the same restaurant which is serving Cantonese cuisine. Here we are regulars. We eat everything that we can get: all sorts of meat, fish, vegetables, shrimp. I'm learning to eat duck tongue, frogs and a kind of small lobster (spicy), get used to it and am increasingly attracted to eating very spicy food, even some that seemed to me strange at first (for example, intestines).

I observe, not only here, that the Chinese extremely like to nibble bones. We would return such a dish to the kitchen and ask whether we had ordered 'bones', but if you order in China 'chicken' or 'pig', it is almost always served as small-cut pieces of bone, carefully moved for minutes in the mouth and be worn away neatly. The same is true for fish bones and fish heads (by the way, in GuangDong or Kanton, this is the prime gourmet dish among all, the body of the fish is for the poor folk, the head for the wealthier, it was said in earlier times).

I also learn to eat crabs. You can order them in restaurants (if you have no chance to buy them yourself at the original site where they are raised), and for most Chinese people they are a delicacy for which they like to spend much money. The connoisseur will accept only crabs from lake YangChengHu (阳澄湖) in SuZhou, these are freshwater crabs, in our view quite strange-looking creatures, and hairy (indeed they are called 'hairy crab'). They are incredibly tasty and, because of the high protein content, very nutritious, too. As always, there are also the clever traders who have grown their crabs somewhere else but water their baskets a day or two at the shore of the lake: Thus, their crabs 'come from the lake' and are ennobled, that is, they will cost several times the price of 'normal' crabs. The true connoisseur, however, can easily distinguish the true from the fake YangChengHu crabs by their taste. Crabs are gnawed with devotion (after eating the bulk of the body) for hours, I can find nothing left in the long thin legs and claws, but for the Chinese gourmet now, this is just the beginning.

At some point I am getting asked: 'Do you like dog?' I reply truthfully that I have eaten dog twice, once in Korea in the demilitarised zone during a crane research trip, another time many years ago in ChangChun. Both times it was o. k., but not convincing. So dog is ordered – it tastes great. The Cantonese way to prepare dog is much more palatable than that in North Korea or North China (which I have to admit, although I would never order dog for myself).

I especially like the vegetables, lotus root, soy and bamboo shoots, and for me, "马齿苋" is an entirely new discovery. It took weeks until we found the proper common Chinese name, because my friends knew only a popular name ("cat ears"), while the right name, ma chi xian, literally translates as "horse-tooth amaranth". It is a kind of purslane, a very fresh and sour tasting vegetable that even grows wild in the ditches of ShenZhen, and in moist places in parks, I have found it myself there; the fine shafts and the fleshy little leaves are very tasty.

So our evening dinner meetings are not only moist and fun but also educational.

Exhibitions

YeDan (叶郸) is a successful businessman, a Chinese who was born and raised in Taiwan but has lived for decades in ShangHai. He was Asian CEO of a European high-tech company and one day – not yet sixty years old – he grew tired of business life. There is after all something else to life than revenues, costs, profits and share prices, and life is too short only for that.

He also knows how to paint, and teaching is his favourite passion.

So, being 58 years, he begins a second and at the same time a third career: In his third career, he is associate professor (marketing and business management) at three universities; in his second career, he is entering the art market, his plan is every year to create a series of exhibitions in various cities, each time featuring another topic. His first topic is ‚Cranes' the second, ‚Rapeseed', the third, ‚Green', and the fourth is: ‚Oceans of the world'. Through mutual friends he meets by chance the German manager of a small chemical nanotechnology company who is also proficient in global crane research.

They talk about cranes, during a visit the German shows him ‚his' cranes in Hamburg, YeDan is thrilled – these are his first wild cranes that he can watch! They talk the whole evening at dinner, until finally the topic of photography is mentioned. Words fly across the table, the German retrieves a couple of photos, YeDan is enthusiastic: ‚Shall we make an exhibition together?'

The German is just beginning to make his entry in China, he has never shown his photos in public, and then if he did it for the first time it should be in China? Can you ever dare to go public with these images that do not match professional standards? But YeDan does not give in.

A few months later, the German is still living in China in ever-changing hotels, the idea of renting an apartment has not yet arisen, but in ShangHai there are two exhibitions: ‚Worldwide Oceans', the first one being in the artists' quarter, the second one in PuDong, in the new, large and modern NanHui Oceans Museum. They display 50 oil paintings by YeDan with ocean motifs and 25 large photos that the German Chemistry Doctor has made during his various diving and fishing trips on the oceans of the world.

The first exhibition is a full success. Local dignitaries and the German consul in ShangHai come along, all of them are giving speeches, the atmosphere is relaxed. The day before, outside the programme, before the official opening, even a few government officials and a minister visited the exhibition, YeDan is not really a nobody in China.

A few days before the opening of the second exhibition, YeDan is sending a scan of an article published in a ShangHai newspaper: ‚They have even printed your name, now everyone will know you in Shanghai!' But I do not find the name, not until at last YeDan explains on the telephone: ‚Your name is in the sub-headline, it is spelled 卫斯林, Wei SiLin.'

Without further discussion, the German adopts that name for himself, it is printed on the Chinese side of the business card, and the players that he will get to know a few months later call him spontaneously 'LaoWei', or 'Old Wei' ("Wei" meaning "guard", how well this fits to his later position in the football team!).

As promised by YeDan, the exhibitions are great fun, moreover, a whole new subject in every way: being a photographer who has for his first time a public exhibition, and then in China! And you get to know some people.

Painter YeDan's topic of next year is 'Children smile'. He will paint in oil hundreds of photos that he either made himself or were sent by from acquaintances and friends, including two smiling German children who were preschoolers then but are now the adult and working sons of the Chemistry Doctor, LaoWei.

» Two images out of 25 from the exhibition 'Worldwide Oceans' – in Antarctica: Gentoo Penguins take a breath during a voyage to their hunting grounds while leaping from the water, the picture shows all the stages: penguins under water, just before the appearance, jumping in the air, during re-immersion. The second image shows the ocean off the Australian east coast in the early morning, long deep waves approach the coast and are breaking on a rock.

How do I best establish a company in China?

We urgently need to establish our own company in China, otherwise we may not be able to hire sufficiently more technicians, above all, we cannot pay them directly. SunLi is initially paid for many months across complex circumventions, and every time something goes wrong, straining SunLi's patience to the utmost and turning me angry. Without a valid business license, we cannot make any business directly in the country, everything would have to pass over the agent's desks, which I want to avoid as much as possible, or it would have to be managed by foreign banks, which the customers want to avoid as much as possible.

Establishing a company in Germany is elsewhere already considered a challenge. The bureaucratic requirements are high in comparison to many other countries. I will assume, for simplicity again, that it is as easy or difficult for Chinese people to found a company in China as it is for a German in Germany.

But when a foreign company, in my case, a small private German company, desires to establish a subsidiary in China, then the hurdles are extremely high. I browse the internet, ask the Chamber of Commerce in Kiel which refers me to the Chamber of Commerce in ShangHai. I search alone and by the aid of SunLi in the GuangDong province – everywhere the same result: It is a very tedious process, you will have to turn to own and local lawyers in any case, you need an officially designated consultant, and have everything translated by officially approved translators.

Based on the individual items I estimate the financial effort on 50,000 to 100,000 €, which is enormous, it was the equivalent of one million RMB, and I cannot yet decide to issue the orders.

For the weekend after the first opening of the exhibition, a trip to NanTong (南通) is planned, YeDan has arranged this and I think naively that this will probably be a tourist city, expecting temples and gardens and archaeological sites. Everything is prepared, a hotel is reserved, the next morning a friend of YeDan is appointed to pick me up.

He is actually there on time, that is, with a large tourist bus in which 20 people are already seated, the remaining 30 gather with me to depart. I do not quite understand … to be precise, I do not quite understand anything at all.

Other than myself, there are several Chinese, some Japanese and some Western-looking guests, YeDan's acquaintance interprets for me what the 'guide' in front tells to the Chinese guests and interpreters: We will get the opportunities for investment in NanTong described and which companies are already located there and which industrial zones are just now developed. The dramatic climax will be the new bridge over the ChangJiang (长江, literally the Long River, outside of China it is called Yang Tse). We get out and admire the civil works and the construction, in one and a half years, the bridge will be completed (by now, in 2010, it is already finished). Now no one needs to take the longer way by ferry any more, the travel time from ShangHai is shortened to a minimum.

All this and much more is demonstrated and

explained to the guests of this bus tour and myself, and at the end of the day when all of us are already exhausted, there is a sumptuous dinner in a large room with many, many round tables. All the time officials pass by, wish us all good luck, gan bei, and many milliards of investment.

So, if I had not yet understood that already, each drop and little drop of baijiu and hongjiu (红酒, red wine) is telling the same story: They want us to invest milliards here! Nice, but – where to get the milliards?

I talk to YeDan's friend who piloted me here: We would indeed like to invest, but actually we first need a company registration, then we may see for the rest, and we got some ideas what to do! But he must also understand that we cannot just after registering enter with millions or milliards here, we are a small company, and everything will go ahead very slowly – if this was also compliant to NanTong's interests in investment?
 Yes it is.
 Well, how can we proceed then?

Well, a few weeks later we have registered the subsidiary in NanTong and received those business licenses that we are interested in. We have translated everything ourselves, with our own resources (SunLi and a staff member of the Investment Office, YangMei (杨枚)), have these translations just officially confirmed (took five minutes and a stamp process) and we did not need any advisers nor lawyers. Together with the officials we have filled in all forms, passport photos taken of me and get everything filed, stamped, sealed and accepted, all in the course of a day, for a fraction of what was previously known to me as a minimum fee. I paid no more than 2,500 RMB for everything, we did not even pay for dinner nor lunch, and then I was general manager of a Chinese company.

The next step is to get the work permit for the German general manager so he can receive in China a salary from his company. The condition for the required permanent visa would be met.

First I have to carry out a medical examination. The staff member, YangMei, who has assisted us the day before with the procedure of company registration is today helping in the health office, or wherever I happen to be there. It is a multi-storey building, on the ground floor you have to register and pay a fee, there are dozens of people waiting and pushing. I am a kind of VIP, for YangMei manages to get within minutes the routing slip and the examination result booklet. I gave her the money for the fees.

Now we go to the upper floors for blood sampling, ECG and eye check. Overall, I have to pass more than half a dozen stations, I decide in each case for that doctor room in front of which the shortest row is waiting. Very quickly I'm learning not to wait outside the door, but to go in and put the examination booklet down on the table. Just as fast I discover that I must make sure it will remain lying on top, under no circumstances I must tolerate it to descend.

In order to do so, you remain as close as possible to the table of the examining doctor and draw out your own book from the heap again if another was laid on top. It is a friendly tailgating competition. All those waiting are interested in what is done to the poor patients now examined and what may be found. And what the doctor says is eagerly commented.

Especially the eye test provokes a lot of laughter if the candidate misinterprets something, guesses wrongly or makes a joke. The doctor joins the fun, there is a relaxed festive mood, here are all of us virtually simultaneously examined. When it's my turn, everyone is anxious to see if I can read the numbers and what I will say. With my first rudimentary handling of Chinese language, I defend myself bravely. Appreciative murmur of the bystanders.

For ECG, there are now a few rules to be obeyed. First, four women are admitted, the door is closed, after which it is the turn of four men, at some point I'm with some others, too. Each group of four will discuss in detail what results the examinations have shown.

At the end of the day, only the blood results are still missing. YangMei will retrieve it tomorrow morning in person, she was promised that it would be it is preferably treated for me ... I enjoy a preferential treatment without any compensation, for once again I cannot even pay for lunch, because YangMei returns to her office.

Then I have to travel to the employment office in NanJing (南京), the provincial capital. After an interesting train ride, we finally come to a modern building that is bursting from a crowd. But not of such people who want to be imparted by labour office officials, but there is a job market in the hallways! Many companies have set up little stalls offering jobs, people go from stall to stall and ask. The labour office is clearly not meant to impart jobs to unemployed people but to help companies fill their vacancies.

I am waiting in the hall, because we have met with a staff member of the Office of Investment in NanTong, she will help us to gently jump over the bureaucratic hurdles. Already she is filling in forms that I finally sign.

During these activities I am interested looking about at the busy activity and suddenly find myself besieged by a TV camera. A beautiful young Chinese woman behind a microphone asks me (but actually SunLi because I do not understand) what kind of job I was looking for at the job market, which of the company vacancies I considered the most interesting.

She is disappointed that I – being a foreigner and thus suggesting such a nice story for the local television – am not at all looking for a job, but already have one and just want to obtain a work permit. I think that's a shame, too, because who does not want to be presented at least once in life on local television of NanJing?

Some time the mission is accomplished, everything within a single day, and I feel a little dizzy thinking of all those consultants who told me how difficult and above all expensive that would be, and that I should definitely get some or other experienced (read again: expensive, but that's the way it was) China consultant, by no means a minor, cheap individual consultant, for these chaps know nothing and have no connections. I got no adviser at all, but via a friend with whom I did a photo exhibition I stumbled into an investment show in NanTong, where I actually thought to have to visit temples and old city walls but not industrial parks, well, and that just set the avalanche in motion.

At the police station of NanTong I finally have to request my visa. We are guided by our new local tax adviser whom also the office has appointed to us, it is a small company ('HuaDa' 华达) advising some Chinese and Japanese companies in NanTong. Soon we had agreed on a price for accounting and tax services (including wages, remitting income tax both for me and for the first staff, soon to be extended). Virtually from now on we can transfer salary payments.

But how is it all to be settled, who will arrange for bank transfers, 'sign' documents for the tax office? For doing any of this we need the company stamp, where should I leave it? Take it to ShenZhen? And lug it to Germany every time, too? Then we can perform any kind of business just by FedEx or EMS, that would be safer for the company (taking those stories into account that were told to me when travelling with Chancellor Schröder several years ago), but probably completely impractical. After agonising musing and much discussion with the new tax consultants I make a decision. I will give to the accountants a leap of faith and the company stamp, and I will allow them to carry out all transactions on behalf of the company, but only after prior approval by me, and that will be recorded. I rely on my ability to govern any problems with the help of my friend, YeDan, and his friend in the investment advisory office of NanTong (i. e. not with the courts). They were my trustees. I was right.

Now HuaDa's responsible staff member assists us in the visa application. A grim police General – we call him in English that way, but only in whispers – is residing opposite us. Indeed he is sitting one metre more elevated while we are standing down at the counter. We fill in the form several times in succession, because every time something is missing or wrong. Finally, HuaDa's employee has to leave for another customer, he does not have that much time. SunLi takes over and succeeds after a while in moving the 'General' to assist us in filling the right fields with the right information.

Now there comes the real terror: I may retrieve the pass not before five days from now ... Say what? I cannot fly without a passport even from ShangHai to ShenZhen, let alone to Germany, my return flight will leave in three days! 'Well, then we cannot issue a visa.'

Now a long discussion begins, we ask and beg. SunLi calls YangMei, speaks words into the phone that I do not understand, only her pleading voice I am able to acknowledge. Shortly after the General receives a call. Suddenly he withdraws without comment into the back rooms, comes back after a few minutes and carries the required documents under his arm, in a large envelope.

He indicates to us that we shall follow him. We share a taxi ride to the police headquarters. It is already closed. We enter through the back door. Only a few officials are still in the offices. The General asks us to wait. We watch him wandering with the documents from one office to another. After half an hour he comes back to us and gives me the pass with an unlimited two-year visa.

He accompanies us out of the back door, for the first time that day he smiles, receiving our effusive thanks but refusing everything else. SunLi tells me now that YangMei had only promised her to call the General, otherwise she could not make us sure of anything. SunLi and YangMei have made friends within these few days, despite the significant difference in age. But even I with my sparse knowledge of Chinese was able to recognise that the two of them got on well. And by the way it helped me a lot to remove all hurdles from my road without my own initiative.

Nature in the juggernaut city

ShenZhen is not a national park, it is not an ecological model city. It is a juggernaut of city with more than 1.7 million cars, China number One in cars per capita density (even before BeiJing and ShangHai! ShenZhen is simply huge, extending across 2,050 square kilometres, that is about one-eighth the size of the German federal state of Schleswig-Holstein which, however, is inhabited only by about a quarter to a fifth of the population (less than three million) in comparison to ShenZhen (12 to 15 million). Here, 30 to 40 times more people are living per square kilometre than in Schleswig-Holstein. The roads are crowded and I am often stuck in traffic jams. Riding by bike to the football pitch just takes me only about ten minutes more than by taxi: the costs saved have already amortised my bike, even if you reckon that it was stolen (apart from the associated health effect, which, however, again saves on the German health care system). A recent study found that ShenZhen has the fifth highest population density in the world.

That does not leave much space for green and nature. Yet it is possible to find some.

The city has everywhere applied smaller or larger parks. There is for example „SiHai GongYuan", the Four Lakes Park, but the literal translation ("hai" means "sea" or "ocean", but not "lake") is a splendid exaggeration, because in this park no „lakes", no "sea" and especially no "oceans" to speak of have been created but merely some slightly larger ponds, yet ponds they are. The first two Chinese characters in the park name 四海公园 also mean "the whole world", and for me, surprisingly, in a figurative sense "to be loyal to his friends." Whatever the true meaning of this name might be – at least the people here love this park, and I do, too.

Another park is called the Lotus Blossom Hill Park (LianHuaShan GongYuan, 莲花山公园), a park extending across 150 hectare, beautiful, sometimes (deliberately) overgrown, comparable in size to the Lychee Park (hardly overgrown, more "orderly", with numerous small squares for many kinds of sport such as table tennis, badminton, etc.).

And then there is the Mangrove Park (HongShuLin GongYuan, 红树林公园), which is integrated into a larger mangrove reserve. I was told that the mangroves had been almost destroyed, for the coastal road, one of the three major parallel multi-lane highways that are dissecting ShenZhen from east to west (and back) was planned right along the coast, but the plans provoked an uprising, so that finally the road was not only relocated a few hundred metres inland but also screened with several metres high walls from the mangrove forest and the adjacent scrub further inland. Along a distance of about six to eight kilometres, the coast is not accessible at all, not even for park visitors.

Seven days a week, weather reasonably permitting, the parks are crowded or just full of people. They meet here to play chess, cards, mah-jongg, badminton, fly kites, let their children or grandchildren play, flirt and kiss, fish, jump around in the mud or catch worms and snails from the shallow shore water, depending on age, preference, situation, season or time of day. On weekend evenings there is dancing, often till late into the night. Many hundreds of people participate in any activity, actively or passively, dancing or watching. The village meets to dance.

In each park people sing and play music on the weekends, there are small and large bands, here is a chorus of eight, over there three musicians are found, in another corner a large orchestra with one or two singers is playing. And somewhere remote you can find one single singer, for example, maintaining one single sound, for minutes, as long as breath will last. Nobody is surprised, everyone may do here what he desires. A practising session in the park, alone with a standard violin, a corresponding Chinese instrument or a flute, playing etudes and stumbling the gamut up and down, is anything but uncommon.

One exception is the YangTaiShan SenLin GongYuan (羊台山 森林公园, approx.: Plain-of-Sheep Hill-Forest-Park), rising some 500 m which make it the second highest hill of ShenZhen. The name derives from the fact that on the flat summit (the "plain") a number of very large rocks is lying, one of which looking like the head of a sheep. At this summit, the Japanese invaders met particularly long resistance in 1937/38, until the Chinese had to submit here as well.

Here you can enjoy real peace, because only few people find this mountain at all (the access is not marked well, and the hill is not very popular), and few people want to "climb" or walk up there. I have done it once, persuading Fang ShiFu to drive me and giving him leave to join me or not – he joined with enthusiasm, he did not know the hill, either. I had chosen a very hot day, no: not really chosen but it happened by chance that I was free on a very hot day between two July days of heavy rain.

When I gathered from the weather report that it would not rain or only briefly, I decided to go there. Temperatures rose to 35 °C, humidity to 95%, and the T-shirt and my shorts stuck to my body. We met only young people, after all, there were holidays and semester break at the university, but maybe there was only a total of 50 people during those four hours that it took us to the first summit (2,470 steps), and back. The second, actual peak (at about the same height) we did not make any more, we would not even try, it would have been an exaggeration.

Not only did we feel the strain on those sometimes very steep stairs. Also the author of a graffito on one of the small pillars that support the railing had probably been close to despair and saved himself into sarcasm: '山上有美女冲啊, shan shang you mei nü chong a!' – 'On the hill there's pretty gals, hurry up, gah!' (There's no girls up there, I checked that much).

We had a splendid view down on ShenZhen and in the distance to the highest hill of ShenZhen (the WuTong) which is a must-see for every resident, I have not been there yet.

It was a beautiful (very demanding) hike, essentially through forest, with very different trees. With almost all of the small groups of youthful climbers we exchanged a few words, many wanted to be photographed with me, the exotic guy, it was very funny.

In contrast, all other parks are always very well attended. Few people notice that among the trees and shrubs and on the flowers and blossoms there is a surprisingly diverse insect and bird life. ShenZhen's population is not particularly attracted by nature nor developing interest in it. For the people, parks are places for meeting and recreating (also oases of calm, though almost everywhere the traffic can be heard roaring more or less), centres of social life in a pleasant contrast to the bustling business life in the city.

To the birds and butterflies it does not matter whether or not they are found, observed and admired. But for me it was a wonderful surprise to find these places.

Few people discovered that right in the middle of the megalopolis of ShenZhen, the Four Lakes Park features not only an extremely well-stocked tea house, but also that this tea house has a nondescript patio at an even more insignificant pond #5 out of the four, not worth mentioning, with absolutely ugly (and partially broken) plastic chairs at no less ugly round plastic tables.

But right there a huge bamboo bush is growing with an incredibly active bird life (especially in late afternoon), above all sheltering my favourite birds from ShenZhen, the red-whiskered bulbuls, being in my view extremely funny birds. I simply like them. Strange that hardly any Chinese in ShenZhen knows about these conspicuous and noisy birds seen in every park, in each settlement where more than ten trees are growing, in almost every road that has a continuous row of trees, and of these there are actually many in ShenZhen!

Only the patient tea drinker who for once does not edit mails and texts on his laptop in a taxi, a bus, an aeroplane or a lounge will notice the following ornithological show: during breeding season, announced by the characteristic short whistling sound, a common kingfisher in brilliant blue plumage comes a-flying, catches a small fish from this inconspicuous pond and veers off toward the surrounding skyscrapers – where may it breed, I wonder? I thought it needs cliffs along rivers, streams, where it may dig a cave? Where does it find this in ShenZhen?

And the common kingfisher is not the only member of its zoological family which you may find in ShenZhen if you do not restrict yourself to licking ice-cream, flying kites or photographing the family: especially in the Lotus Blossom Hill Park I have seen relatives of the kingfisher every time I have been there, and still I wonder: Where and how do they breed in ShenZhen?

In the Four Lakes Park it seems to be the same (or a very similar) species that we have in Germany. Sometimes it shows up only briefly, fishes out of the tiny pond some – perhaps dirty – little fish; sometimes it misses the poor prey and then sits down on a "raised stand" which is suspended above the water, just a few metres from myself. I am deeply happy every time I can witness this.

As much as I curse myself every time for not having brought a camera just then but just this stupid work laptop! And whenever I come with a camera, the kingfisher will let me down. But the images in my head – I'm working on e-mails, on a presentation, on a patent application, having an excellent green tea in a glass, sitting at a quiet spot in the park, at a small pond, a few metres off the bulbuls are romping in the bamboo, before me a kingfisher is sitting on a branch of bamboo – I will not forget that.

» **The kingfisher with the freshwater shrimp**

Finally, I have good luck. The light is unfavourable because of a heavy cloud cover so that I have to operate my 400-telephoto lens without a tripod and thus slightly too long exposures, the resulting images are slightly blurred. But after processing I discover a surprise: The kingfisher is not hunting small fish, but freshwater shrimp!

During almost each of my visits to the Lotus Blossom Hill Park ("LianHuaShan GongYuan"), I was able to observe large kingfishers, much larger and differently coloured than 'my' specimen, and sometimes I could take pictures.

Everywhere you can find butterflies. This is probably the most difficult to photograph, especially of these busy guys are aloft. They do not follow any track, they flutter here or there, they stay a little or they don't: who can tell, how can you follow with the camera?

There are amazingly many species of butterflies, small and large and very large, modestly plain or colourful or strikingly stunning ones. It's fun to try to photograph them in flight, and it is fun to exchange a few words with some of the many people who watch and enjoy my "hunting". Again and again I am asked to show them my camera, because they have small compact digital cameras to photograph their girlfriend or their children, but I am using a large, heavy digital SLR of the kind professional photographers are applying.

In late spring and summer there are many places in ShenZhen, not just parks but wherever there are meadows and trees with a small depression, where after heavy rainfall a charming chorus of frogs begins to sing. A football match under floodlights after a tropical rain can be a game with cheers by Frog vuvuzelas! Unfortunately I never managed to see any of these frogs, even those who are every 30 seconds booming an incredibly loud, low individual "hhuuoooonnng" sound like a ship's horn. Accordingly, I never managed till now to photograph this ship's horn frog (or other), it is very shy. I imagine that it would be at least 20 centimetres tall, but maybe it is quite small? No less impressive are the cicadas' orchestras which perform particularly in parks but also in smaller groups of trees and in the afternoon make a deafening noise. And would you, if you did not know better, expect such volume from such tiny creatures?

In Germany I have seen fireflies for the last time 45 years ago. In ShenZhen, I can watch them in the summer in some places almost every night.

"HongShuLin GongYuan", the Mangrove Reserve, is a special place. It is not only an urban park, but a national park, the smallest national park of China. It lies in a bay across from HongKong, where at the other side there also is a mangrove reserve. Thousands – and in spring and autumn, when the migrating birds are passing by, tens of thousands – of birds are living and resting here. Here I have seen the only fish eagle I ever found in China moving above my head, most interestingly toward the inland. Also I have seen there the only spoonbills ever, and I did so more than once. These are black-faced spoonbills, a very rare breed, very endangered and occurring only on East Asian coasts. Just a little more than 2,000 individuals are left, spread over at least eight separate populations.

The many herons, avocets and wading birds are wonderful to watch, especially at low tide when the tidal flats are laid bare.

A really unusual feature is the botanical garden ("XianHu ZhiWu Yuan" 仙湖植物园). I visit it at least once a year, in contrast to the parks of which some are within walking distance, other are easily accessible by bike or bus. It is farther away and quite large, extending across 590 hectares. Therefore, I take almost every time a whole day off for a visit, and I can only do that very rarely.

The botanical garden is located in a hilly area of ShenZhen, which includes the highest hill ("WuTong") of the city area. The park was planned and created simultaneously with the city itself, the pristine nature has been incorporated as much as possible. It covers fifteen different sections, divided by type of plant. This is not man-made display garden with labels on each plant, but a territory developed out of what was already there and a large area where serious botanical research and conservation are performed, particularly in terms of endemic plants, which are those that occur only in southern China. Thousands of species of trees, shrubs and flowers are growing, so to speak, all by themselves. It is breathtaking.

I am astonished again and again that this large protected area attracts ordinary people, including especially those who have no interest in "nature", but just want to relax, meet, have fun – school classes, student gatherings, companies, families, youth organisations, individuals and groups of friends.

In the centre of this park there is Fairy-Tale Lake, "Xian Hu". Although this is indeed is a botanical garden, simple "pleasures" are offered, too – you can go pedal boating on the lake and having fun, and lots of young people use it extensively for racing and sprinkling each other with water. The garden's purpose is to enhance understanding of nature and the aims of its conservation. The many herons and other birds that live here do not mind that the many young people here do not pay attention to them but just photograph each other and enjoy endless fun. When writing, I notice that all these people are often picnicking on a central meadow, but although it is not really prohibited no one will drink beer or other alcoholic beverages, never I have seen drunk people here, which indeed would not be surprising with groups of youths, corporate outings and the like, but here it does not appear to exist. Yet there are no other guards or supervisors visible who would ban anything.

The range of southern Chinese and southern Asian plants also includes more than seventy palm species and more than sixty bamboo species. Some palms I am able to distinguish – but seventy of them? Or sixty kinds of bamboo? I cannot tell.

In another area about 200 rare and endangered plant species have been settled. I consider most impressive those corners where shade-loving plants are thriving, here it is dark and cosy. The air in ShenZhen often suffers a humidity of 90% or more, and after ten metres outside the house you are completely wet from sweat. Here in this cool corner it drips down to a certain extent. Ferns, begonias, orchids are found, and for me, best rest and relaxation.

Although 170 species of lotus flowers are advertised here, I have found the loveliest ones in urban parks. In my Four Lakes Park or even more so in the Lotus Blossom Hill Park, it is simply overwhelming to see how the lotuses, together with water lily, sometimes completely overgrow the ponds, span a vast umbrella of many colours and attract insects in such abundance that their whizzing almost seems to drown the nearby traffic noise.

And if you watch attentively, you may observe in-midst the sea of lotus flower the Chinese versions of the wagtails or my friends, the red-whiskered bulbuls, fluttering back and forth and hunting for food.

I am not surprised that the Botanical Garden also features all kinds of mango trees and 30 species of lychees, more than may be familiar to the highly literate fruit seller, ChaoMiao (whom I will introduce to you soon). Although lychees are among my favourite Chinese fruits, I have never seen the different species growing on trees, except for one species that I also buy from my fruit seller. Here, as in the parks, people are allowed to harvest them themselves and take them home (in one park, you pay, I think, twenty RMB, or about 1.5 Euro, and you may fill your bags, in other parks you may take as much as you find).

I love strolling around in relaxed fashion, camera in hand, sometimes I take images of ferns, sometimes of palms or of desert plants and cacti. I always watch people and enjoy their active social life in this botanical garden, even though they do not "seriously" want to study the botany, let alone the birds and insects, but only their friends, their girlfriend, their granddaughter. And, I ask you: In which botanical garden in Germany may you just go fishing? Not only from the bank, but even from a boat?

And in what park in Germany may guys (in that case that I could observe they were about seventeen years) climb into the trees and pick mangoes? This way I have even noticed for the first time what mango trees are indeed looking like, I have spoken with the guys and got two fruits for a present, still green, they ripened in my apartment and tasted delicious.

» **One of the many bees that are interested in the lotus flowers.**

» Lotus flowers in the Park of Four Lakes.

» A grandfather is playing Go with his grandson at the fifth pond of the Four Lakes Park, right in the back that huge bamboo in which a large flock of red-whiskered bulbuls is screaming and spending the night.

» Male red-whiskered bulbul with minor

» The whizzy red-whiskered bulbuls are all the time in motion and make a hell of a noise.

» A butterfly

» Butterfly, flying

» A species of swallowtails.

» Young people are posing for photos with their friends at the botanical garden at Fairy-Tale Lake

» Countless "I was here" pictures are made at a memorial for Deng XiaoPing. He initiated and accelerated the economic reforms, for which he is named father of the boom city of ShenZhen, and he himself planted this tree.

» Which one of the four beauties is the most beautiful?

» Two visitors to the Botanical Gardens go fishing on Lake Fairy-Tale.

» Two youths harvesting mangoes in the trees of the HongShuLin Park.

» In the Four Lakes Park chess and much more is played like everywhere else.

» This older gentleman in the lychee park watches a music video playing on his laptop, sings to it with microphone and speaker, to his left are notes in case that he does not know how to go on, and it does not bother him that he has no listeners, they are standing 20 metres behind him and listening to another, larger orchestra elsewhere, no one seems to be disturbed by the musical interference.

» A thrush-like bird in the lychee park

» A white-throated kingfisher, about twice as large as the European kingfisher, in the Lotus Blossom Hill Park.

» The smaller common kingfisher, sitting on a pergola of the tea house, …

» ... and taking off...

» ... to the next hide.

» Very hard to detect in the city, not easy to be photographed: the brown shrike.

» Even harder to detect, still more rare: the black-faced cuckoo shrike, mainly prevalent in Australia, that it showed up in a Chinese city was a huge surprise for me!

» This little bird is seen in parks quite often, but taking pictures is challenging, for it is persistently in motion: the Japanese white-eye.

» Another surprise: in a ShenZhen park, on a pond, I met some black-headed mountain finches, relatives of the European bullfinches and grosbeaks. The mountain finches actually live in the mountainous regions of Kazakhstan, Afghanistan and in the high mountains of western China.

» A little egret on the sea has recently caught a small fish in flight by scouring across the shallow water and plunging his bill down at the right moment; on the photo you do not see the head, but the reflection in the water reveals head and beak and the fish in the beak.

» The black face spoonbill, a most rare species anywhere in the world, lands near the coast at the „HongShuLin GongYuan" (Mangrove Park) in shallow water ...

» … a second one joins, and they spoon up in the shallow water near the mangroves for food by pushing the half-open beaks laterally through the water. As soon as they feel something delicious in the beaks, they close them and swallow.

» The peach blossoming in the botanical garden offers for a few days a stunning red flowerage. The first blossoms appear before the first leaves.

» Everywhere bees are buzzing, roaming for nectar.

» Not only the individual blossoms are impressive, but also the abundance of peach trees (here shrubs throughout, rather than trees) offers the viewer a veritable red flower ocean.

» The peach blossoming enjoys all over China a long tradition. Peaches have been cultivated here for several thousand years. Only about 1000 years ago they came to Central Europe. In China the peach is a symbol of long life. The peach blossoming has yet another meaning, though: an unmarried person (being at least a bit superstitious) looking for a partner shall walk three times around a flowering peach tree, then her wish will come true …

Minor entrepreneurs

ChaoMiao (朝苗) was born in ChengDu (成都) in the province of SiChuan. There she goes to school, both their parents are postal workers without much ambition. At home everything is OK, but not very exciting or stimulating. She is in love with books, reading all day. But because she only reads and otherwise does not learn, her final grades are not enough to be able to attend a university. She would be rejected everywhere.

Her boyfriend lures her to ShenZhen: ‚There you can do everything, be everything!' She wants to continue learning, studying, finding out about the Chinese literature which is so rich! But while her boyfriend is determined, graduates on an engineering school and finds a job, she is still searching and cannot find her way.

Her friend has soon enough of feeding her, his income is not princely, but sufficient, yet he wants to get more and in that feels restrained by his girlfriend. He kicks her out. Now she is on the road, must immediately find an apartment and speaks first to her friends. One invites her to sleep at her apartment during the first few nights, but soon she has to find her own place.

Her friends ask around, one of them knows a young woman who lives with three others in a larger apartment, one of them is just moving out, a room becomes available. The room is a few square metres wide, equipped with very basic furniture, but it is enough, ChaoMiao is satisfied.

Her three flatmates are working, she now has to search even more determined, so much is obvious to her. The four of them talk a lot during evenings, sometimes they meet with young men, alone or all together. Other young men join them, one of them has already one or two eyes on ChaoMiao. He also has no regular job. They talk.

He proposes to start up a business together. ‚What business?' – ‚We can sell fruits on the street!' – ‚Where we should get the fruits?' – ‚I have a friend who is working for a wholesaler, we buy there in the morning, we drive around and sell on the street.'

So they set out, with a bike that has a front display case and a stable stand. Soon they buy a second bike and find a road in NanShan (南山, a quarter of ShenZhen), where they gain a loyal clientèle. ChaoMiao finds that she has taken it well – she can read for hours while she is waiting for customers, only when it rains, she has a problem. But then they have no customers, either.

To accommodate for the rain they have to think up something. But first there is a little different turn: ChaoMiao moves out from the young women's residential community, and with her fruit dealer business partner she has found a cheap simple two-room apartment in NanShan, they move in together and ponder whether they should marry. ‚Let's wait a little, we don't know each other well enough yet.' – ‚But I mean it serious', her partner says. ‚Wait, I won't run away,' she says.

It goes on like that for a few years, they save very carefully (except for the books which ChaoMiao buys and devours but resells in second-hand book-stores). One day per week ChaoMiao visits her favourite temple, she insisted on once per week not having to be on the road and selling fruit.

On this day she is always found in the Book City (书城 ShuCheng), the great, fantastic book-store in NanShan which is her temple. On four floors is offered here everything the book lover is looking for, whether old or young, male or female, child or adolescent, lover of old or new books, preferring digital or analogue, and interested in no matter what literary or technical specialisation, up to musical instruments, music sheets, CDs.

She would like to come here on Sundays, too, for then there are the most interesting things going on, but on Sundays they have the most customers on the road, meaning they have to wage priorities.

Like all Chinese, she loves to poke around in this Book City and to spend hours sitting on the floor and first carefully examining today's pre-selection of books. To do this, they want to be read in peace! She is by far not the only one here, everyone reads his or her books in advance a bit before buying.

And on Sundays the corridors are full of children reading, chattering, running back and forth, and that she finds so beautiful but can rarely enjoy (only if it rains quite awfully). It is perfectly normal, no seller would intervene here, not even against children at play ('Hush, will you be quiet, this is a book-store, you have to be quiet!' This is a sentence that does not translate into Chinese and does not exist in Chinese).

She buys at least one book a week which must be thick, or maybe three thinner ones. For she has much time for reading when waiting on customers, she reads everything of Chinese literature, ancient or modern.

After several years, the two fruit traders decide to open a „real" business: They buy a small minivan, not new, but used by a former shady taxi driver, a neighbour who cannot drive any more because of a back ailment. They get it for cheap cash, remove the two rear seats, insert wooden boards, buy five as much fruit, present it in the back and position themselves at the same intersection where they know their regular customers.

Now they can sit in the car during rainfalls, either in front or in the back under the open back door, sales are increasing. ChaoMiao can indulge her passion and read if the customers do not flock. Until late into the night.

ChaoMiao may be atypically fond of literature, but reading is a passion for most of the Chinese. She knows other road entrepreneurs, they see each other, they meet, but the various business groups keep to themselves. The literature-minded among the road entrepreneurs read for themselves, ChaoMiao at her fruit car, the bicycle carriers on their vehicles. The bicycle carrier entrepreneurs/card players meet on Sundays and public holidays and play cards among themselves, as well as the waste disposal contractors keep to themselves, though they are competitors, yes!

Some groups are sitting on the street, others take their carts. If someone needs them, they immediately jump and drive off. All of them are not so much competitors as they are partners, and it is always better for them to have the ear to the ground. Some transportation or relocation orders can be dealt with by two or three only, anyway.

LaoLao (姥姥, "Grandma"), as she is affectionately called not only within the family but also at work and on the street, is now 80 years old. Her husband has been dead for a while already. She was born to the old ShenZhen, spent her life as a fisherman's wife, first for decades on the various boats that she and her husband were driving over time, then at the sale of fish and seafood which her two sons brought ashore. Together with other fishermen's wives and fishermen she sold at the coast of SheKou where with the growth of ShenZhen increasingly affluent people gathered to get the very freshest (and very cheapest) goods, day in, day out, seven days a week each.

In recent years, this has become more arduous on the sand, often in the rain, so she moved to the market in SheKou, which is covered, and where in addition to fish and seafood of all types every other kind of food is offered that the customer may need and want to buy fresh – meat, vegetables, fruits, spices, live chickens, frogs, turtles, oysters which are grown under wooden rafts in the bay between SheKou and HongKong.

Her two sons are daily out with their small boats at sea, unless a typhoon is approaching. They are satisfied to work individually, not as hired fishermen on those big ships that are moored in the fishing port of SheKou at the quayside, these huge ships on which some eight or ten men are working! No, they do not make themselves dependent. Sure, they have never been able to make any great leaps forward, and sometimes when the fish did not want to be caught or when the customer did not want to be caught, either, resources got scarce, but they never gave up.

Two years ago it had been very bad when that typhoon hit HongKong and then raged across ShenZhen. All boats were securely moored in the fishing port, and the eye of the typhoon moved just across them. There was an eerie silence for more than half an hour. But before and after the passage of the eye, it was a huge storm, even in the port the waves beat metres high, several small boats drowned, including one of the boats of her sons. It took days before they had pulled it out of the mud again.

Each of her two sons has a daughter, one being more handsome than the other. The one – she always calls her „XiaoMei" (小美), my Little Beauty – helps her on the market. Grandma LaoLao is always proud of how the men look at her granddaughter, yes, she really is beautiful. And LaoLao has nothing against the fact that some customers are now apparently buying from her as well or only because of her granddaughter. The other sells the daily catch on the small fish market at the beach, and she is very pretty, too, she is called „XiangMei" (香美), you may translate that as the Fragrant Beauty. Whether this stuck from the smell of fish that is sticking to the whole family (and is not a bad thing by itself), or from the fact that after a shower she might smell so pleasantly, Grandma LaoLao does not want to comment on that, because after shower not many people have yet been able to examine her second granddaughter with respect to her odour, that she will surely hope.

Actually, Grandma LaoLao had hoped a bit that her grandchildren would turn to a different career. But as very young girls when they were fifteen years old and then slightly older, they have only hung around with the boys in SheKou, the manners were turning ever stranger, like that it did not use to be. Sometimes they were even for a short time with foreign boys or later even with adult and older foreign men! That was really impossible, who knows what happened! But now they are both just over thirty, both are married decently, and because they have learned nothing else they are also fishermen's wives and sell seafood. But Grandma LaoLao is now also a little proud of that, and she does not know what she should be more happy about: what is now or how it might have been if her grandchildren had learned better and taken other jobs, perhaps in a clean supermarket or in a bank?

Good thing she has always admonished her granddaughters. Even today, she does it every now and again, ‚for safety, you never know,' and she reminds them of the inglorious times. The grandchildren will groan in unison: ‚LaoLao, that was last century! We were little girls then!', and they are not completely wrong about that, and Grandma LaoLao responds: ‚You're still little girls!', about which granny is objectively wrong!

Ever again she is happy that her sons are not as crazy as many men in their environment. Everyone wanted to have only sons, but her sons were also satisfied as they each got a daughter, and so in quick succession. Both love their daughters. And if you look closely, being a woman has always been the better option in life, Grandma LaoLao silently muses, and particularly now in modern China where there are fewer and fewer women.

The few young girls are being courted even more than she was back then, how wonderful that ought to be! But what about the millions of guys who cannot find wives? Grandma LaoLao is not someone who constantly thinks about politics, if she is honest, she does so almost never. Much less she thinks about population policy. But when she hears that there will soon be not only millions but tens of millions of young men in China who cannot find wives because there are simply too few women, she is turning thoughtful and even more pleased that she is having two such beautiful granddaughters.

But will there be enough countries to which China's surplus in guys may emigrate to, are there perhaps countries that have too many women? Then we could make up for that internationally, she muses, as we export so many Chinese products and import oil and iron ore, we could theoretically import women and export men, „of course only on a voluntary basis!"

When Deng XiaoPing was still alive, he who unfortunately died much too soon, he would surely find a solution. He has turned poor ShenZhen into this huge modern city, too.

Following Grandma LaoLao's line of thought, we might actually come to believe that all women in China are finding a husband extremely rapidly, and it ought to go down with the devil if he should be Mr. Right, too, after all, there are plenty of them.

But unfortunately the world is not so, even in China.

Here we see ZhouYing 周颖, a good friend of SunLi. ZhouYing subscribes to the idea of "Self do, self have", everything she does and knows herself. Her bachelor of engineering allowed her to become self-entrepreneur with a small shop that is trading electronic components. Then she took on the distribution of a Canada based manufacturer. Now her office is too small, she has to move, because nine employees do not want to squeeze into 25 m² and listen to each other during loud phone-calls. Her major supplier, a very specialised high-tech company based in Toronto, also frequently sends along the founder and managing director, sometimes the marketing director or the chief financial officer. They need to have room as well.

ZhouYing is a powerful woman, she is successful, not outright beautiful but not ugly, either – and yet she has no boyfriend, no one whom she could or would marry. Now she wants to go to the Canada for at least a year – whether she will find someone there? She would like to win a foreigner as a friend and husband.

MaLi (马莉) is a friend of ZhouYing. MaLi does not live and work in ShenZhen, but in BeiJing. During her studies she has a platonic relationship with a student, she will let him off after he tells her one day: 'No one on the road turns after you, no one would recognize you, you're so average.' Apparently he wants to suggest she should be grateful that he is so merciful to her, but she interprets otherwise and enables him to move together with prettier girls. Her ex-boyfriend later marries one of her best friends, the two women remain in contact, but any attempt of her ex-boyfriend to reconnect is even less than ignored by her.

After the bachelor and master in engineering she quickly made another master in „theoretical physics", to then apply for a PhD in a field of astronomy, currently she is working on it. Along the way she works part-time as a translator for special literature (the PhD scholarship is a little short, she says) and for herself and her family and some friends she handles the daily purchases and sales in the stock market.

MaLi has two computers in operation at the same time, at the one she's working for her PhD (with right hand and left brain), on the other (with the vacancies) she is chatting (MSN, QQ), trades in stocks and makes translations. Any outsider might get the impression that she was 24 hours a day (and night) online, but this is probably exaggerated and hardly can be controlled, unless you want to go online yourself in the middle of the night and check out on her.

Without a doubt, MaLi is highly intelligent and academically successful. But apart from a years-long relationship with a man who did not decide between her and another woman, she was not able to establish in recent years any relationship with a man.

ZhouYing and MaLi are two non-comparable women with completely different appearance, demeanour and professional activity. Both have in common that they are intelligent (the second one most highly) and successful (the first one most financially). Chinese men do not like that, or: There are not many Chinese men who want to get involved with active, intelligent, confident and successful women.

Of which there are more and more in major cities – in BeiJing, there will be hundreds of thousands, in ShangHai as many, in ShenZhen probably half of that.

All friends and acquaintances of ZhouYing and MaLi make every effort to find them suitable partners, but successful procuration has failed so far because of two constraints: not only the men who are afraid of strong women, which in China is perhaps not different from any other country in the world, but also the two women who consider any proposed men too soft, too stupid, too dull, in every possible way not good enough. MaLi and ZhouYing have just high expectations ...

Procuration efforts run hot at times. An old college friend from BeiJing calls and asks ZhouYing if she could recommend someone in BeiJing. 'But she must be very very pretty, as a picture!', that is the lower limit below which should not even start to suggest. ZhouYing is not able to procure any 'very very pretty' girlfriend, sorry. But whether her classmate might recommend someone for her friend, MaLi, in BeiJing? No, sorry, all the others are either off the market or will "under no circumstances" have a woman who is scientifically so far above them.

For ZhouYing in turn, MaLi may do anything as well, because she does not know any foreigners.

ZhangMiao (张淼) is again another "case". She is very much with foreigners, because she is working all day as a freelance translator for conferences, travels, documents. First, she does not have time to look for a boyfriend, second, she is interested in foreigners only in view of their role as customers, not in any other possible roles.

She, too, is self-confident, critical, knows her own mind and is no appropriate partner who would wait on hand and foot for a Chinese husband wanting to be her lord. So she is another example demonstrating the problems of modern young women in China when trying to find suitable partners, even though they occupy a niche market. We will see that for men it is not that simple, either.

ChenLi (陈荔) is an independent artist (photography and visual) and lives in ChangZhou (常州). She is a friend of ZhangMiao, they have studied English together. ChenLi was for years with her boyfriend from college days, but somehow he disappointed her. She separates from him and discovers then that she prefers lesbian. First, she kept that secret even from her college friend ZhangMiao, but then she and her lover "make out". For several years they live together openly. Homosexual relations are by no means unusual in China any longer, at least not in the big cities.

Of course, not all the minor entrepreneurs of ShenZhen constantly worry about relationship problems. First of all they are laborious, brave, active and willing to take risks. Some of them do because they have had no other chance (ChaoMiao), others because they cannot imagine to work as employees (Grandma LaoLao and her sons, or ZhouYing and ZhangMiao), still others, such as MaLi, because they want to work in addition to their regular jobs, others again because they want to be rich, and ChenLi because she made her hobby into a career.

HaiQiang (海强) is someone who wants to get rich, but at the weekend he is football player in the "LaoNiu" team. There, he is the fastest and safest ball handler and can play all positions. He has an eye for goal, can play both outside positions and also organise the defence. If he is absent, the team is only half as strong. He plays football with the very same enthusiasm that he invests into his business. After he finished his studies, he has had an idea: He wants to sell high-purity cleaning and maintenance product for floors and windows, and his market shall be the electronics industry emerging in ShenZhen (and vicinity). He has no idea about this market nor of cleaning products. So he looks around, visits companies, asks what they need.

He perceives that these products are so far sold at rip-off prices. HaiQiang calls them "European prices," which is for him equal to "overpriced". He will cut the price by half and yet generate excellent profits. Everything with him is self-made – he looks for suitable staff, they are building the necessary equipment for the cleaning of commercial products (which as sold are not suitable for the electronics industry) and begin to introduce prospective clients to first samples for testing. Since he radically undercuts the current prices, the interest is large, he soon sells commercially relevant quantities.

After a few years, he is a wealthy (young) man, has 150 employees, he invites all his LaoNiu friends to the inauguration of a new company building so that they learn to know his staff as well. It is a casual happy gathering with loads of food, HaiQiang splashes out, serves lobster for everyone till nausea (and not just lobster). Without envy, everyone in the team recognises him as "our richest friend," they all know he has made it himself.

In contrast, HuXie (胡偕), as he is called at Tian Long, is rather dull. He barely manages to keep afloat with his business. He produces imitations of Adidas and Nike sports clothes, but because he is not the only one by far and because prices for imitations have hit rock-bottom, his is a tragic, dreadful business. HuXie lives up only when the team enjoys the joint dinner on Saturday night and when playing cards.

Our Korean player-coach in the TianLong team is a trader for rice. When you see him play football or hear him speak (both ways are reminiscent of a steam roller), you can hardly imagine that he is selling rice during the week. One might rather think that he was a building contractor, a foreman, a dealer of used cars or the like. He can talk about rice varieties and their differences as sophisticated and subtle as (legendary) Greenlandic Inuit about varieties of snow. He buys rice that is grown in northeast China and sells it in the south of China. ("Only the rice from the North is really good because it grows slower!") And once a year, he asks me if I would not like to import his rice to Germany (which I, being a chemist, consider myself perfectly unsuitable for).

ShenZhen is an El Dorado for minor entrepreneurs, whether they operate their business mobile or in rented premises.

There are thousands of hawkers offering fruit, drinks, honey, trinkets, self-carved handicrafts, clothes, laptops, mobile phones, haircuts, shoe and clothing repairs, transport and television repair services or fake tax receipts. They do business on the pavement, addressing drivers who are stuck in a traffic jam or chasing customer on their bikes (apart from hand-line readers and other charlatans who are sitting on plastic chairs for kids, making their living quite decently).

There are fixed street markets set up and there are hawking illegal markets which dissolve as soon as danger looms but a few hours later are as active as before.

There are buildings that offer markets on several floors under one roof, this can be a tea market or an electronics market, of which there are very many. The electronics markets are a typical phenomenon of Chinese entrepreneurship and flexibility. Here, the traders (mostly young people) rent a booth or "box" and offer their commercial products (mobile phones, laptops, computer accessories, GPS, digital cameras and optical equipment). If you enter such a building as a newcomer you are struck down, struck by hustle and bustle, decibels and diversity.

If you commit the mistake of not deciding immediately but trying other vendors (or even another market, next door or in a cross-road) first and then to return and buy that thing at that third booth in the first market, your attempt will fail: You won't find the booth again. What floor it was, are we in the right building? If so, in which corridor? It is obvious that you can trail these markets only using appropriate maps or expert guides, otherwise you are lost.

In nondescript side lanes of these bustling markets you may find (with patience and risk tolerance) ingenious craftsmen, if not artists, who may fix any hardware problem in any type of laptop. They will use either original parts, provided they are in stock or can be obtained quickly from friendly dealers, or they craft something suitable. If necessary, the laptop will be completely disassembled, without plan, without any assembly instructions.

The process resembles an open-heart surgery, only the boss of the repair crew performs such operations, his staff is allowed no more than to carry out the disassembly and reassembly and easy soldering. Nothing may go wrong, for there is a 30-day warranty. When LaoWei for the first time observes such an operation at his laptop up close, he does not believe that the poor device would ever be put back together correctly and work again as intended. He is mistaken, and becomes a regular customer.

An odd kind of market is the begging. Everywhere you may be besieged by beggars, in roadside restaurants, in the car at the semaphore, as a pedestrian on the pavement. No doubt there are many horrible stories behind, you see people with disabilities, leg or arm amputees, begging for their living.

But there also young children addressing you, sent by their parents (or by organised beggar gangs?). You see young mothers carrying their babies or small children before the belly or on the back, begging every passer-by, they can rend any heart of stone.

How to distinguish who really has suffered a bad fate and does not know how to make ends meet, or who professionally operates the begging? And the latter kind is not at all infrequent. Our Saturday dinner we fellow football players usually celebrate in a roadside restaurant where there are several such restaurants lined up like a string of beads. There are (as elsewhere in other districts of the city) certain beggars marking their territory.

One of my football friends once met a beggar whom he had given a small amount in the evening late at night again, with customers in a karaoke bar (in China called "KTV") – only that the beggar now had exchanged his 'working clothes' against a suit that was proper for KTV. I myself have several times seen two beggars from another territory in a Seven Eleven store which had set up a lounge for breakfast tea, coffee and snacks, exercising their "business meeting" in the morning.

So everyone can find his place, everyone has a chance, take it or miss.

» The literature-addicted fruit seller before her mobile fruit business.

» Children (and not just children) sit down in the breathtakingly large bookstore "Book City" (ShuCheng), on the floor or in chairs, or they stand around, reading extensively before they decide.

» A craftsman combines a break for smoking with productive work.

» This chicken seems to be suitable for sale.

» The shoemaker seems to be in gaol behind the bars, his wife lures customers and takes care that everything is paid.

» Juice is pressed from this liquorice, it is tasty and supposedly helps in any possible health issue.

» There are combs offered, the two experts try them first before mummy may decide.

» Mobile hairdressers in the street.

» If the bicycle transport service providers have nothing to do, they take deep naps on their "comfortable" vehicles (this man has not moved for more than two hours),

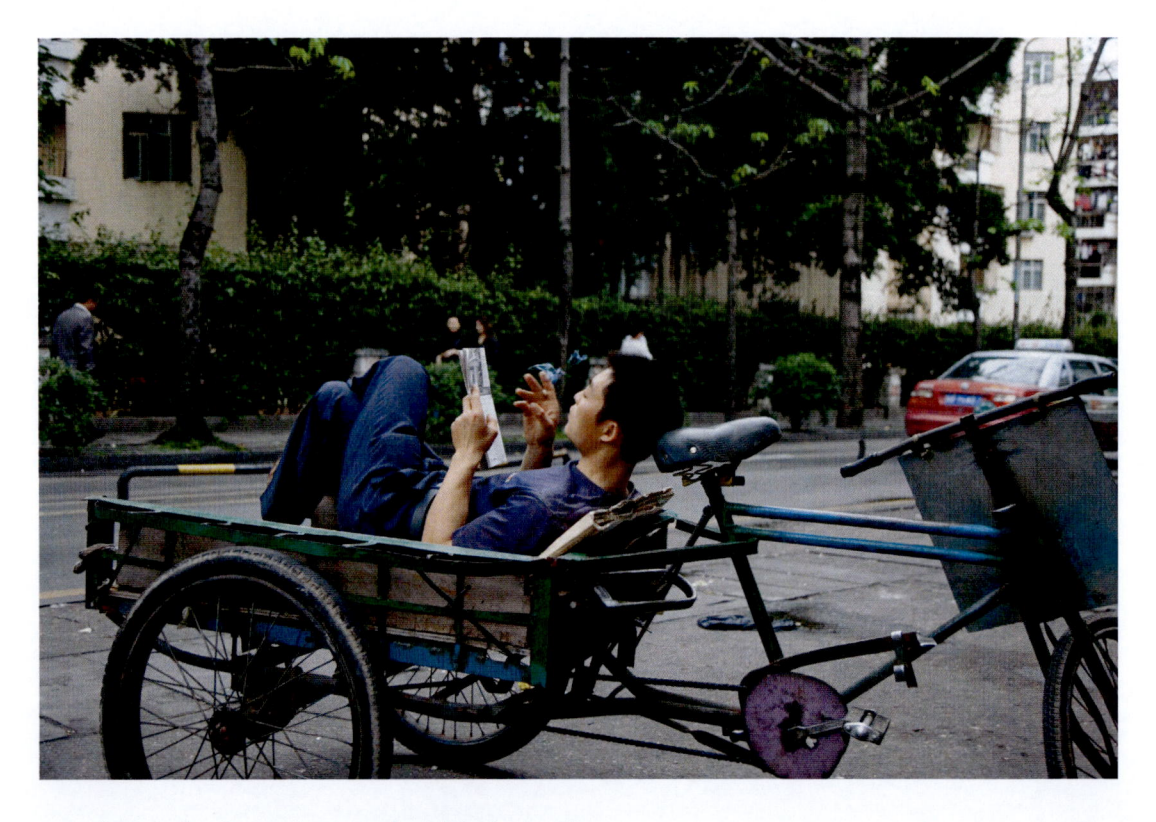

» or they make themselves comfortable for reading.

» A fortune-teller with a client.

» On the market: A large fish is cut into manageable pieces for a customer.

» Grandma LaoLao and one of her two beautiful granddaughters.

» Fishermen on the way home.

102

» After the typhoon: one of the many sunken boats in the port.

» The second of two beautiful granddaughters successfully negotiates with a customer on the small fish market at the coast.

The staff

But China is not all entrepreneurs, not even just independent street-folk like vendors, cobblers or barbers.

Although Chinese are very reluctantly working in dependence of others, most of them do it, anyway, no different than other people elsewhere in the world. To the benefit of those companies who offer vacant positions, including our own subsidiary in China. Now in all the guidebooks you will read very quickly and in the first place the same thing that you hear from all the China experts, being that the loyalty of Chinese staff to the company employing them is close to nil (if you want to have it euphemistically). You cannot even hire new people as fast as the staff switch from one company to another. Be happy if your own staff at least do not constantly work *against* the company employing them!

Well, I had to try for better or worse, for we needed to hire technicians, desiring to provide technical services in China, producing for our chemical processes that we develop in Germany, and exporting to China. So we searched and hired.

In the course of the past six years, we have hired and fired about a dozen young men and women, with six of them remaining at the end. These six cooperate as a solid team, they are precious gems and very loyal and committed.

We have not found them immediately; at first, after SunLi had become my first employee, we hired a number of staff who were slightly or fairly decently speaking English. But before long they gave in to the pressure – the pressure of problems, the pressure and the attacks of criticism from Chinese customers, the requirement to be available and respond within minutes and even at night, sometimes until well past midnight.

The secret of success in my view: I gave up the requirement that our staff should be able to speak and write in English.

Irritatingly, I heard and read later: Many Chinese companies, including HuaWei, do not hire Chinese who lived at some point during their life in the West, as a student or even professionally, nor any who had worked in China for a company with Western background. Their reasoning is: anyone who has been there is spoiled and wasted. The claims were to western standards, demanding to work a maximum of eight hours per day, free weekends, holidays, wages, benefits, protection ..., such claims are not satisfied with HuaWei.

There is another group of claimants: technicians and engineers who speak English well enough. They want to work in foreign companies. Cisco, IBM and Microsoft are offering good conditions, unfortunately most of the Chinese whom we first employed believed that our company was as rich and suffering equally little problems, that they could work with us as they believed they might work for Cisco, IBM and Microsoft.

And definitely the work requirements of HuaWei and Cisco China are different, fundamentally different. And our needs for manpower were as fundamentally different from those which are sufficient for Cisco and IBM China. So we have relied at the end on something completely different: You ask reliable friends, they ask around and recommend reliable acquaintances, no matter if they know to speak English, or, more precisely: they could hardly speak English, but performance, loyalty and competence were of importance. From now on I only hired staff who got a good judgement from reliable people, thus, in the end, former colleagues of former colleagues or former staff of customers.

And this finally solved our problem: these staff are still with us. Some of the previous we screened out. I cannot remember all of them, there were too many.

LiHai (李海) was lazy and cowardly. Whenever there was a problem to be solved, either the bus was late or the highway completely blocked for hours, so that 'it is no longer worthwhile even trying to drive to the customer.'

LuQiang (陆强) lasted less than four weeks with us, the stress at the customer was too high for him.

ChuFeng (楚峰) had acquired a German doctorate in chemistry. He could never accept the fact that our customers thought so rarely in scientific terms, that on the contrary they often had to be taught in basics. Nor could he understand that in a German company in China he was not supposed to work in accordance with German rules ("eight hours, overtime pay, no work at night and no work on weekends"), but according to the rules of the Chinese market, ultimately simply complying with the requirements of our customers, seven days a week for 24 hours and troubleshooting "right now", not in two weeks. We parted amicably after a year.

MaiDi (麦迪) was just too slow in every respect, and whatever she did not want to do she shoved off with a remark that this was not within her responsibility. As a last resort she was sick and "at least today" could not do that job.

So the search for staff was anything but easy, searching and screening was worth doing, however, and I have learned a lot from that. Some generally accepted opinions, such as: "Chinese people are all so extraordinarily eager," or, "Chinese people are disloyal to the employer," or, "You have to supervise Chinese in any respect, or they will steal everything, they are so tricky" appear to me not any longer such universally applying. All of this I do not perceive that way. At any rate I lost no employee whom I wanted to keep. All the others who had not proven themselves I gave every chance to improve, operating with transparent messages. Finally, those who did not fit us in their style of working went by themselves, I did not have to fire anyone.

Chinese employers and staff may, on average, be cleverer and trickier as Germans, I cannot judge that. As long as ingenuity and trickiness are applied for the benefit of consumers and company, I can only be grateful. Of that I have seen many examples. But unfair tricks and financial schemes (for example, charges of fraud or bribery, phony invoices, of which some amount vanishes on a black account) are to me an abomination, I would not witness them neither on the assets nor on the liabilities, and I have not witnessed any in my company, but I do know all too many examples from other companies in China.

In such companies ethical principles do not seem to apply. If the company leaders themselves fiddle with customers, exploit their suppliers, keep playing them off against each other and perform dirty tricks wherever they can, perhaps as well circumventing the tax office, who shall then expect internal loyalty and honesty from their staff?

WuJiao (吴姣) is a young woman in love with life and hard work. Since I do not want to have any nepotism in my little Chinese company, I emphasise that we will not employ her (she is a friend of SunLi). She works in a company that organises all types of events – company parties, product launches, large family gatherings, official receptions for prime ministers or dignitaries.

She is efficient, fast working, straightforward. This is not appreciated by her immediate superior who is fiddly and happy to blow up her work with words and reports more than is compliant with reality. With WuJiao it's vice versa, she uses very few words, because the work was indeed done and can promote itself.

Her superior starts to bully WuJiao. Minor and ever more vicious taunts spoil the day, until she quits one day without having another job. Now she calls all her friends, they arrange to meet for dinner and discuss the situation in detail. WuJiao actively applies to many companies.

Soon she is invited to Walmart, the interview is positive, she is only requested to send a certificate, then she will be hired. But where to get a certificate? The former company, and especially her former superior will issue none, at least not a positive one. WuJiao and SunLi get the idea to forge the certificate themselves. SunLi is as well available for a phone interview in a neutral tone, praising the virtues of WuJiao.

WuJiao is hired. Less than three months later, she quits: 'It's mind-numbing there,' she says. 'We just fill in papers forcing our suppliers to speed up deliveries and lower prices, one supplier is being blackmailed by alleged promises of another, that I will no longer comply with.'

Again she is out. Soon she finds a job as a teacher. After six months probationary period the contract is not renewed. Allegedly the students are not fond of her. She has grown too small, her stature does not promote her enough. After some back and forth her contract is extended after all.

WuJiao also is still looking for a friend. Despite the lack of women she does not find Mr. Right, and SunLi's various attempts at referring her are of no help, either.

Jun Yang (军扬), "Laptop Jun", an employee in a software company, is a very remarkable man. He is an old college friend of SunLi and an expert in computers, especially in software. Whenever I have a problem with my laptop (which is not uncommon), Laptop Jun will help. He never allowed himself to be even invited to dinner, if I would put water or tea, he only takes a few sips, the fruits that I'm offering will be left lying, he works on and on without a break.

Once there was a giant problem, it was difficult at all to locate the error. Laptop Jun could not be sent home, but by two o'clock in the night he sent me on my couch ("Go sleeping for a few hours!"), at six o'clock in the morning I woke up, Laptop Jun was still busy, 'I 'm almost done, I found the error, I shall go home and then in the company." He did not even allow me to make a breakfast for him.

Laptop Jun does not only give me aid, or SunLi, he helps everyone who needs or wants his help. Free and immediate. When he speaks, you think of machine gun fire. Meanwhile, my Chinese is quite o. k. for daily use, but his speech, ten times the rate of even an ordinary Chinese, is a profound challenge.

He is a genius and an incredibly nice guy. But he has no girlfriend.

SunLi has referred him already to two or three women, but each of them he "lost" – one because the girl doesn't like his boring way of caring, which is to make her computer powerful with all the fancy software while the girl has quite limited interest in computer performance, and another because he never told her that he found her actually quite nice (he insisted she did not tell him anything, either …).

Now, however, one last attempt has been made by SunLi and another friend of hers who has a colleague whom they both consider a 100% match to Laptop Jun. SunLi has arranged their meeting and appealed to Laptop Jun's conscience: 'You have to speak with her, you have to take the time, you cannot just work, and if you are bound by some support work for somebody else – tell her!'

Her friend meanwhile informed the colleague: 'He is a very nice guy, but he has trouble communicating. When he's not talking to you, that's no refusal, that's weakness and uncertainty.'

This time it works, the two marry in the summer. Actually, of all relationship problems I have so far witnessed this was one of the few which could be solved by all the matchmaking activities among friends and families which are endlessly notorious in China, one of the few that is known to me as having been successful.

LangLang and me inaugurate a new concert hall

One Friday evening I am sitting, as I almost always do, in a restaurant at the streetside. I like to sit outside at evenings (when I get home in time and it's not pouring rain) to eat or work at the laptop, and to observe life around me during dinner or working breaks.

This evening my observations are interrupted by a call. SunLi asks me: ‚Would you like to attend to a classical concert? The problem is that you have to queue for the tickets tomorrow morning, you cannot just buy them. LangLang will perform and play, no idea what.' I do not learn anything more, consent, however, and are informed: It's her friend WuJiao who has had this idea, and SunLi has no desire to queue for the cards, nor does she feel like attending the concert.

So I am just a substitute, so that her friend will not have to wait alone, let alone go to a concert without company, I am supposed to be the escort. I'm still thrilled by the idea. I am addicted to classical music and interested in the new concert hall and in witnessing a concert in China. The next morning, I'm half an hour before WuJiao at the meeting point to get me fit into the already growing queue, two hours before opening of the box office, I go to the organizers' table, ask for an explanation of the procedure, I get the number 169 and line up at the end of the queue which soon grows even longer behind me.

In Germany, I've never been queuing early in the morning to get pre-sale tickets for whatever concert. I have never before bought tickets for a classical concert (and I only attend to classical music or to jazz) without knowing what is on the agenda. And I have never visited a concert of LangLang in person, I don't like LangLang. He boasts a big show at the piano, he is arrogant, but I want to hear music, without any show.

However, I'll do it, I'm curious. The several hundred meters long queue makes three turns, the organizers have spent little plastic chairs, many people are sitting while waiting. Children run around and have fun. After an endless time the cash registers open, the children collect the chairs with delight and help the helpers; at some point it's the turn of no. 169. After a brief telephone consultation, we buy three tickets, for SunLi now wants to come after all. I pay for all the tickets, insisting. I'm getting more and more curious about the concert.

While visiting the new concert hall (which displays a surprising architecture) along with hundreds of enthusiastic families and their children, I am tracked down by local ShenZhen TV, for I am apparently the only foreigner here. So if I was not allowed to perform in NanJing before millions of viewers of the local TV, then now at last in ShenZhen, in front of yet more millions, how exciting!

I am asked what I think of this new concert hall, by which I am very impressed, by design, acoustics, architecture ... as if I had any idea. I hope I have not been talking complete nonsense.

In the evening I'm as excited as anyone who appears for the first time in front of millions on television. Especially since it is in China.

I am sitting at the telly, the tension rises, the show starts, and at once I get myriads of phone-calls – many of my friends and some of the staff seem to have watched the show at dinner, and now they discovered me!

A few days later, the concert is taking place. There is an elaborate pre-opening ceremony, the French architect of the building is assessed, the mayor is celebrated, cannons shoot something similar to confetti. Before the concert the audience talks, laughs or phone-calls loudly – then there is a message: Turn off all phones, no more talk!

The concert begins with "Les Préludes", then LangLang enters (after a grand piano was rolled in) and plays Chopin's Piano Concerto No. 1, it is very beautiful. After the break, my socks are knocked off by Rachmaninoff's famous Piano Concerto – highest standards of technical virtuosity, combined with moving most strikingly everyone who would listen even just a little bit.

But LangLang does not begin playing. He waits. He hears people talking, rustling, it bothers me, too. He turns to the audience and speaks very seriously with them. Now everyone is quiet. The concert begins, it is one of my favourite piano concertos. I am melting away.

Around me there are hundreds of listeners, the majority of which (unlike me who knows it almost by heart) probably is not familiar with the concert. Most of them are perhaps for the first time in a classical concert. LangLang has pointed out to them that one is supposed to listen, not to talk, eat chips or sunflower seeds, nor to phone around. They obeyed LangLang, and were carried away by him.

I am very impressed by everything, by the audience, the atmosphere of curiosity and open-mindedness, with all the children and families, and by LangLang who presents himself to me here in a totally different manner than I know him from television in Germany.

Later, in Germany, I have once again the opportunity to attend to him in a concert, together with an international youth orchestra, and once again he has really impressed me: It was very surprising to see how easily, naturally, casually he treated the young people who were only a few years younger than himself, but by orders of magnitude less famous, and as well us in the audience! How easily all broke and started again at a moment that was not played to the satisfaction of the conductor. I've changed my mind about LangLang at least about 50%.

» The interesting architecture of the new concert hall building.

» The children frankly marvel, the adults are more relaxed, although they are also impressed.

110

» SZTV is interviewing me.

» Shortly before the concert: The mother tells her son what will happen now.

» LangLang playing.

» After the concert, he talks to the audience.

I am trying to learn Chinese

During my first few months in China I felt like amputated. Nothing, absolutely nothing, not the least midget I could catch without an interpretor. No check-in in the hotel, not one order in a restaurant, not a small purchase of fruit on the street, apart from such "transactions" that were done with hands and feet.

It was obvious when I rented an apartment: The life and work here I cannot persevere if I will not at least learn a little bit of Chinese. And anyway I want to know the country and its people better and not only to work like an outsider and guest here, but "immerse" as well – and that is only possible when learning the language.

I bought books and computer programmes and kept stumbling along the first few difficult steps: the phonetic transcription system (pin yin), sounds or sound sequences of otherwise identically written syllables, fundamentals of the (relatively simple) grammar and the first Chinese characters.

For the holiday week centred around 1 May I am finally booking a crash course in a Mandarin school: five days, five hours a day, a teacher just for me. It is expensive. She is surprised that I want to learn the Chinese characters, too (‚But the other foreigners don't want that, and it is very complicated!'), yet I insist. And as I have already developed some of the basics myself, we are making good progress.

Enough! I want to have two hours training once a week, but it's only possible on weekends, I would prefer Sunday morning. The private school offers me two possible dates, either Wednesday at 3 p. m. or Friday at 11 o'clock, ‚then most of the aliens have already left for the weekend – you don't?' No, I am not leaving for the weekend Fridays at 11 o'clock, indeed not before 8 or 9 o'clock in the evening. During the week my working days take more than 12 hours, not rarely up to 16 hours. And often I am with clients on Saturday mornings or working through subjects left unaddressed.

I cannot participate on Wednesday or Friday in a Chinese language course. So for now I have to try advancing by autodidactic lessons. But it does not work, I am making hardly any progress.

Finally, about two years after my one-week crash-course in May, I discover in a store where I am often buying a print inviting to a private Chinese language course in my home area! I call the lady, LiLin, and she is willing to give me lessons on Sunday mornings.

This works well for two years. I am her most faithful student. All the students set out with enthusiasm, no one except me wants to learn the characters, too, most of them falter after three or four months. First, the hours are scheduled less often ("I have too much work to do!"), then they cease altogether. The initial euphoria turns quickly into disappointment when after the first advance further progress comes more slowly. Thus says LiLin, and she knows, she has taught aliens for many years in Chinese.

I do not understand why many other aliens do not want to learn Chinese at all, they would not even try. No question, it's exhausting, it's completely different from any European language. But if you are living here you would at least want to say or understand something, if only the most primitive basics?

One of our customers is a joint venture of an Italian and an American company. The son of the Italian "Cheffe" or boss lives with his family in China, establishing the joint venture. We get to know each other at various business meetings, find by accident that we are both football aficionados, and he invites me to a football game. He is living in a settlement where only aliens are dwelling, we are playing there on a small pitch, seven vs. seven, not a single Chinese but only Italians, Scandinavians, French, but no German except for me (and everybody is much younger than I).

He is a very good and aggressive player, trying at all costs to dunk goals against me but fails for a long time because in the tiny goal matching the tiny pitch I am even better than in the large goals, but eventually he succeeds. At least one goal thus I allow him to pass (not on purpose, obviously). So we are both satisfied at the end and having fun. After the game, I wonder how he gets along with his family in China. Initial attempts by his wife to learn Chinese soon faltered, ‚We do not have enough time, there is too much business with the children, etc.!'

Cheffe jr. himself has never bothered about learning even any single word of Chinese (except for "Good day", "Thank You", etc.). Like most aliens in China, he only crouches over his work, and after work he preferably sits together with his peers (apart from his family), where he needs to learn, of course, no Chinese.

His plant manager, an American, is a very interesting person: Whenever I talk to him, he criticises China and the Chinese around him. The craftsmen are all bad, everybody is late, everything is supplied too late and in too poor quality, service is atrocious, at his home everything breaks and nothing is ever repaired, workers and staff are terribly unreliable and all the time must be either fired or leave anyway on their own.

Strangely, such experiences I have not had till now. Are we speaking of the same country? I have found very good companies as suppliers and partners, and staff who are reliable and deliver the best work and are endlessly helpful. Did this guy have just bad luck? Or is his perspective limited by prejudice? To snap at the Chinese in the company the manager does not need no learn Chinese, on American it has the better effect anyway, and if the Chinese understand only a quarter of it, the damage is not so serious, you might say.

Occasionally I notice on flights within China some foreigners who seem to speak fluent Chinese (in any case, far better than I do), read the Chinese newspapers ... Then I am annoyed about my too-slow pace, my inability to understand Chinese sufficiently that is spoken at standard speed. It spurs me to learn even more intense.

So my learning speed, in my view, is far too slow, but I must also consider that I am now twice a grandpa who learns just slower than young spring-chickens can. At least I know now about 700 characters, on the computer I can write in Chinese everything that I can speak and understand, but I cannot read as well by far.

All the more it makes me angry when a training lesson drops from the schedule. One Sunday LiLin does not appear at all, I do not reach her by phone, not even during the following week. Is she gone? During the week I search the web and find an alternative within a few days – ZhangMiao.

Another few days later I find out that my first teacher was with her boyfriend on the road. I am angry that she had not told me in advance, she had just forgotten and apologises verbosely. Yet I am definite: I will not tolerate that, I want reliability, at last she understands but I am not going to change my decision. Her final words are: ‚I understand now that you really mean business and want to have in any case the lessons, no matter what. I'm sorry, I will observe this more from now on with my other students.'

ZhangMiao has since been my teacher, she is very professional and makes me feel progress in conversation, grammar and characters. I can perform ever better in daily conversation, but technical or business subjects I may still not treat in Chinese. Once Chinese have the impression that I speak their language (because my pronunciation is quite good), they start to talk enthusiastically, setting off at high speed, and cannot be disrupted by ‚man man shuo!' (‚Talk more slowly, please!'). And then I get nothing but a few dispersed words.

But at least I can deal with the daily life itself quite well by now, including dental visits, shopping, talks on the street, communicating with my football friends. I am able to trade Chinese SMS messages with my friends and my shady driver. My biggest difficulty is understanding. I can pretty well express myself (albeit with limited vocabulary and often un-Chinese sentence structure) and will be understood, but often I do not understand the Chinese, partly because they use words I do not know, but for the most part because they cannot be persuaded to speak slower. They think as I am "so good" at talking Chinese, I will understand just as well their own Chinese …

Fruit Seller ChaoMiao, the one who only became fruit seller in order to properly having time to read, introduces me into the diversity of "lychee" (Chinese: li zhi 荔枝, to be pronounced *li je*, with a final schwa sound that is located back in the throat). Who in Europe knows that these fruits are from the province of GuangDong and that ShenZhen virtually is the global capital of lychee? Sure, I have seen these trees in almost any park in ShenZhen, and they are in many settlements, but I was not aware that they were planted really systematically on the slopes of the hills and mountains in and around ShenZhen, and then harvested and exported into all world! Except, of course, for the tons of lychee that are in ShenZhen sold and eaten at every corner.

Who knows that there are at least a dozen varieties, not to mention the Dragon Eye, one of many li zhi species? ChaoMiao always tells me in all detail, she is happy about this alien who is struggling with Chinese and wants to learn about her world. One day she shows me a fruit, asking me if I was familiar with it. I deny, she tells me it was a 'pi pa', and I ask her to show me the Chinese characters (we do that with my Chinese cell phone: 枇杷), then at night I look into my Chinese-English PC dictionary and find that I do not even know the English word – loquat!

But even that hurdle is low – it is an Asian variety of medlar! First, I confuse the word with the mistletoe, known from the magic potion in the Asterix cartoons (reasonable, for in German the mistletoe is distinguished from the medlar by a single consonant only: *mistel/mispel*) and which I cannot imagine to bear edible fruits, but the medlar is indeed a completely different plant, and what kind of fruit it bears ChaoMiao has taught me. This fruit is wonderfully acidic and fresh, ChaoMiaos marketing campaign was a complete success with me.

Far more difficult to be investigated was a different fruit, "shan zhu" (which ChaoMiao persistently pronounced "san doo", but I found out after unspeakable troubles that this was not standard Chinese pronunciation, but standard Chinese I need to understand or to type into my cell phone what it might be). 'Shan zhu' 山竹 literally means Mountain Bamboo, and I thought for one second that it constituted perhaps the fruit of the bamboo. Far from that, it has nothing to do with bamboo at all. It is a delicious fruit that you have to peel out of a hard shell that is 3 to 4 mm thick, and then you will eat a white, soft, fleshy (containing some seeds) interior which consists of several parts and has a fruity and refreshing sour taste. The fruit is imported from Southeast Asia. In English, this fruit is called mangosteen – *mangostan* in German – from the shell tea can be prepared, moreover this fruit is also used for medicine since ancient times.

Grandma LaoLao is no such simple conversation partner, and her beautiful granddaughter is very quiet. LaoLao is speaking Cantonese, which is as far away from Mandarin, the standard Chinese that I am trying to learn, as Oz is from Oxford English; sorry, this is but my personal impression and not meant to be scientifically exact, true connoisseurs may think otherwise and forgive me. But Grandma LaoLao makes an effort, she tries to speak Mandarin, and little by little I understand better and better.

The bicycle transportation services are a funny breed. They have no easy task, certainly they do not earn very much, make ends meet just about so, I suppose, but I have never seen even one bad-tempered man or woman of this profession. On the contrary, they like to communicate with each other, with others, and – if I address them – even with me.

And they can perfectly relax on their uncomfortable vehicles.

I consider my biggest success that I am able to talk to taxi drivers, including my precious Fang ShiFu, about everything (about his exploits as a lorry driver, for example), for Fang ShiFu is speaking primarily Cantonese, and most taxi drivers in ShenZhen are blessed with all the dialects and languages, which China can boast, and of these there are a great many. And I'm a little proud that I can talk to engineer Su about birds and how to photograph them, and to craftsman Wang on bicycles to be repaired (and more).

In hospital

As you may remember, dear Reader, I have had my first encounter with the Chinese health system in NanTong where I had the mandatory medical examination before getting a working permission. This way I had already acquired some basic knowledge which I urgently needed. Without it, in a Chinese hospital you will fight a hopeless last stand (if you are able to stand, that is).

In the meantime I had gathered some additional minor experience from getting injections against hepatitis and during a medical examination of my knee that for a while had made trouble. But now there was a different problem.

During my winter vacation I had slipped and fallen on an icy descent, and from that a painful spot at the right elbow had remained. During the next weeks, a blister turned up there. I felt increasingly uncomfortable, and the sore elbow restrained my actions in goal-keeping. For inevitably you drop sometimes on your right elbow: A goalie after all cannot choose just to jump and roll towards the left only!

Finally I decided to get this elbow examined in China during a free forenoon. Chinese hospitals – at least those I know – are similar in structure to those medical centres that in Germany are called *Polykliniken* or General Hospitals. In China they are known as „She-Kou People's Hospital" or „NanShan People's Hospital".

There the People first accumulate at the registry. You pay a basic fee, and then you receive an examination log booklet which will hold the individual diagnostic findings. Once I had gotten that far, I felt on familiar territory: Just find the bones department and then use the book to make sure that once it will be your turn.

Well, yes, like that it works here, too – the door is standing open, some people are waiting inside, it is someone's turn. I put my booklet down on the others. Well, the physician has something different in mind: He looks at my booklet, then he looks at me, then at my name, he addresses me, nods at me – and stows my booklet away, below the heap.

Before I start complaining I try to think about that and decide to wait until the next patient will enter, whether walking, limping, carried, or pushed. And so the next booklet turns up. The physician looks up and into the patient's face, examines the name – and stows the booklet away, below the heap, under mine.

Well, well, this man has no particular objection against me, he has just established a FiFo system – first in, first out – unlike in NanTong where they work according to the LiFo rule: last in, first out. After all, a patient has to be adaptable and proceed according to individual custom.

A line of patients is waiting there before me. Some of them have brought their x-ray images. That of the patient who is currently treated has been fixed at a light box. Now the physician explains the diagnostic findings. If some among the interested audience cannot see the x-ray image properly because they are standing too far at the side, they advance to the centre of the room and happen to comment on what remarkable things they are seeing.

While the physician is examining my elbow I can be sure to attract the attention of everyone around – especially as they may test my handling of the Chinese language. But since I am able to say 'elbow' and 'swelling' and 'fall on ice', I pass the test and am honoured with approving murmur.

I am sent to the x-ray department. There I have to pay. After a while it is my turn, I take the image back to the physician in charge, and he explains to me – beneath a chorus of thoughtful murmur by the audience – that a small part of the elbow bone has splintered off, and this probably has caused the swelling.

He wants to puncture this, he says, if I should agree to that. I do agree, and finally we leave this public space, and I am getting punctured in another room where they provide injections and other niceties. Four 'nurses' are busy there, discuss the matter, suggest to the doctor what better to do, but he holds sway and proceeds in his way. Out of the swelling at my elbow he extracts a light-red, watery liquid.

Now my arm gets bandaged. I receive a couple of recipes; the pills are supposed to prevent inflammations and improve the general strength. I can buy them at the ground floor as soon as I have passed the row of waiting persons at the counters of the issuing office.

Just a few months later, during a football game, I get injured. It is Saturday evening, and we are playing under floodlight. At a distance of eleven or twelve meters from my goal, our left defender, hardly challenged at all, suddenly squares the ball to the right. I mean, it was a totally meaningless thing to do, for not even our right defender was dozing off there somewhere, there was not even an opponent! He did not intend that as a return to me, neither was it a square pass to the sweeper (who was at that moment about two meters outside the box), it was just plain bullshit. At once I start running after the ball, one opposing striker approaches both me and the ball, feeling that he got an advantage a) because the ball is approaching him off-key ahead b) because he is less than half as old as me and probably thinks: 'Now it's easy to outplay this yeye' (爷爷, this 'granny' – the striker knows me, and I know him to be an extremely fast and tricky young player).

But Granny YeYe is fast as well, especially in defending the goal. Today he has heroically stopped some balls already, and this time, Granny YeYe is one tenth of a second sooner at the ball than that striker. So, where the ball had been one tenth of a second before (but kicked away be me) there are now two things: the inner side of my shank and the striker's shoe. Very soon, a third thing adds: an acute pain below the rim of my shinpad.

For minutes I feel so much pain that I am unable to get up. At last I find that nothing seems broken, I do get up and (first mistake) continue painfully to play for another ten minutes, till the half-time break.

Then during the break I willow my trousers, remove the shinpad, and discover that a considerable swelling has developed, a giant bruise spreads along the shank (at least it is not an open wound, I think). I tell the other players that I will not go on playing but rather ride home to cool my leg there (we do not have a cooling spray or ice near the field).

Some players offer to drive me home and bring back my bicycle later-on. But I politely reject, not desiring to mean any trouble to them or to spoil their Saturday evening. So I get on my bicycle and head off (second mistake). The distance that I have to ride is not very long: about 14 km, and usually it takes me a little more than half an hour to get from here to there. But now I turn ever slower. My right leg cannot tread any more, the pain gets worse, I have to willow the trousers, they rub and squeeze. The injury swells significantly.

Along the first part of the road there is no settled area. This is some motorway or bypass along the coast, just a construction area. Only seven kilometres further-on there is finally a residential area where I can find a pharmacy. I tell them my problem and receive a cooling spray, ice, and Chinese medical plasters.

No way that I would continue riding that bicycle. What to do now? I walk along the road, leaning on the bicycle. Some businessmen and craftsmen are sitting there around a table. They drink beer and play cards. One of the players, craftsman Wang, recognises me. Once he has repaired for me a bicycle chain that was ripped on the way riding, another time he pumped lots of air into my tires and spread oil on the chain.

Craftsman Wang addresses me, and his wife, LuLu, offers tea and more ice for cooling. I need a car that would take me home and my bicycle, too. Craftsman Wang knows what to do: He phones someone, and five minutes later a tiny minibus approaches – a shady taxi driver who has never before taken a bicycle aboard. He objects.

Craftsman Wang convinces him. Together, he and his neighbours try tucking both my bicycle and the seats until at last everything, bicycle and me, fit into the minibus, ready to go. Five guys tried everything to help me. Craftsman Wang asks me to tell him later under any circumstance what had happened about my injury. I promise to drop in soon when I will be able to ride that bicycle again, and to tell him news about my leg.

Back at my apartment, some neighbours assist me in tucking the bicycle back out of the minibus. I pay the driver twice the usual charge. Leaning on the bicycle (for the lack of proper crutches) I limp to a nearby shop. The sellers know me, I am allowed to remain outside the door and tell about my problem; at once half a dozen sympathetic viewers gather around me, examining and commenting on the swelling.

The sellers know that I am playing football (the more because I am still dressed like that), and they understand why I ask them for more ice and some cold beer. I cannot pay, however, before tomorrow, for I never take much money along when going for a football play, and I have already used up my today's budget for the pharmacy and the minibus driver (lucky that I can tell all that in Chinese!). Well, no problem.

Now I am cooling my outside with ice and my inside with beer until late night arrives. And the whole Sunday I continue cooling, the only interruption is my lesson in Chinese. In the afternoon finally I am able again to step on the ground quite well.

At Monday I take a plane to ShangHai. I have some appointments there and in KunShan, and from ShangHai I go on to Japan (third mistake: no visit to the doctor). At least I keep on cooling that leg during almost all the flights, in almost any restaurant, in any hotel. It is Friday night when I return to my apartment. The swelling is immense. The blue bruise has turned more colourful, but I can step quite normally and walk without pain.

At the weekend I call my driver Fang ShiFu, telling him that Monday morning I would like to go to the hospital and get an examination. He objects against my wish to visit the SheKou People's Hospital: 'That is not enough, you will have to go to the Central Hospital! I have a friend there, he will help us.' And so, we phone three-way with SunLi, for I do not understand everything at once.

SunLi is relieved that I do not want to go alone to the hospital, even though Fang ShiFu is anything but an interpreter. But with me telling him slowly what it is all about, and with him patiently interrogating SunLi, sometimes by SMS, sometimes by phone call, he is yet able to assist me in using proper Chinese for Chinese people.

At Monday we set out in early morning; we want to arrive at the hospital 'before the real rush' and it is a drive of about 40 km. Two facts, however, we underestimated: first, the traffic, second, that the rush wants to be there before the rush, too, so that everyone is there already when we arrive early enough.

The traffic and the additional time that we needed to get to the hospital as wanted was at least useful to find out something when talking to my driver: his friend was not a physician at all as I had believed, but he was an electrician. I seeeee... (How is an electrician supposed to help me in a hospital?) He is Fang's friend because his 20-years-old daughter from his first marriage has a boyfriend whose father, well, happens to be that very electrician.

The hospital is revealed to be a small town behind walls. The access way is the first ordeal – if you do not pass it you seem to have forfeited your right to get treated. On the territory of the hospital there are dozens of buildings, most of them being about 20 to 30 years old, which means that they derive from the founders' age of ShenZhen. Streets are narrow and blocked – no chance to find a parking space here.

I guess that Fang ShiFu will have to drive (or 'crawl') in circles while I will err across the hospital with his friend, the electrician. I should have gone to that hospital that I was familiar with ... Meanwhile, Fang ShiFu busily phones with his friend and I understand that he apologises for being late because, etc., and we are now in front of this and that building, and, please, which street do we have to take left or right to find building F20.

Suddenly we stop at a turn. Plastic 'traffic cones' (or pylons) are set up there for cordoning off. A guard hastens to put three pylons aside. We drive in. Someone approaches our car and welcomes Fang ShiFu heartily – seems to be that electrician! Indeed he is. So we got an invisible VIP passport and a reserved parking space.

Now we walk through various streets and buildings and corridors until we arrive in an entrance hall where people have to register and pay the basic fee – no: where other people have to, for we only cross it (which is hard enough, for hundreds of people are standing, waiting, pushing) and then squeeze into one of the closest elevators nearby.

Upstairs we find a door before which a guard is standing. On the door there is written clearly and readably (in even for me readable and perfectly understandable Chinese characters) that there is no entry. But after exchanging a few friendly words with the electrician the guard yet allows us to enter.

Our friend the electrician leads us along sickrooms to a consulting room, equipped with four physicians and six nurses. He addresses a doctor who seems to be the boss here, one Mr. Song DeLian. But the other doctors and nurses as well as our friend the electrician call him "Da Song".

The physician examines my leg, murmurs, wrinkles his brow, asks me where I had gotten that from, and I explain to him in my crude

Chinese what had happened. 'Didn't I meet you just a few weeks ago?', he suddenly asks. 'In Xia Sha Cun, my native village? Didn't you photograph there?" And indeed, that is true, but how did he perceive and recognise me?

He had seen me from the corner of his eye, walking around and photographing people who were playing cards or majiang. That does not happen every day, he says, and very rarely foreigners come to his village. We talk a while (as far as my Chinese allows) about the 'village', his parents, his origin.

And after a few minutes he decides that I should get an ultrasonic and an x-ray examination. For that, we have to enter the proper departments and pay in advance. First, the ultrasonics. We arrive on a floor where several dozens of people are standing, waiting, pushing and desiring to deliver payment. Well, that can take a lot of time …, but not with my driver's friend, the electrician. I handle to him the money, he approaches the cash-counter from aside and chatters to the 'nurse' through the discontinuous glass screen. This 'foreign guy' (by that he means me) got problems, he must get help, that much I understand.

Suggestively, he reaches my money through the gap in the glass. Two or three patients later he has made it. We gained twenty minutes or so.

The ultrasonic examination is not very spectacular. The result reads 'blood bulge', if I interpret that correctly. I know those characters. That is a blister in which blood has accumulated, in other words, an impressively huge haematoma. It is quite hard, not as soft as the other swelling at the elbow that I suffered from some weeks ago.

Next comes the x-raying. We get one floor further and find it thronged with people. Here it will never be my turn. But our electrician squeezes himself through to the counter, and at once things start to look very different. He seems to know the fellow at the counter quite well; they chat, my money for paying the x-ray examination vanishes behind the glass screen at once, and then he tells me that I should not wait here but return to the entrance hall and leave it towards the left where I shall wait before the door. We do so. This door is locked. He vanishes.

After a few minutes the door opens from the inside. Lo and behold! there is our electrician, smiling. How did he do that?

Now I am inside the ultra-modern x-ray department, let us say: stepping from behind right into the centre. Each room that I can see at passing it by on the corridor is cramped full of the most recent devices. We enter a room in which the x-ray physician is monitoring everything. Someone is lying on the examination table, and of course we can hardly send him down from there (though our electrician seems to ponder even that). But just after the examination that was already taking place is finished it is suddenly my turn. And I do have a bad conscious, for outside there are more than 100 people waiting, and with the aid of the electrician I have just overrun them from the rear …

But even a bad conscious may allow to get good x-ray images, as I find (anyway, bad conscious is not detectable by x-rays and does not hide away in the leg, as far as I know). For just after the x-raying our electrician hastens there and back between the various rooms while I am waiting together with my driver on the corridor, fixed and immobile. From every room we hear his talking and laughing together with the x-ray guys, and finally he waves a huge envelope at us into which the images are wrapped.

My x-ray images and myself are then returned to the chief physician, Dr. Da Song. However, it is just his lunch break – no problem for my electrician. He knocks at Da Song's office door behind which the chief physician probably currently rests his head on his desk and takes a nap. This is a popular way of sitting in China's offices during lunch break – a position in which I could hardly sleep for a second, but Chinese people can do it for hours.

The chief physician emerges with somewhat sleepy eyes, as expected, but not at all angry because of us disturbing his lunchtime break. We meet in that huge consulting room where we had started earlier today.

He explains to me slowly and patiently (because of my limited handling of Chinese) that my bone had not been injured but that there was a severe haematoma. And that there were two possibilities between which I might decide: either I could get a small operation including two or three days of staying in the hospital, or I could wait till the swelling vanished by itself, which of course would take longer.

I decide for the slower way because I would not want to remain lying in that hospital … just insecurity (because I probably did not understand everything) and just prejudice. So the consultation is finished, but now it is the nurses' turn. They talk at me, for after all, it does not happen very often that a foreigner drops in here, and with the popular electrician as his hospital guide and with the foreigner talking a little bit of Chinese as well, they may just talk to him. I tell about Germany, and everyone wants to get invited there. So we have much opportunity to laugh.

The chief physician, Da Song, the electrician, and my driver meanwhile discuss my case in detail. I do not understand anything for the discussion is a) too fast b) in Cantonese and c) drowned in the nurses' chatter. But in the end I grasp just that far that initially, Chinese remedies should be applied to me.

Then we drive back. On the way home I learn (slowly, because of my limited Chinese) that this friend is not just any simple electrician but a kind of Electricians' Manager and more than that: Somehow he is also engaged in the trainee programme for new staff of any kind, but that part I do not understand exactly. Anyway, he knows almost everyone in the hospital, from the guard of the parking place to the chief physician, and he seems to have done at least one favour to everyone there, for everywhere he is heartily welcomed; and his attitude is not demanding but very friendly and comradely.

During my next stay in Germany my familiar sports physician will confirm the diagnosis and also tell me that while I was in China it would have been recommendable (for the blood in the huge blister was still solid) to make an 'erasion' that involved a considerable section, and a stay in hospital; but now, four weeks later, the filling substance had sufficiently liquefied – turned paste-like or like a gel – that an erasion was no longer necessary, but a squeezing through a minor section would do.

I will decide to get this done in Germany, being relieved that in China I got the proper diagnosis after all. The 'squeezing' will turn out to be not comfortable but tolerable (though much less entertaining than the examinations in China).

I am tempted soon to offer a beer to the opposing striker who is still tormented by his bad conscious, because of the experiences his assault had provided me with. Without his awkward kick I would never have met this electrician/trainer-friend of my driver nor the chief physician, Da Song, who in his village is called Xiao Song, and all the curious tale of what happened in the hospital and especially in the x-ray department I would have missed. How much I gained from this injury!

But then, is it wise to offer beer to an opponent who inflicted upon you a severe injury? Could that not be mistaken as an invitation to do it again? Ah, I have to consider that …

We do not yet return to my apartment but (after visiting a pharmacy) to Fang ShiFu's apartment. He applies the remedies that we bought before and rubs them into my extremity while his wife cooks a meal and his little son entertains me with his toys.

We eat together. I try to convince his son that he should eat a bit of vegetable for it is really healthy. ('No, it's not good!' – 'Yes, it's healthy, give it a try!' – 'No, this isn't good food!' – 'How do you know if you didn't try?' – 'It's not good!' At this the dispute ends) This was very funny. Just my leg does not make me laugh again yet.

Stock market hype, top and flop

HaiQiang is a young man in his early thirties who within a few years built a medium-sized enterprise, selling high purity cleaning and maintenance products for the electronics manufacturing industry. ShiTou is about the same age, he is a software entrepreneur and has only three employees, as successful but claiming that HaiQiang is „our richest friend." Wang LanBo (王蓝波) is an employee, 39 of age and thus quite old for this circle of friends, he married when he was 38 („I've always been too busy, and, alas, you can't meet anyone in ShenZhen') and immediately conceived a son, he is working for a company that is developing and supporting software for trading in options for stock markets, for example, for the stock markets in HongKong, ShenZhen and ShangHai. LaoHong (老红, "old Red", a nickname the team uses to call him) comes from Inner Mongolia, is foreman on construction sites and changes his employer like other people a fresh shirt. LaoZhang (老章) is in his mid-thirties, and together with a partner he set up a small restaurant chain in ShenZhen.

They share a love of football (having played for years, either in "Lao Niu" or "Tian Long") and money. They have the unwavering will to become, if not rich, then at least well-off, to drive good cars and to turn money into even more money.

After football all of them will meet for a joint dinner. The discussion – depending on the current situation, unless wife, girlfriend, lover or divorce is a current topic – may even focus on the stock market. In 2007 (when all of them were still four years younger, hence some of them even below 30), this is the hottest issue. Up to a dozen players are sitting at the round table, chatting with each other and enjoying the simple good meal and beer, and being together. And discussing about stocks.

'Recently I've invested in Wuhan (武汉) Iron & Steel, they're looking forward to a frenzied boom because here in China we're investing so much in infrastructure.' – 'Bullshit, look, they're marking time, there's hardly any progress with them!' – 'Sorry, but you haven't got any idea, of course you mustn't invest right now, but you should have done so last December, by January you'd had to buy latest, now their stock is already at an all time high, I've made a profit of 30 % since then!' – 'So will you keep the stock, or will you sell?' – 'Don't know yet, but latest if the profit is 50% I'm going to sell.' – 'I don't believe in steel stocks, financial stocks are better, look at how BeiJing Capital is rushing forth!'

The only player who (albeit limited) can interpret English and back, WangQiang, is soaked in sweat. He also invested in the stock market, and so he enthusiastically participates in the debate, but LaoWei wants to get a good enough grasp of the debate, too. A difficult balancing act for the inexperienced interpreter, because the debaters don't wait with their arguments until the interpretation is finished.

'LaoWei, have you bought any shares?' – 'I have not, and I will not.' – 'Why not? Look at how we all get rich here!' – 'If shares are discussed at football dinners, there will soon be a crash. I would not like to be present then.' – 'But before that you can take the profits!' – 'You buy mostly too late, and when you make profits, you take them too late, at least I am afraid that that was how it would turn out for me.'

Like that it went on for a whole year. Then suddenly everything fell quiet around. The benchmark ShangHai Composite Index had crossed the 6000 points mark, doubling within one year, increasing by a factor of six within the past two years, that's enough to cause euphoria, 'It will go on like that.' But toward late 2007 the decline began, only occasionally interrupted by some minor highs that immediately stir the optimism of the football friends again.

In the last quarter of 2008, which then also reaches a temporary low with the global financial crisis that was induced by the collapse of Lehman Brothers, the Index (and the courage of the football players at the round dinner table) drops to a low point, losing against the peak of the year before about two-thirds of its value. The gathering is open about the balance sheet: All of them except one have lost a lot of money, they had entered too late, got out too late (if ever), not taken any interim profits.

Hindsight is always wiser. This is no different in China than anywhere else in the world, take for example the New Market in Germany in the late 90s of the last century. The only question is how long the cunning will last and whether during the next hype you can detach yourself from the horde of lemmings.

Noise

No reader will be surprised to learn that it is noisy in China, this is (correctly) stated in all the books about China. Of course, here too this accounts „just" for the cities, but except for rare cases and the first few months in China when I spent my weekends in a charming village outside of GuangZhou, I am all the time in cities, living in ShenZhen as well as working for there and from there.

And if I am in China, I am spending every weekend in ShenZhen, I don't or don't yet travel – which I may be sorry about later – at all in the countryside. The reader will have noticed that I prefer to play football games on Saturdays and Sundays, driving by bicycle back and forth, celebrating extensive dinners with the friends, sometimes floating on beer, learning Chinese on Sunday mornings and, weather and work permitting, going photographing on Saturday mornings.

I am (or rather was) chronically, almost hysterical, allergic to noise. My family always rolled their eyes when we were sitting in the evening or on weekends in the garden and I (correctly) could predict that latest within the next five minutes, a lawnmower or a leaf blower would go off. Then my spirits were at rock bottom.

I'm a devotee of lonely and quiet nature. Sometimes I was alone, sometimes with my family, once with one of my sons on a weeklong kayak trip through a deserted area in northern Sweden/Norway, spending wonderful times in a remote territory, mainly in the north of our globe, but also (because of diving or the cranes) in southern climes. However lonely, every now and then the loneliness was ripped apart by helicopters, private aircraft, motor boats, chain saws or other unspeakable engine noise (except for the boat-trip in northern Sweden).

Then I got hysterically angry, wishing myself into even more offside wild, and that I turned into reality – to hit at one (1) engine there, too.

But this is now China. I admit that the turmoil in the streets, the bustle and chatter in the restaurants, the masses of people everywhere, the scramble and yelling and shouting, the loud mobile phone calls (even louder than in German Intercity trains!), the debates across the street inmidst the noisy traffic and the constant honking of the car drivers have early on terrorised me unspeakably.

But gradually I got used to it, I understood why it is so and not otherwise, maybe I am jaded, but I do not think so. Now, when I come to Germany every four to five weeks, I enjoy the peace, not noticing any longer even the lawn mowers. I confess that I have not yet become addicted to noise, but I can tolerate it now, even with road noise I can sleep at night to some extent.

On my bike trips to the football pitches (up to 14 km either way) I have learned to relax, despite the seething traffic all around me, despite the honking, the engine buzz, despite all clamour and confusion.

China has toughened me to noise, not immunised but made resistant. And more and more I understand: Everyone needs to find his place and audience among this milliard of people, and this is often to be done through volume, working itself up.

The foreigners in China seem to adopt this, especially Americans (who do not need to adopt it in the first place). Well, Americans are not really the most quiet of peoples, but in China – here they are louder than the Chinese. Whenever more than three Americans are together in a restaurant, you can be sure that they will predominate all Chinese people. And all listeners – if they understand American, because English was not enough – are ready to note: All these Americans are disproportionately talented showboaters.

This is not even matched by the loudest of Chinese, they are generally much too modest, not all of them but most of them. With Americans, it is the other way round.

Toothache

Spending that many years in China it is perhaps inevitable that sooner or later you will get a toothache. Once an old filling leaves my tooth for good. Each and every one advises me: ‚Get this done in Germany, or why wouldn't you go to HongKong?'

I wonder, why indeed? Do all Chinese people of ShenZhen walk around with toothache and never get it cured? That is not my impression so far. But frankly, I confess: I do not want to go into one of these dental practices which can be watched from the street through a large window; I know that in China everything is public, but I do not want to be treated in full public view at my teeth.

So I'm asking around, I get all sorts of recommendations, one of which sounds appealing: There is said to be a new group practice in FuTian, a district of ShenZhen. There I go on a Sunday morning after having arranged an appointment (with SunLi's assistance).

For those who still do not know: Service in China, especially southern China, is to the delight of any working man. Anyone who – like me – never has any time to spare will in ShenZhen face no trouble in yet achieving everything, other than in Germany where as soon as you have found some time you will also find that the others have run out of it. Everything is possible to get at almost any time, even this appointment on a Sunday morning.

The practice is new, and as I sit in the treatment room, I'm convinced: This is a modern dental practice. Wang QiongHao (王穹浩) is a young, compared to me even a very young doctor, about the age of my sons. He quickly lays me flat on the chair. But he cannot speak English. My Chinese is limited. We manage somehow – until we suddenly realise: He can speak French! Me too! What a surprise!

Now things become most funny, because we fluently and enthusiastically communicate in "Chinçais" (that's the French-Chinese equivalent of "Chinglish"). Whatever he does not know in French, I can understand or tell in Chinese, and vice versa. It was a wonderful synergy. He is a Chinese from HongKong (his Mandarin is quite fine, though), has studied and practised for a time in Paris, then joined a practice in HongKong, but there was no more success. ‚The competitors are destroying everything, dumping prices and quality.'

The gang of four physicians decided to move to, and start anew in ShenZhen, where everything is new and they may escape the competition in HongKong. The practice is better equipped than anything that I have known in Germany.

The repair of my tooth means no trouble. But Wang QiongHao has instilled confidence.

About a year later I get a real problem: nagging toothache. I call the practice, but don't remember the name of the doctor ... Sorry, please. When registering, I ask (in crude Chinese) for being treated by that doctor who speaks French. ‚No problem, tomorrow at 4 o'clock, is that all right with you?' – ‚Sorry, I would like to come next Sunday at 10 o'clock, it that possible?' – ‚No problem!'

This Sunday it is a real ordeal: root canal treatment, complete dental revision, ceramic crowns, four sessions altogether. Our Chinçais is perfect, with one caveat: He can talk normally, I have to keep my mouth open with ten tampons inserted, that way speaking Chinçais is not so easy! Four hours after the sessions I play as a goalkeeper ... straining all my resources. It is a tough challenge, but I enjoy to meet it.

I have rarely – or more precisely, never before or again – endured so inspiring (albeit serious) and modern dental treatments (has the X-ray image of your root canal treatment ever been shown to you right on the dental chair, and then copied on demand to an USB stick?). And then with a somewhat swollen jaw I kept away the shots from the goal ...

» One way of getting teeth treated in ShenZhen: A dental practice with unhindered showcase view.

The "China capital of crime"

The following you will not read in any China guide, you may perhaps not even find it on the Internet, but all inhabitants of ShenZhen (and acquaintances from ShangHai or BeiJing) whom I know will tell you this: This city has the highest crime rate in all of China. I'm always recommended to be most cautious right now, as this or that festive day was imminent and this usually makes the crime rate – which is already so unfortunately high – soar even higher.

I know hardly anyone who has not been robbed. In the bus suddenly the bag has gone amiss, in the subway the back pocket is slit with a knife and a wallet „removed" (lucky that the slitting of the pocket did not violate the buttocks, too!), the entire backpack was stolen during a football game, and bags hung from the shoulder torn off just so. My bag pocket, too, was once ripped on the bus, but I don't have my wallet there, so first, I felt relief that I was not robbed, second, that the knife did not stuck anywhere else in my buttocks, which might have happened on this bumpy ride.

As much as I feel affection for China and the Chinese – I'm far from believing that the rate of crime in China was low in comparison to other countries. On the contrary, I believe that in all levels of society, from the road to schools to corporates, the government and police, it is more or less equally widespread as in all other countries of the world. I don't arrogate a judgement on whether there is more or less crime in China than elsewhere.

Why wouldn't there be "normal" crime to be expected in a country where many companies have forged baby food, where no one is surprised about having bought ineffective or even toxic drugs, because even the pharmacy fell prey to the criminal swindler company? In a country where corruption has become so overwhelming that even the government was forced in recent years to massively intervene and to condemn to death and execute the head of the national drug registration authority, a fellow who wrote approvals preferably depending on the level of bribery than on efficiency. Likewise, for example, the former deputy police chief of ChongQing, the largest city of China, who at the same time held a key position in organised crime.

And ever since my driver told me that there was more and more child abduction in ShenZhen, above all in front of schools and kindergartens in good locations, and that it had become a kind of industry to demand ransom, and that the parents would not like to see their children driving alone to school and prefer to pick them up afterwards – ever since I have no reason to doubt that ShenZhen is no paradise on earth. But that I should always be very careful.

To the football pitch I never bring my normal backpack („my office/property") containing my laptop, external backup drives, passport, credit cards, wallet with money, but instead an older, less valuable backpack with sports stuff and drink, house keys (secondary) and magnetic front door card (secondary), no credit card and only a paper copy of my passport, just in the event that I should run into a check and would have to identify myself, which has not happened yet within five years. If I'm robbed there, I will manage and only replace my door lock for safety's sake. On the football pitch – as opposed to one of my Chinese friends – I have not yet been robbed.

I do not know how many murders are committed in ShenZhen, compared to Hamburg,

Frankfurt, London or New York, in total it seems to me that the police is always very relaxed here while it seems much more present in ShangHai, much more rigorous in Germany and very overwrought in New York. If you ever see coppers here – and they are really a very rare sight! – they are just for a chat, drive their girlfriend home or shopping on the police motorcycle (preferably with warning light, yet at least no siren) or compose a text message on their phone, presumably to that girlfriend that they have just taken home.

I do not understand how in such a juggernaut, in this city clutter, a crime could ever be solved – on the other hand, all the Chinese tell me that nothing remains concealed, no one can hide, because all the Chinese are very curious and talkative and weird secretive people would be noticed immediately. I have no doubt that the Chinese do take a very active part in the lives of neighbours, for I witness this myself almost every day. Once our employee, SunLi, was pregnant, and twice within a period of several weeks we ate dinner in a restaurant close to my home. And some time later, when I was eating there alone, I was asked with polite interest when „my wife" was going to get „my child", and whether this wasn't surely exciting, was it? Because of my limited knowledge of Chinese it was hard to explain that she was not my wife and the unborn child was not my child, but that she was an employee and married to a Chinese. In another restaurant where I was occasionally a guest, during a period of years thus „more often", I had once as well been eating with SunLi, and some time later I was asked whether „my child" was now born and whether „my wife" was now in her home-town as was custom, and whether it was a son or daughter and how everyone did fare ...

Back to crime. I am convinced that there is in ShenZhen a remarkably high rate of petty crime and certainly of organised crime. I think ShenZhen is less than New York a capital of serious crime. But I do not know.

I have also been robbed – but fortunately so far only once. My first bicycle was stolen after more than a year of cycling. My former Chinese teacher, LiLin (李琳), had warned me that I had better avoided purchasing ‚such an expensive bike', because she was curious as well and asked me what I had paid for my bike, and she was speechless for minutes when I mentioned the exorbitant amount of „RMB 1600", being about 160 €.

She had a foreign couple as her students in learning Chinese, and their bicycles (both bicycles! And not even expensive ones!) had many times already been stolen before Starbucks. ‚But were they locked and chained?' I ask. No? Then it is not surprising, for such bicycles would indeed be stolen in Germany as well, I tell her. Really? Yes, really, I confirm, and I would always lock my bike not only in Germany but also in China, even tie at something with a chain and, if possible, keep an eye on it.

She thinks buying cheap bicycles was preferable, for if they were stolen I could easily buy another. I disagree, claiming that I want to go properly on a sensible bike and that on weekends I had four times to ride a pretty long distance to the football pitch, and I did not know whether I could do that on cheap bicycles. She replies that she was understanding that much; she had three Japanese students, too, who were learning Chinese, and each of them had bought from Walmart a cheap bicycle at a price of about 10 % of my bike, one collapsed after 500 metres, the other before reaching the residential area, the third one a few days later. Well, there! That's exactly what I had in mind.

With my Sunday team I join dinner as always;

and as always I fix my bike on the parking lot, at a side gate which is not moved for any reason, by threading and closing my massive (actually hysterically voluminous!) lock around two thick iron rods and then to the rear wheel and the frame.

This evening, after eating and drinking, I want to liberate my poor lonely bicycle and take it home, but it's gone! The two (not too thin) iron bars of the gate have been severed with a hacksaw, and then, probably, my (even more solid) chain lock was as well cut. The thief(s) must have observed that the bicycle was chained at the gate behind the cars more or less every Sunday, and that behind the cars, in the dark, one could indulge in heinous actions unobserved.

I get the boss of the restaurant and my football friends, showing them the mishap, but they can indeed do nothing more than pitying me and telling me that this all too frequently happens in ShenZhen. A few days later I am buying a new bike, even one category higher and more expensive, and this one I do not even allow to be (locked) in front of the house, it is now always in the middle of my living room.

However, I have no major concerns about my safety in ShenZhen. I am always careful and aware, but not scared. Many Western (European, but especially American) business partners ask me if I really had no problems riding a bicycle in ShenZhen, with this traffic and crime so threatening? No, I don't have such problems, I am very aware when driving (not unlike Germany), trust that in case of doubt I can call for help or go away quickly or run away, I do not feel any more threatened than, say, in Hamburg or Frankfurt Central Station. I was told that some senior managers of major U.S. companies feel constantly under threat in ShangHai, even in the car of their own branch. I think that's really hysterical. In New York I feel more threatened than that.

Whatever, for Sunday night football dinner I take my new bike from now on always into our private chamber. For of course – I have not yet mentioned that – our team is occupying on Sunday not public restaurant space, but one of four special rooms for specially loud guests, as we are. At the Saturday evening dinner, we are usually in a roadside restaurant, and the bike is – tightly locked – standing next to our table. On Sundays, neither the service nor the boss nor my friends criticise that after football I carry my bike upstairs and into a corner of our private chamber while the first cold beer is served. (青岛！冻的！快一点 'QingDao! Dong de! Kuai yi dian – A cold Tsingtao! And hurry up, please!)

Serial suicide at Foxconn

Ten days after the small surgery on my injured leg, I return to China. At the weekend I would like a ride by bicycle again to the football pitch and just watch, for once. On Saturday, about an hour before the scheduled kick-off, the rain deteriorates into a terrible storm, an artillery of drops of centimetres size descends on Shen-Zhen, even the lightning is hardly to be seen in this dense torrent, the thunder is hardly to be heard in the loud crackle of the warm (sub)tropical downpour.

A circular text message to everybody updates me – the game is cancelled. So I hope for Sunday to bring better weather. On time in the early afternoon I drive by bicycle, in spite of a few small showers, and remember near the pharmacy on half the distance that I was asked to tell craftsman Wang at the earliest opportunity what's news about my leg. And sure enough, there he sits outside his shop, drinking tea with a neighbour and his own wife who has finished providing the passers-by with snacks for the lunchtime hunger and is now waiting for the afternoon and evening hunger.

I brake, he invites me to sit down, LuLu gets a tiny cup, I get every few minutes freshly brewed tea: hot water on the leaves and let stand for 15 seconds, then pour. Like that I also use to drink my green tea. I show him the leg, tell (as far as my Chinese permits) what has happened since that night six weeks ago. And that I plan on next weekend for the first time to play football again. Not today, today I will just go watching and eating with the friends.

After my story and my involvement with my words of thanks (refused with much force) for their help I want to ride on, but craftsman Wang is hemmed and hawed, he wants to tell me something else. He asks me if I understood "duan jian", 短见. Accidentally, I know the words for reasons of topicality – they mean "suicide", but the literal first meaning is "myopic view," or "myopic", but only in a figurative sense, not in the language of the optician. Isn't it remarkable how "suicide" is expressed in Chinese? There is yet another Chinese word that literally means "self-killing", but craftsman Wang uses "myopic" – the one who is in a valley cannot look afar, he has to get up on a hill to look ahead and see that one must not kill himself.

But this was not what craftsman Wang wanted to tell me, he first wanted to make sure that I would understand (which I did) if he would now tell me the following story: Previously he had received a call of his former neighbours from his home-town (they call each other every few weeks), her son has moved about a year ago to ShenZhen and works in LongHua (龙华, a district of ShenZhen) at Foxconn. Do I know Foxconn? Of course, I was there several times already. There is a huge company, a city within a city.

300,000 people live and work there, only for Foxconn, in any of the Foxconn divisions. It does not look there (for me at first glance) any different from many other places in ShenZhen, It is not the district where I would urgently like to move to, but it is not repulsively ugly, either. There are uglier ones.

The neighbour's son has taken his life the day before by jumping from the roof of the residential building. His parents are desperate, they do not know why. There is no suicide note. Their son had sent each month "a lot of money," he was very frugal, supporting his parents. Last time he had been home for New Year. This young man is the eleventh in a series of suicides in the course of a few months. This was known to me even from German media, and in China as well it was hotly debated when I came back a few days ago.

Craftsman Wang claims that he had offered to the parents at the time to employ their son in his workshop, but he could not pay as much as Foxconn offered. 'I think he killed himself because he had no girlfriend,' says LuLu. Her husband disagrees, because of that you don't kill yourself, and besides, there are enough young girls at Foxconn in LongHua, anyone can choose among them very easily.

I agree, because there and in other mill villages there are always many young boys to be seen, at the arm a girl, walking around after work, and there is certainly more than cuddling to it. Those people do not look unhappy. 'I think he had problems at work,' craftsman Wang suggests. Foxconn is Taiwanese, and the language of the Taiwanese managers can be very rough.

I cannot oppose that. Some of our customers are Taiwanese companies, too, and some of the local managers certainly have not attended to any staff management seminar. Even in my presence, Chinese employees have already been dismissed, I cannot imagine that it was that pleasant. The famous "saving face", which supposedly is in China a sacred and important principle, is no topic here at times. And the thought passes through my head that as well the American factory manager at the Italian-American joint venture is a very rude man who has also mercilessly (and even unjustified) criticised an employee in my presence who suffered this stoically, without response. A couple of minutes later I clarified the facts via a long linguistic detour, earning a secret grateful smile from the unjustly criticised fellow.

But do you kill yourself because of such a thing? The reason for the series of suicides in the media was seen at Foxconn, in the working conditions there, that I cannot evaluate. It is one of the first topics I share with the Chinese colleagues at dinner. They think it is on the one hand a reflection of problems in Chinese society, no wonder with all the upheaval, the growth, the gaps or rather abysses between city and country, rich and poor. And the greed for money.

On the other hand, we should not overrate it, because Foxconn is a gigantic enterprise, and the suicide rate was below the average rate in China. While still at dinner we research with our mobile online laptops. By using Wikipedia we quickly find out that the suicide rate in China is 13 per 100,000 inhabitants per year. This is somewhere in the global centre-field, with Germany rating slightly higher (18), the ranking is topped by Russia (58), Japan (35), Finland (31) and France (26). At the lower end are Peru (1), Philippines (2.5) and Greece (6). Extrapolating the Foxconn suicides per year and 100,000 people, these are also about 6 cases.

This cannot comfort the former neighbours of craftsman Wang, nor himself and LuLu. He claims again that he could have prevented the suicide, and he and LuLu as well had once started business from the ground, working 24 hours a day until they no longer could, and then they established their own business. 'I've made him an offer he refused. Why did he want to go there, just because there's more money? Because he could earn more with overtime? Money isn't everything!'

Craftsman Wang is desperate.

On the ensuing drive to the football pitch more thoughts are passing through my head, something that I overheard a few days ago, it matches somewhat LuLu's theory on suicide and the male-female search-and-find trouble that seems to be so common. At a dinner with Chinese colleagues during which we also talked about the suicides I was told what was an absurd story from my point of view:

China's TV is running a show where men and women may find each other. 24 young women are standing behind a podium whose frontside is lighted. A young man enters (by elevator, "floating down from the heights") who is looking for a girlfriend or wife.

Now after the first impression – the guy is questioned a little by the moderator: Where is he coming from, where does he live, why his hair is cut so strangely, the candidate has to give some witty answers – the girls shall decide whether or not they are further interested. Those who are no longer interested switch off the lights at their podium.

Then the man is first asked about his profession, his income and his financial status (one or more apartments?). After this part, if necessary, some further candidates switch off their lights. My football friends told me that someone who apparently truthfully said that he was a baker glared at once into 24 switched-off lights - he was in the truest sense out of the game, Darkness had seized him.

After this part, biography and personal interests are being asked for. The ladies can ask questions now, interrupt, argue, the show is anything but austere, the audience is amused, laughing about all sorts of pokes and puns. The moderator is witty, aggressive, but also well informed, trained in psychology, not at all superficial. An "observer" is his sidekick who interferes without previous notice, paying a remonstrance to either the moderator or the candidate or one of the girls (ladies), exposing someone to ridicule or making a substantial comment.

In the end, maybe three lights are on, now the candidate may choose, asking the girls this and that, and selecting.

In this phase, my colleagues tell me, one young woman had eliminated from the game because on the candidate's question, 'Who wants to bike through the city with me, talking and viewing everything?' she replied, 'I'd rather sit in a BMW and talk to a man about love while crying.'

Now, the next candidate in the case I was told of said to the same woman (who was again with two others on the shortlist) that she might cry with him in the BMW, he was a millionaire (even as a millionaire, or perhaps because of that, he had relationship troubles?) and he could offer her several BMWs to choose from.

She decided (probably for other reasons) against him and in a later round took another BMW driver.

Relentlessly I commented that that was "sick", IMHO, and the Chinese in the round nodded approvingly. China has thus on the whole developed well, one might say (sarcastically) that while in Germany we have been offered for a long time already all sorts of embarrassing shows on all channels, here now stations just feature "High Earner Wants a Wife" (actually the title is a word of wisdom in an old Chinese stylistic tradition – "four-letter words": "Fei Cheng Wu Rao" 非诚勿扰 – a crude translation might be: "Be serious, don't be annoying" or, closer to the point, "If you aren't serious about it, don't annoy me"). One of the group said in such programmes people were stripped bare and it was hard to bear looking at how cheap they do private things in public.

At once someone else contributed another "sick" story from current society gossip: a wedding is ready, the future husband has rented eight Audis to drive the family to the restaurant where hundreds of guests are waiting.

The bride leaves the house, perceives the eight Audis and asks her fiancé why he had ordered Audis and not BMWs. He takes refuge in the white lie that only Audis were available, but the bride does not concede. At least for herself a BMW has to be rented, verily it ought to be a 745, and on the spot. Even the brother cannot persuade his sister to move away from her position.

Then says the fiancée that he had now got to know her a little better, and that he will return all eight Audis without ordering a BMW, as this was no longer necessary. And the guests should now begin to eat, but he would not be there. That's pretty weird, but – according to the Chinese who told me – after all, not yet the rule, however, it also reflects a "sick trend."

But as long as the suicide rate in Germany is higher than that of China, and China's more than that of Foxconn, one could rest assured, here and there. Craftsman Wang and his wife, however, especially his former neighbours, don't look at statistics.

I ride on to the football pitch, lost in thought, arrive just before kickoff. The pitches are partially flooded, it had indeed rained a lot the day before (remember the game was cancelled) and so until late night. Only half of the pitches are being played on, of our team only eight players have appeared, the others apparently were afraid of getting wet. I will not play yet, not wanting to take a risk that the wound should burst which is still fixed by a plaster, and I have no goalie equipment taken along, no gloves, shin guards, elbow pads, no shoes, just open sandals without socks, shorts – I was only prepared for bicycle riding and watching! They harass me, I give in. On our side, the referee will play as well while whistling the same time. Someone from the opposing team lets me gloves. Now we are ten players.

On sandals I am standing, in puddles in the goal, having previously arranged with my friends that I will not dive for the ball, they should not criticise me for that. I cannot express "to dive" or "to throw myself down" in Chinese, instead I claim, 'Today I will not fly', which causes uncontrollable laughter: 'Today, he won't fly, but otherwise he can.' All right, I'm not going to get criticised that today I cannot even fly.

Two minutes later, my intention not to dive is forgotten. Five minutes later, I look like an eight-year-old who is playing happily in the mud, and I am indeed happy! Only at one action I take back my right leg, not willing to risk that the opposing player would kick against – 0-1. But I can prevent a lot of goals, the referee even makes a goal for us, and when he is once fouled, he whistles while lying on the ground, everybody laughs, there is a free-kick, no protests. During the game, a prolonged rain unfolds, dunking everyone who had not yet been thoroughly wet before. The final score is 3-3, my friends are satisfied with my performance and would like to thank that on occasion I was yet flying, that I even played without any equipment, I am satisfied with myself, too. My sandals are wet, I am completely dirty, from top to bottom, and that way I am going home by bike for showers and laundry.

Life is not just the pursuit of money. On the contrary.

The injury break I had used a few weeks ago for photographing my team when playing. On this occasion, there was also an opportunity to observe and telephoto how groundkeeper Fu trained his little five-and-a-half-year-old son in playing football. When he realised I was taking photos, he asked me to send them to him via e-mail.

A week after the unexpected "sandals game" I come again for a Saturday's game. Groundkeeper Fu notices my approach, waves and thanks profusely for the photos. He asks me to his office, now one of the photos is a wallpaper on his computer. He invites me to tea, we talk, in thanks for the photos he gives me one of his special tees for a present. He is a real tea expert.

The game is interesting. I notice when playing that my condition has worsened from before the injury. I was driving my bike a lot, but that's different than running, throwing myself down ("flying") and getting up. So I have to perform a morning jog again, which I had not been able to for weeks, either. But I feel good, I also padded the injury under the shin with a bandage.

My warming-up is always very important. I have to get a lot of shots on goal from short and medium distances so that I get the feeling for the ball, shutting off the conscious part of my mind and begin automatically and without thinking to catch, punching, plunge into the corners. That is also the main cause of relaxation for me: All the business, technical or scientific problems, often haunting me yet when biking to the pitch, disappear at the latest when warming-up. But during a football game the conscious part of my mind is in standby mode, I use to claim; I must not think, 'when will the ball arrive, do I jump now or soon, do I have to run outward now, when will I have to plunge?' If something like this happens, it's always already too late. While being the goalie my brain has a "timeout", it may decide for me without any conscious participation on my part, then I am at the height of my power, then I am also subsequently recovered very well.

Often – especially in summer when there are 30, 35 or 40 degrees outside and, preferably, more than 90 % humidity at times – I'm already entirely drenched in sweat after five minutes. From the bike ride I'm coming completely wet, but change my clothes. After the game, both sets are wet: my keeper stuff and my light biking dress. "Wet" meaning: you can probably wring one litre (or two) of sweat out of my clothes. Although on such days, and of them there are not a few a year, I drink at least three bottles of water during the game, it will take till late evening and several bottles of beer until I have to pee again.

At the beginning of my goalkeeping career in ShenZhen, when I still was not adapted to this, it seemed quite possible that after the warming-up – when I got maybe 50 or 60 shots on goal within 30 minutes, jumping, plunging, back up, retrieve misplayed balls from the rear – I might suffer a faint. This was demonstrated by the fact that my viewing angle, otherwise extending across 180 degrees, had shrunk to only 30°. That was very irritating, but happened only sporadically and only at the beginning, obviously my metabolism has become more resilient.

Today we play once again in the evening under floodlights. I do not like that, the light is dim, rather similar to the floodlights on training courses of the German regional league teams. I can hardly anticipate the shots, high balls often come out of either the dark or directly from a light, there's less time to react. The flood lights of the neighbouring pitches are blinding me. But I like the bats. Nowhere in the world I have ever seen bats as close as with my football games in ShenZhen under the floodlights.

We are playing against a team which is on average at least five years younger than ours (about the difference to my age I will not speak now). They are incredibly quick, to make pressure, they sometimes walk through my back line as if the defenders were but slalom poles. But they cannot overcome me. I just got extremely fast reactions.

We succeed in countering with three goals while only receive two of them, I believe I have kept two "untenable" shots about which my team-mates told me afterwards that they had seen them in the goal and did not expect that I could prevent them.

Most fun for me is the so-called "one-on-one situation," but it is very dangerous: if our defence is overwhelmed and the opponent's striker is alone approaching my goal, I need to get out. I must dash out even before the shot will come, I must anticipate the emergence of the situation intuitively and catch the ball as early as possible, or grab it from the striker's foot by diving into the grass before him. Today, this happened several times, ten times at least. Only twice I was brought low, in most cases I win and have the ball, my right leg I did not withdraw.

After the end of the game, as we sit on the lawn chatting, exchanging clothes and drinking some water, about a kilometre's away from us a fireworks display, well visible, is launched from an amusement park. They do that every Saturday evening at half past eight. I call out: 'They are celebrating our victory, how nice!' Roars of relaxed laughter – after all pressure from the opponent which we withstood we do deserve those fireworks!

It is a long and very moist dinner. We sit at a side street restaurant, it is a balmy early summer evening, many people are strolling around loud and cheerful. The team celebrates me as "the best player of the day". 'We would've lost without you today, lost 3-6 rather than winning 3-2.' It's true. We have some situations again to reminisce. I tell the story from the hospital, everyone knows this large central hospital, but none of the team has experienced something similar there. About midnight I take the bike (probably with more than the tolerable blood alcohol) several kilometres to my apartment, it's a wonderful feeling to have overcome the injury.

» **The football groundkeeper trains with his son.**

» Before the start of the games he always prepares tea, invites all referees and occasionally me.

» Such wonderful teas with flowers that unfold when one adds the water, you do not get on the football pitch, but with me in my apartment.

The 2008 Olympics

Latest in early 2008, after finishing the celebrations at the beginning of the Year of the Rat (or is it the much more appealing mouse? I did not then find out, the images in this year rather seem to indicate a mouse, the Chinese word for rat and mouse, at least according to my dictionary, is the same), there is only one topic in China: the Olympic Games in August this year.

BeiJing has prepared for them; border security was reinforced, visas restricted, imports for our products as well became more complicated on a daily level, YouTube and Google Picasaweb (the photo albums) were no longer accessible. The latter affected me most, for on that website I was making my images from China accessible for my family, colleagues and friends.

Regarding safety, China prepared for not having to take any risks, at that time particularly, Muslim terror attacks were most feared. These aspects reflected in the German media.

From inside China, things looked different, people were just thrilled – Olympics at home! Everyone spoke of how exciting this was, how perfect everything was prepared. 'Are you going to BeiJing?' No, I did not intend to.

The torch relay begins, becomes politicized by merging the Olympic idea with the Tibet issue, people in China, my staff, customers, friends, neighbours and guests at the restaurant, react upset: 'Why do you disturb this peaceful torch relay?' – 'Why is even a disabled athlete in Paris getting assaulted?' – 'What has Tibet to do with the Olympics, what do you know at all about Tibet?'

I did not know much, too little, I could not participate in debates but only accept the charges, representing the French, Americans and many others who have actively tried and succeeded at least in part to interfere with an internationally unifying event or the prelude to it.

My friends harassed me, 'What does Germany want? What does France want? Tibet belongs to China since thousands of years, why is this now an issue in the Olympics? Do you know what was going on during the British occupation of Tibet, how the upper-class has suppressed the people? Why, if the Basque Country or Catalonia may not be independent, should China give Tibet to the Dalai Lama?'

I don't know, I try to get informed, and become thoughtful. My football friends are very committed in their talks to me and let me know: Before the People's Republic of China incorporated Tibet again into the state, it had been a feudal society since centuries, also later under the British Government, with a minor upper class, with serfs (i. e. slaves) who had to serve the feudal lords (and the Dalai Lama). The serfs were deeply in debt with the feudal masters, they had no rights, not even for their own life or that of their children, they received no education.

'You know that Tibetans are now one of many recognised ethnic minorities? They aren't subject to the One-Child Policy, they do have right of access to all higher education institutions, get admission to universities and such under easier terms compared to us, the Han-Chinese.'

When the torch relay arrives in China, the debate falters and is replaced by euphoria – at last, the Olympics finally arrived at the people, not abroad, not only in the media. On 8 May, the torch shall pass through ShenZhen.

On 9 May my flight back to Germany is booked. I arrange myself so that on 8 May I will not have any customer meetings. I want to watch the torch relay. But how and where? I'm asking around, browse the Internet and find out eventually which route is taken. With 40 kilometres, this will be one of the longest parts of the global torch relay event.

Suspecting that everywhere there will be a terrible crowd, especially in the centres of the municipalities through which the relay is passing (each district in ShenZhen has indeed more inhabitants than Berlin!), I wonder how I will most cleverly manage to be present and watch without driving into the centres. I choose a place that I know from my rides to the football pitch: Bin Hai Da Dao (滨海大道, in translation it means something like "Coastal Boulevard") near the Hong Shu Lin mangrove reserve (红树林公园) at the coast. There are few residential areas nearby. So I go by bike and notice along the way that I was absolutely right: It is incredibly crowded everywhere, people stream toward NanShan centre with pendants, flags, painted faces, happy euphoric smiles, shouting all the time at each other: '中国加油, Zhong guo jia you' – 'Push the throttle, China!' They laugh at me, talk to me, wave happily at the biking foreigner who is travelling the opposite way, away from the centre. 'Poor fellow, there's nothing going on where he's heading for! Doesn't he want to watch the torch relay?' some might have thought, and how wrong they were!

I finally get to the place on the Coastal Boulevard that I have in mind, and sure enough, even here it is crowded, but you get to the curb, even close to the barriers, because no family with grandma, grandpa, mother and grandchildren can hike to here. They have to go either by car (but then four hours earlier!), by bus or by bike as I did! Otherwise this place is too far away outside the centre of the district NanShan. Many others have also come by bike.

Here are young people, entire companies (by bus) who, as I gradually learn, know someone who will carry on the torch for 100 or 200 m.

In the morning it was already made clear that the torch relay would not start at the originally scheduled time, but only when the torch would have arrived at the summit of Mount Everest. For that reason, in many places in ShenZhen – especially near the start and finish areas of the relay, huge screens had been set up.

The arrival on the summit was broadcast live on Chinese television and at many places in ShenZhen. I watched this in my apartment before I left. It was very impressive. After this race to the top, I left for the place I had chosen, for by now the torch relay had started in ShenZhen, too.

All spectators had to wait, as was to be read later, and there were at least three million of them. Many companies had given the day off, the families had gone, it was a huge city party for millions of families and friends along at least 40 km.

The traffic is still flowing normally on the Coastal Boulevard, but it is gradually thinning out. It's hot, very hot in the bright sunshine. It feels like 40 °C, but a look into the historical weather data for 8 May 2008 in ShenZhen reveals to me that temperatures rose to no more than 31 °C that day, humidity, 89 %, but virtually no wind. Therefore it felt so hot! The humidity is what makes the heat so hard to bear.

The Chinese around me are in high spirits, ever again chanting battle cries! Finally, the traffic on the six-lane road calms down, one can assume that it is now blocked, so the torch is coming soon. Not yet. First a few inquisitive cars and cyclists approach who somehow managed to get on the closed roads, waving flags and honking from open side windows, roof vents or riding one-handed. When they drive past the thousands of spectators, they reap applause and battle cries as if they were already the torch bearers.

The coppers are smiling, enjoy themselves, do not interfere. They even do not interfere as more and more viewers climb across the median of the six-lane road, a wide grass strip with trees, shrubs and flowers, because they also want to participate.

Finally the trek approaches. First, the car of the sponsors with the most beautiful young girls and women whom they could collect. They are followed by a bus – from it emerge the torch relay runners, they are positioned by the organisers every 100 m, with a not yet burning torch in hand. The spectators along the barriers reshuffle because they want to be at exactly that 100-meter section along which their idol is running. The torch bearers are athletes from the city, acquaintances of the company, neighbours, friends. Each individual torch bearer has a fandom of dozens to hundreds of people. There is a sizzling, effervescent mood.

It is rising to the peak as the burning torch arrives and the next torch is lit, the runner "runs" at a modest pace, this is not about speed but about symbolism. Three stages I can watch close-up, the next ones are already farther away, after a few minutes the show is over. It's like catching fish: The fishing (waiting for fish) takes hours, disembowelling and preparation, half an hour, the fish are eaten within five minutes.

Later when I show my friends and staff the photos, especially those who live in ShenZhen and also were observing the rally are surprised: 'What, you were that close? We've seen nothing, it was all too crowded!'

Four days later, the confident, continuously euphoric mood was suddenly tilted, when in SiChuan Province, a major earthquake occurred. Olympia had disappeared completely from the media and from the debates. It was a cold and also painful acid shower.

All of China mourned, all of China donated intensively (me too), all of China suffered with the emergency measures, all of China wept with the mourners (including me), many volunteers set out to help. All of China (me too) watched the media several times a day, in the company, after the football game we discussed it regularly – how do the rescue efforts proceed? Extent of damage? Could other people be saved? What do the survivors do, how will they find their way back to life? For what reasons did especially schools collapse like houses of cards?

Olympia was out of sight, out of mind. The torch relay was interrupted for several days, but then continued with a different route, and with a different mood and purpose. The message was: "Now more than ever", matching the disposition of the nation. Olympia was increasingly associated with the earthquake, the spate of help grew stronger day by day. SiChuan was only visited on the penultimate day, before the arrival of the torch in BeiJing.

On the eighth of August at eight past eight (the "8" is an important lucky number in Chinese superstition) the opening ceremony begins. I plan to watch it in some restaurant during late dinner, supposing that in all the restaurants tellies will be set up. I wouldn't like to watch the ceremony alone in my apartment, but all of my friends and colleagues are with their families and closer friends.

I'm leaving early, two hours before the event, because I still want to work a little bit outdoors, the weather is fine. However, I have the vague feeling that I might have problems finding a suitable restaurant, not because they have no television, but because they might be too crowded already.

But all restaurants are empty, completely empty. Nice, then I can choose the best one, yes. Far from it. Wherever I ask, I am told: 'We are completely booked.' So I committed a silly mistake. Well, in that case I decide to go into a large restaurant which I usually do not like to visit that much (only with foreign business partners whom I invite) because they offer "international kitchen" and therefore a few foreigners go eating there. But even here: 'We are completely booked.' Meaning that the other foreigners are smarter than me, and I am really annoyed not to have thought of that!

As it is now getting late and I can think of little other opportunities, I talk (Chinese scatting) at the waiter with the patience of Job. I can arrange for getting a single table carried in for me, gladly helping them with moving other furniture, pushing some tables together a bit; my table will be at the edge, yet I will have a good view of the big screen. There the broadcast is already set up, it has turned dark. In ShenZhen, dusk is falling all year round at some time between 6 p. m. (winter) and 7:30 p. m. (summer), as the city is located about 100 km south of the Tropic of Cancer. Around 21 June at approximately 12 o'clock noontime, the sun is here in the very zenith. Accordingly, night is falling sooner than in Hamburg or northern Iceland. Now, in August, this is an advantage for the transmission of the opening ceremony in the restaurant.

Just a few minutes before eight o'clock, the restaurant suddenly gets crowded abruptly – only Chinese people, not a single foreigner! Strangely enough, but no other foreigner had tried his luck, no one else had asked for a seat, it seems I was really the only guy in ShenZhen who did not know that today there was only a place to get if you registered in time. After all, everyone knew when the Olympic Games would start, there was an endless count-down, and how thoughtless I was! But as well lucky.

The opening ceremony begins. The Chinese around me are hooked, they cheer at each other and me, I'm excited together with them. 'Zhong guo jia you! (中国加油)' Now the national teams enter – and we are all gripped by the scene: YaoMing (姚明), the world-famous basketball player, two metres and thirty-two tall, is the flag-bearer of the Chinese team. Next to him, sometimes hand in hand, there is a nine-year-old boy half his size running alongside: LinHao (林浩), he survived the earthquake right in the epicentre.

When he had freed himself from the collapsed classroom, he ran back and saved two of his classmates. He was injured, and during the Olympic parade of nations, the patch on his head was clearly visible. Altogether, ten out of his thirty-two classmates had survived. While they had waited for rescuers and paramedics, LinHao again and again started singing, animating his classmates to join so that they did not fall into depression during the endless waiting for rescue, water, food.

Many Chinese are crying next to me, I cannot help but digging out a handkerchief.

Later I read in a Chinese online news magazine that the boy would almost have not been there as intended, for some of the guards had not been informed that he was to participate and tried to detain him because he was no athlete and did not belong to the team. The problem was solved. Eight seconds late to the plan, the two unlike flag bearers entered the stadium.

During the Olympics nothing is as usual in

China. Schedules are deferred, staff are late ('There's a terrible traffic jam, you know' – 'Guess not! It's rather my impression that you were watching the coverage at home!'), business lunch does not revolve around business but only the number of previously won medals ("medals" referring to gold medals, silver and bronze are for losers and not to be counted) and the possible opportunities for this day. Often there is no talk at all, because everyone is staring at the TV sets that are installed in every restaurant, in every corner, and on all sides, too.

People who otherwise show a limited interest in sports suddenly watch weight-lifting as if banned by magic (this being a discipline of which none at the table is an expert), and there's a great hooray in the restaurant when the Chinese athlete has propped the next heavier weight.

When the Olympics have passed, there is a great void. No one knows what to do now during the evening or what to discuss in business meetings, the Olympics are over.

» Just in the centre of the district NanShan more than one hundred thousand people are gathering along the road where the torch relay will be seen, however, 95 % of these people will see nothing.

» I am standing amid enthusiastic fan-groups waving red flags on the Coastal Boulevard that is connecting NanShan to the centre.

» A young father lets his daughter sleep at his shoulder, the heat and her exhaustion do not restrain his excitement.

» The road is now blocked, which does not prevent some cyclists from performing their own show, challenging the audience to rapturous enthusiasm.

» Also, some drivers managed to circumvent the barriers and move ahead of the relay trek with flag, horn, and fanfare.

» Finally here comes the first car, enjoyably equipped with pretty girls.

» The torch runner right in front of my viewing point. Next to me, his fans are beside themselves with excitement.

Encounters in the botanical garden

During one of my first visits to the botanical garden, I met the Chinese pond heron, a small, strikingly coloured heron of a species that I did not know before. They are there everywhere in the trees and near the water. At that time I witnessed something that made me observing for two hours, deep in thought, while my camera was most busy. Across, on an island in the Fairy Lake, two young herons were pursuing an adult bird, begging constantly. As the young birds were fledged, the parent bird was apparently finally decided to start with education and to inform them that the time of baby feeding was over. They harassed the adult, it fled again and again or banished them. On one occasion a young bird perched on its back, this was too much for it and it hid in the bushes. The young birds wandered around, searching, did not find it and flew away at last.

Then after some time it left its hiding place, sat on a low-lying branch and within minutes had caught a small fish. To my surprise, it flew to my side of the lake, landed only about seven metres away from me in the tree and turned the fish (by raising its head abruptly, slightly opening the beak in very controlled manner and tossing the fish upwards) so that the fish finally slid down the beak into its throat – now it could swallow, otherwise the fish would not have got down.

It was an exciting, rarely observed thing, especially so much close-up!

Today I visit the Forest of Petrified Trees where more than seventy different kinds (probably more than 500 specimen) of partially giant fossil trees from all over China are on display. An impressive site that I enjoy almost on each of my visits.

I notice a large group of older people with big cameras on tripods, equipped with even larger telephoto lenses. I already have a very decent professional camera, such as I also perceive among this group, but my 100-to-400-mm zoom lens really is a toy, when compared to the 400, 500 and 600-mm-telephoto lenses presented here.

All of these guys are apparently ten to fifteen years older than me, they are standing in small groups around a large bush, a shrub with bright red flowers, at a distance of only two or three metres. But why on earth do they need such telephoto lenses to photograph the bush and its flowers? I am standing there some time, not sure whether to leave or to consider interesting what is going on here.

After a little while, I decide just to address those people. It seems that no one understands standard Chinese (Mandarin), i. e. that Chinese which (if I may say so) I am trying to speak. They all speak Cantonese of which I hardly understand a word, and vice versa probably. But one elderly man understands me at last and replies, being able to talk Mandarin.

Before I can ask curiously what they are doing here, I am asked myself, because my equipment isn't looking unprofessional, either. First my camera is examined (with approving murmur), then the lens (mild frown). Now I am asked where I come from, which is usually always the first standard issue, but now subordinated to the more technical subject, what am I doing here in China (interpreted by the fellow in Cantonese, for those around him), whether this was my first visit to the botanical garden, how long I have been already in China, why I am learning Chinese and so on. Next, I am offered something to eat, they have all kinds of fruit here, which I must not refuse.

Then we address my subject. I learn that they are waiting here for a bird, apparently a rare bird of which they know that it shows up here from time to time, but when? I learn that this bird feasts on the flowers – is that a hummingbird? I don't know the Chinese word for „hummingbird", so I paraphrase it – no, it wasn't a hummingbird. A sun-bird maybe? I translate freely from the English: "tai yang niao (太阳鸟)", no idea whether there is a name for this family of birds in Chinese at all, but I am lucky. It is exactly the term for a sun-bird – no, they aren't waiting for a sun-bird, either.

So, we are trying to get more specific. I ask for getting the name pronounced very slowly, writing it in phonetic notation into my mobile phone, character for character, and let the fellow decide which character has to represent what syllable: "zhu bei zhuo hua niao." As soon as I read the characters (朱背啄花鸟) I understand: It is a bird (niao) with a crimson red back (zhu bei), doing something that I do not understand (zhuo) with blossoms (hua). Later in my apartment I am able to find out this with the help of the Internet and my digital dictionary: In German this species is called "scharlachroter mistelfresser", that's "scarlet mistletoe-eater" if translated word by word, and "zhuo" means "to pick", so in English this bird is named "scarlet-backed flower-pecker", which is closer to the Chinese name than the German one. Anyway, this bird does not occur in Europe.

But still it has not shown up, we continue standing in the dazzling sun, the professionals around me wear caps, their cameras and telephoto lenses are protected with blankets or overcoats. I learn more from my opposite, including his name. He is Mr. Su, once working as an engineer and now retired, for a few years he has been just dedicated himself to bird photography only.

Engineer Su, and others, too, with his interpreting assistance, ask me many things, about my wife and family, grandchildren (because I mention this), occupation, housing, travel. This drives me to do research as well, and as there are some women among them I wonder if his wife has joined them, too – no, she is not at all interested in photography, let alone in birds, she is playing in an orchestra. I ask if she is playing in a professional urban symphony orchestra. – No, she's up for an amateur orchestra which is most of the time performing in parks. Of course, of such things I know! Certainly I've seen his wife already there! That pleases him.

In this way, I learn more:
The group is a special bird photography group in a Pensioners' Association that is supported or fed by the city of ShenZhen – of course I did not understand exactly how it is organised, but in any case they are pensioners, many of them wear a vest with the embroidered name of their group. They have a website where they display their photos and discuss them together, they drive around together to take their photographing opportunities, enjoy life and fill their memory chips. They meet more or less regularly, especially if someone finds out where some peculiar bird may be observed, then they will all be there and try to take the best images.

Finally, our flower-pecker does no longer splash out. It approaches on-flight, the talks abruptly cease, frantic activity begins, the clicking of digital cameras around me fills the air. While I trigger more selectively, the others seem to keep on it with automatic fire. I'm moving slowly, though, looking for the best viewing path through the branches, being most mobile with my zoom lens and without a tripod.

It is an exceptionally beautiful, stunning little bird. Not only is its whole back bright red, but against its otherwise pitch-black feathers there is set on its back an irregular, ragged strip of beautiful scarlet colour, "zhu bei" is exactly the right description! Hard to photograph it. It is bouncing back and forth, and if at last it is just sitting still at times, sticking its beak into a flower, then it is posing just behind either a branch or twig, or a leaf or a flower is concealing its head, or, if for once it is brightly within view, it hops off at once. I understand now why they are waiting for such a long time and do not just come here some day: Not just hours or days but weeks may pass until you have achieved a really good image.

I inquire whether they know how many individuals of this birds are here – they have no idea.

Quite contrary to my initial plans I remain there for several hours. The group makes waiting fun, I do not regret to miss other places today. Little by little I am learning to know other group members, including a married couple (both in their late 60s). They have the latest, most professional camera from Canon (I have "only" the generation before that), in automatic shutter mode the new model acquires a lot more shots, so they inform me. Both of them have bought it immediately after launch in China a few weeks ago.

Engineer Su, however, is still more than satisfied with a model of the ante-penultimate generation, it is a slightly inferior model in comparison to my camera.

The woman has "only" a 400 mm-telephoto lens, her husband has a few weeks ago bought a 600 mm, her's was quite all right, she thinks, but her husband was insatiable.

We have fun, laugh a lot, I'm over the moon to have found such a pensioners' group of bird photographers in ShenZhen, and I confess that I am surprised to see that retired people commit to bird photography in ShenZhen, and what's more, with such professional, expensive, high-quality equipment.

The flower-pecker shows up several times. Later, in the work-up of my photos, I can see from the pattern of red colouration that there were four different males visiting us today, plus a female that was not so nicely dyed but rather unimpressive.

The pensioners' group I have unfortunately never met again so far. Too bad. Maybe I should have shared addresses or telephone numbers or joined them, my age is not so far from their level. But since they have a website, I can still catch up later.

» The two young birds annoy the adult bird.

» After it has hidden and gotten rid of the two adolescents, it can catch a fish and swallow it just in front of me.

» The pensioners' bird photographer group in the forest of petrified trees, waiting for the special bird.

» They talk shop all the time, engineer Su is explaining something to his friend.

» The experts verify to make sure everything is properly set, because for this is no time when the bird shows up.

» The collection of petrified trees from all over China is impressive.

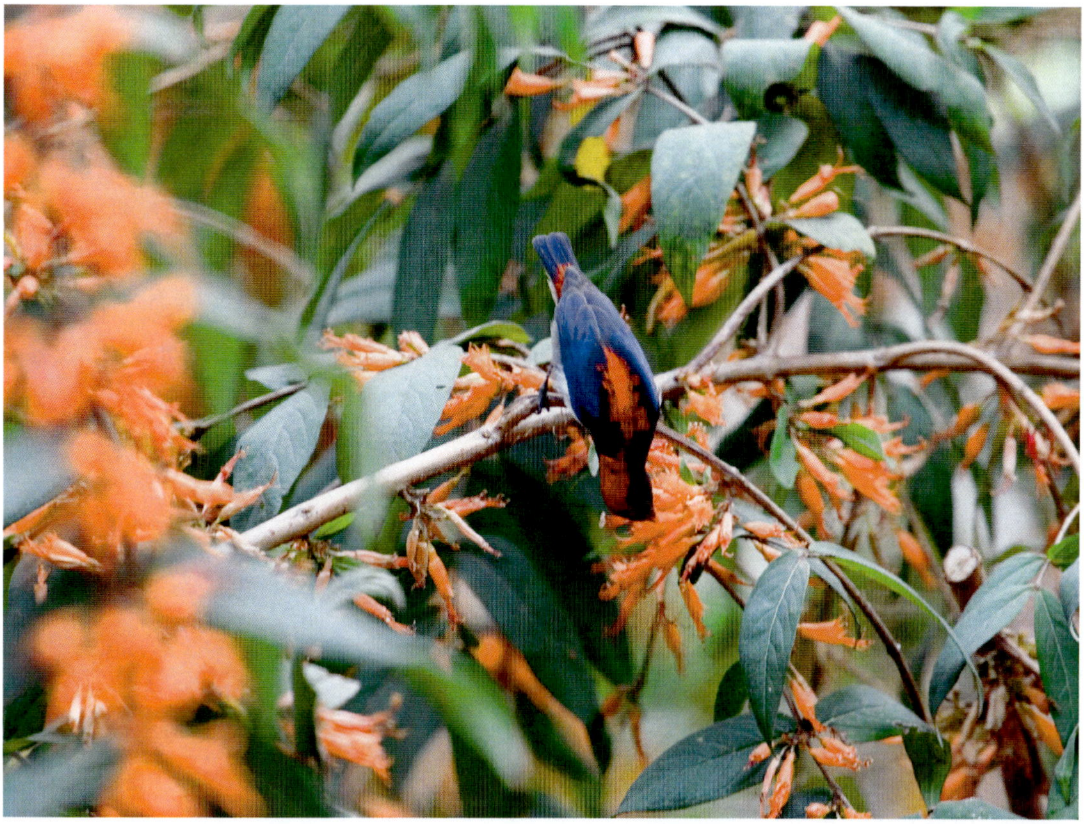

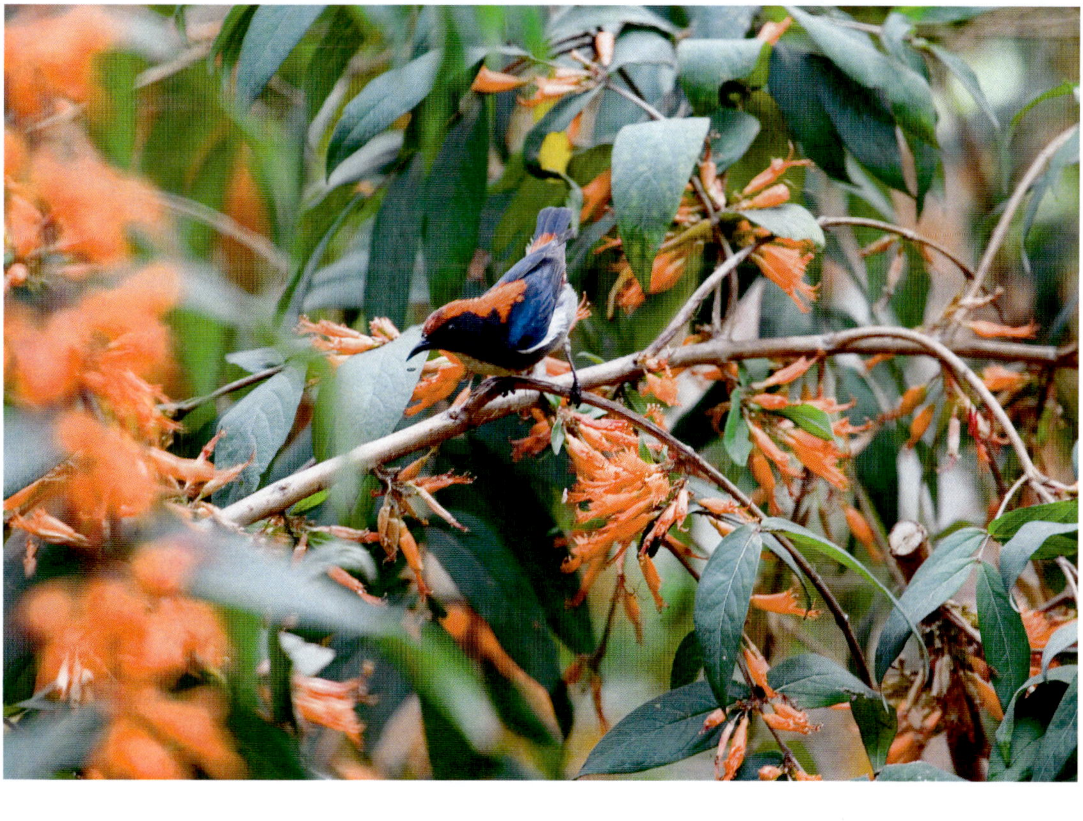

» Finally there is the scarlet-backed flower-pecker, the contrast of its plumage with the red colour on the back is overwhelmingly beautiful.

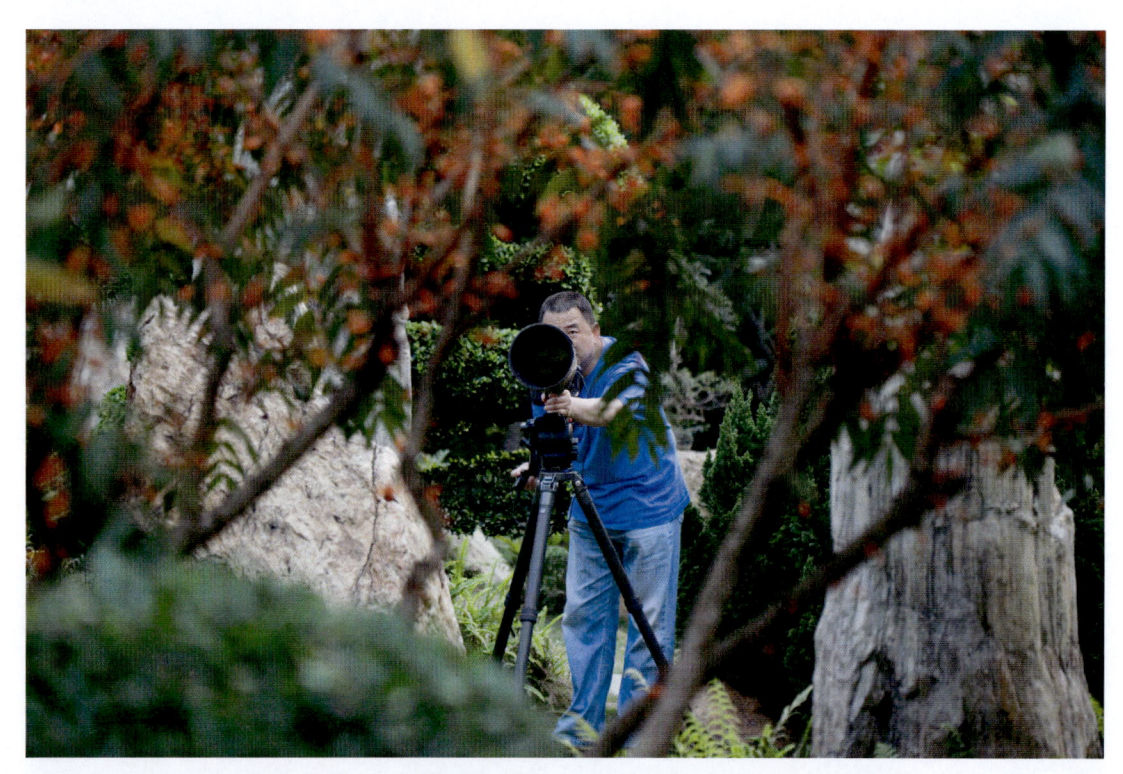

» That's how we photographers are looking from the flower-pecker's viewpoint.

Getting and raising children with joy and sorrow

Engineer SunLi is the mother, Engineer Chu (褚) is the father of HaoKang (昊康) who is more than a year old. Wang LanBo, a programmer, is the father of SunMing (苏铭), he met his wife Wang QingFang (王青芳) only a year before the birth of the child, and married her. Both just happen to have the same surname "Wang". Chinese couples have no common family names, "QingFang" is a first name, promising clear and wonderful scents.

SunLi and Wang LanBo have little in common, apart from the fact that they do not even have the same sex, they have never met, they do not live in the same neighbourhood, actually they only have one thing in common which they do not even know: They have a mutual acquaintance, LaoWei; SunLi for professional, Wang LanBo for footballing reasons.

And they have something in common with many other parents in China: one child, a son, about the same age. For LaoWei this is an opportunity to unobtrusively make comparative observations.

In both cases the parents did not mind the sex of the child. Ultrasonic checks are made in China, too, but physicians are not tolerated to reveal whether it be a son or a daughter. Sometimes grandmothers who absolutely want to know whether it will be a son try to make a deal with the doctors, but at least in these two cases, the physicians kept tight. Too often female foetuses are still getting aborted in China, even in advanced stages of development.

Chinese grandparents are generally very much involved in the care and upbringing of the grandchildren, also nowadays in many cases they still assume even the sway. SunLi's mother came to ShenZhen immediately after learning of the pregnancy, and most of the time until birth, and months after, she dwelt in the not very big apartment of the married engineers couple. Of the eight months before the birth she spent only two weeks in her home-town, her working husband, the future grandfather, had to cope alone all the time. QingFang, however – whose mother was only occasionally, for a few weeks, in ShenZhen during pregnancy –, like many other expectant mothers moved three months before the expected birth date to her parents in her hometown. Now Wang LanBo, the future father, had for months to cope alone. For the birth, he went for three days to his wife and his parents-in-law, he did not get more days off by his company.

In the first six months after birth, SunLi dwelt in her own apartment with husband and mother. For three months the mother in law was there as well, making things crammed, all SunLi had to do was to breastfeed. But in any case the family was together. LaoWei visited them two or three times, and under critical (and then appreciative) glances of the two grandmothers (and later, just the maternal grandmother) he demonstrated his grandfather's skills to move a tired but exhilarated baby to fall asleep at his shoulders. The foreign "YeYe" (grandpa) was accepted and we compared notes of grandparenthood, as far as the Chinese language sufficed.

QingFang, however, lived in the home of her parents, her husband, the young father, remained alone in ShenZhen, he had to work, only occasionally he flew to the home-town of his wife at least sometimes, just to see his child.

After weaning, SunLi's mother decided to fly with her grandson back to her home-town. SunLi was not amused, but what should she do about it? She resumed her work, and her mother wanted to return home for having personal disputes with her husband again, not just on the phone, to restore order in the apartment and to discuss everything in detail with her friends at home. This she has been missing in ShenZhen. SunLi was sad – her baby was gone.

"In the old times" everything was easier, as it has been all over the world. In most cases, marriage was within the same town, the son often remained near his parents, but not too near if could be avoided. A plausible rule is evidence to how close parents should stay to the children: "一碗热汤的距离 yi wan re tang de ju li", "as far as a bowl of hot soup", so far that you can still bring along a warm soup without it cooling down (in Spain there is a corresponding rule of life: "one cardigan away," we should therefore live as far or close from our parents that you have to pull over a cardigan if you want to visit each other, but no more than a cardigan). Those days have passed for most, both in Spain and in China, now people live mostly in separate towns, farther away than a cardigan or a bowl of soup.

QingFang returned with her baby to ShenZhen about six months later, the family was finally united, the father was happy.

SunLi managed to convince her mother that she would return with the baby to ShenZhen after three months of absence. But things were almost beyond repair: Her own son knew her no more, she could not calm him when he screamed, in the beginning he did not even tolerate her to feed him from a bottle, only grandmother was allowed to do that. It took many weeks till some order was reinstalled and she, the proper mother, was again accepted by her infant son. Now also the strange-looking foreign "YeYe" was a reason for the little one to be afraid and even to precautionary cry a little whenever LaoWei came to a visit, but after a while the stranger was accepted as a playmate after all. This has also prompted SunLi's mother to reconsider her opinion of the "somewhat too exploitative" boss of her daughter.

Wang LanBo did everything what a modern young Chinese father is doing, he played a lot with his son, all went well. When the little one was just over a year old, QingFang, the mother, decided that she wanted to work again. Soon after, the toddler was brought into the home-town of the mother and has since lived with his grandmother. Programmer Wang had all of that imagined differently. But his wife and his mother-in-law had already decided everything without him, as they told him how things would proceed from here …

SunLi's baby grew up and quickly turned into a toddler, crawled and babbled and began to walk. Mother and father went on well with him, but granny ruled the roost. Finally she decided that she had now been long enough in ShenZhen, she would now go home and take the child with her. He was just a year and two months old, and mother and child (and father) were again separated from each other. Engineer Sun had all of that imagined differently. But her mother and her mother-in-law had already decided without asking her how things would proceed from here.

SunLi and her husband had long before pregnancy bought a second home, there their grandparents were supposed to live, sometimes with, sometimes without grandchild. The apartment is just minutes by car from their own one, so they can move quickly from one to the other. That would be comfortable. But SunLi's father has to retire first, till then, the plans cannot be implemented. Till then, the second new apartment will remain empty, waiting for grandparents and grandchild.

At least the engineers couple does not have to pay bank loans for the apartment. Engineer Chu earns very good, HuaWei is paying above average, SunLi earns well in LaoWei's company. Of course, they haven't yet accumulated as much money as a great apartment in booming ShenZhen will cost today, but both parents are contributing all their savings, all their own pensions, and so the engineers Chu and Sun only need to take about 10 % of the purchase price as credit, paying it off within a few months.

It is perfectly normal in China that close relatives, and even more distant relatives and close friends, lend each other enormous quantities of money at no cost and without a written contract (such enormous quantities that it even has economic importance and thus is an element of the financial sector which clearly distinguishes China from most other countries). No one would ever think of not paying it back. In any case, Engineer Chu will support his parents fully when they will have grown old, engineer Sun will support her parents, too. For parents, it's not a risk to invest their savings into the second apartment of the young couple, either they will dwell there or they will definitely be funded if the pension should not be sufficient. China's state welfare system is meagre and full of holes, if at all existent, but the private family social network is tightly woven and strong.

Not only in terms of the social network, China is very different from Germany, but also in terms of what is common or not in the rearing of children. Beginning with the notion that young mothers are not allowed to leave the apartment for the first one month after childbirth (after return from hospital), may not have a shower, are forced only to rest, eat, drink and breastfeed a baby (if I got that right from my football friends, that's **really** everything they are tolerated to do, even my friends were not allowed to do anything else besides …). The grandmothers hold sway.

In many families, even the babies may not get out at the open air. If they live with their grandparents in colder regions of China, they are wrapped in warm clothes in a way that perceiving that with German eyes we would be worried to death – how are they supposed to move? They barely can, not to mention learning how to crawl.

But ultimately, they will learn, and they all learn how to walk. According to our understanding this may in part happen a little later "than usual", but many Chinese toddlers are dry much sooner than our German counterparts. First of all they learn (through imitation) very early to squat in most stable manner. For us, the squatting position in general is unstable, if not painful. Chinese squat to relax, it is the next thing their young children learn after walking.

I am tempted to think that Chinese have developed other knee forms than we have, for my knees cannot stand this for long. But the squatting position is not only helpful to relax (at least for Chinese), but also for the completion of digestion.

So we are almost at the point of understanding why Chinese toddlers get dry faster than German ones: during the day they are (unlike our babies and young children) not wrapped in nappies but dressed in thin pants with opened crotches (from far forward to far back), being just cut apart. As soon as the first signs are visible that the child is going to pee (or worse), he or she is either prevented from or, if able to can stand and squat autonomously, urged to squat, so as not to soil the panties.

The apartments are usually not covered with carpet. The toddler can thus do business just on the floor, the tiles are then wiped clean. The more the child finds out about the physical reactions, relatives will encourage letting them know when to bring the pot, the child squats and exercises control over the call of nature – and thus it is not uncommon for 12 or 18 months old children to be almost "dry", at least during the day (at night they get nappies.)

These are obviously for Chinese parents and grandparents the smallest problems.

SunLi ponders this way and that how to balance work, family constraints, and her role as a mother which she has not even assumed properly. The alternatives, a "nanny" or a "minder", as we would call them, she has ruled out so far. There is a lack of confidence, she does not know anyone who knows anyone who can be trusted in this matter. Her network cannot help, no experience in this subject present.

SunLi is afraid that her son might be abducted and sold. Apparently it happens in China every now and then that nannies steal and offer the entrusted children for sale, or that they do not pay enough attention and the child in their care is kidnapped. China is large, and children apparently can disappear. Chinese television news and newspapers occasionally report on such cases, and organised crime specialised on child abduction does, alas, exist in China, too. (In 2010, China installed a new system of special investigation teams to more effectively combat this human trafficking.) In ShenZhen, in one of my favourite parks, only twenty minutes of walking from my apartment, a baby was abducted not long ago while the caring grandmother had only a few minutes not been paying attention, chatting a little too long with other grandmothers and looking the other way …

SunLi wavers back and forth, while her son lives a thousand kilometres away with her mother, and while the mother-in-law interferes in the raising, too. One thing is clear to her from the daily phone calls: HaoKang has his grandparents, all four of them, completely under control even though he is hardly one year and a half old. If he wants something or does not want it, and if any of four does not behave as he expected, grandpa or grandma is penalised with love withdrawal: He refuses looking at them for quite a while, turns pointedly to another grandparent who will be vying for his favour immediately.

Grandparents and parents in China desire that their children will fare "better" than they did 50 or 25 years ago. Therefore, many children are coddled in China, as SunLi perceives with worry. For in China, only girls should actually be pampered or raised in "substantial environment" while boys have to learn the hard side of life, according to a "rule": 女孩子富养, 男孩子穷养, nǚ hái zi fù yǎng, nán hái zi qióng yǎng: to raise girls rich, boys poor. Girls shall learn about the beautiful things in the world, broaden their horizon, not the least in order to prevent them from falling prey to the very first young man who would offer her no future, they must instead by picky. Boys shall learn to assert themselves in the harsh cope.

We may doubt whether all of this is well and good, even more justified are doubts whether boys are really brought up today like that. Engineer Sun and programmer Wang are (entirely independently) more and more worried, more and more concerned: How do and how can they design the upbringing of their son, especially, how to retain influence (if they have any)?

In addition, the very tough competition in China makes them fear. Right now already they are afraid in their son's place that he will find things as hard as they did, or perhaps harder still, whether at school or later, in the university (if me makes it to there at all) he will achieve a sufficient score. They hear and read of many parents who launch into a targeted education of their children as early as infancy. And from that a service industry is growing, such as found in HongKong already: English courses offered for three-year-old, they shall as well recite poems and read and write at least a few hundred characters latest when they are four years old. And piano lessons they must have no later than with five years. Do they really want to do that with their son, go through all the stress?

But how else should he get a job, if he fails to provide above-average performance? They do not so much conceive of opening his own business, they seek for themselves and each for their son something "safe".

At the same time they want to spend a "nice" life, and the meaning of "beautiful" they grasp from daily television and more often and in more detail from the web. Here, in countless forums, experiences are exchanged that Chinese students and expatriates have made abroad. Full of envy (and the envy is not covered up) they present to each other detailed photos revealing what kind of houses, with large and beautiful gardens, are there to be acquired in the U.S. or Canada or Australia for what pittance, compared to the premium prices for an apartment in the 20th floor of a skyscraper in ShangHai, and this arouses envy.

Programmer Wang learns from Chinese residing abroad that the pressure to compete and perform is incomparably lower in schools and universities in the United States, Canada or Australia. 'Why would my son go to school and later to university under such pressure as there is here in China, why wouldn't he have it easy, as easy as, for example, children in Australia, Canada, who are constantly praised for how great they were doing this or that, no matter how great it really was?'

About this some critical comments might be uttered. But programmer Wang is no educational politician comparing education levels of various countries, and he does not intend to become such. He does not mind that a terribly high percentage (probably between 25 and 30%) of the American students, acclaimed to the skies, will later stumble through life as so-called "functional illiterates", read: more than a quarter of young people and adults in the U.S. cannot grasp simple messages when reading nor write in simple words. Australia does not look much different, even in Germany, we have according to estimates four million functional illiterates (some sources claim twice as much). So much for the success of learning without pressure. That's of course not what programmer Wang would like, but he does not want to know about it, either.

Like many millions of well educated and active young Chinese people, he is comparing information picked out from the internet, forums, blogs and other sources, written by overseas Chinese. They tell of amazing six weeks of annual holiday, as well as many public festive days, no overtime, little or no pressure to perform, the family has two cars, you drive at least once a year on holidays for three or four weeks, anyone who wants to can attend University essentially for free, except for some subjects, there is no selection by school performance, no ranking, if you are unemployed, the social network is supporting you, you do not have to go begging – who would not like China to be like that? Work less and earn more, work less, yet have more – who wouldn't?

So programmer Wang and his wife dream of Australia, and the dream turns more vivid as, months before the birth of their son, a befriended couple plans to emigrate from ShenZhen with their then five year old daughter to Australia. For one year the debate is raging while the little one has been living for years with her grandparents in BeiJing, connected with the parents only through almost daily phone calls and visits every few weeks, in one direction or another.

One day, the decision is made, the friends will go to Australia. And within a few weeks the decision is turned into reality. The husband, research manager of the Chinese subsidiary of a Japanese company, quits his job, without having another in Australia. His boss, a Japanese, cannot hold him back, he is very saddened by the loss of this powerful young man.

Even during the pre-move they learn this: The Japanese boss of the Chinese subsidiary company has himself been agitating with the top man in Japan, to achieve that his former research manager in China would now get a job with the Australian subsidiary of the Japanese group. And that's what happens – for the friends of programmer Wang things have gradually worked out in a way they could not have dreamt of any better. With a "small" caveat: the former research manager who is now, in Australia, only product manager, complains after a few weeks already about the lack of requirements, it was dead boring, whether he came or not came, was working or not working, did not make any difference.

Programmer Wang now dreams even more sincerely of Australia, for he is still working under stress.

» In a park named "QingQing ShiJie" (青青世界, "Green World"), offering many activities and interesting places for families under the label of "Nature and Ecology", there is a playground full of old, traditional toys, here is an old heavy barrow made of wood and iron. The children consider it great (many adults too).

» In the botanical garden, the grandmother plays with her grandchildren who have something fished out of the Fairy Lake and throw it in again and again and to fetch it another time.

» Discussion among experts in the park.

165

» Grandpa and granddaughter are tired.

» This Muslim grandfather is sitting on the street outside his shop, talking to his grandson.

Odd: a World Cup with 33 teams

No matter where the FIFA is holding a World Cup, the largest fan base by far is found in China, spending a month as glued to the TV every day, at home, in restaurants, in public places.

China is crazy about football. I meet many people in China who know by name the players of all sorts of clubs in Italy, Spain, Germany, England. Only by their respective Chinese names, that is, thus the German national player Schweinsteiger is simply called "Xiao zhu" (小猪) which would about correspond to his German nickname "Schweini", i. e. "Piggy", because the transmission of the name, Schweinsteiger, into Chinese is too complicated. The Chinese give to any foreigner a name that plugs into the Chinese linguistic system of syllables. Thus the name of the player Lahm is rendered "LaMu, (拉姆)" Löw becomes "LeFu, (勒夫)" Klose will be "KeLuoZe (克洛泽)". There is simply no word or syllable that would end in "m" or "f" (the way the "w" in Löw's name is pronounced in German), Chinese cannot at all pronounce a term like "Lahm".

They observe the European football leagues; CCTV 5 broadcasts on weekends plenty of live games and even more summaries and comments, my friends know more about the league than me, even in the German Federal league they can assign more players to their respective clubs than I do.

When the 2006 World Cup began in Germany, in China all hell broke loose. There was no restaurant, no public square where the World Cup was not celebrated 24 hours a day. Whenever we visited clients, and no matter where – whether in the evening in the restaurant or somewhere on the road or in a „pub" (if you can call them like that in China), we were glued to the live broadcast or a repeat or a match analysis, whatever there was. And the Chinese people bet like mad, asking me on what they should bet. How should I know the outcome? I am not an octopus and my name isn't Paul.

Who (other than hard-core football fans) would watch in Germany a game like Paraguay vs. Trinidad & Tobago? Who would watch the game if Germany was not even represented at the World Cup (as China wasn't). In China, though, the restaurants are crowded, every good action is clamantly commented, any missed goal registered with disappointment – for either side.

My friends have watched more football games than I, beginning at night (e. g. midnight or 3 o'clock in the morning). During the semi-finals and final, I was fortunately in Germany. When we get together on weekends during a World Cup, there is only one topic: the World Cup.

When Germany lost in the semifinals against Italy, the whole of China was over the moon, for the Italian national team is very popular, for Chinese football aficionados, the Italian football league is a prime focus of interest. Germany is not popular but respected and recognised. Italy is loved. I received half-baked compassion.

When Germany turned out third, I received kind and gentle good wishes, telling me I should not fret too much, the Germans had been outstanding, just not quite enough, for Italy had been simply unbeatable. When Italy won the world championship, China was euphoric. No matter at all that Italy played poorly and rather was the luckier one …

During the Euro 2008, it was not very different. The Chinese bet, watched all the games, even in the middle of the night while I restricted myself to those in the evening and to the summaries of the night time games in the morning, during breakfast.

But now the World Cup 2010 is held in South Africa. First, I think that the football craze has lessened, there seem to sit fewer people in the restaurants in front of the TV now, but I am wrong. It's the preliminary round games, such as Algeria vs. Slovenia which this time do not tear the Chinese off their feet. But in truth they are electrically stimulated, want to know everything, and research everything on any team on any website.

As North Korea loses 1-2 vs. Brazil, immediately a lament is struck up: North Korea has at least scored a goal against Brazil! And China, 2002 in Korea, how badly had this gone? And then everything is getting compared what China and North Korea ever achieved against any team in the world, or didn't.

There is a website where all this is related – and it ends with a joke: ‚Stop insulting North Korea!‘ For how can you compare a football giant like North Korea with that football dwarf, China?

„The" Chinese (at least the ones I know) are not at all interested in Chinese domestic football, not even in the national team. They do not expect anything. There are web pages containing lists of potential pretexts for coaches and players (and media) for why this next game was lost as well and what was to the disadvantage of the Chinese team with regard to the opponent: „The grass was too high/low/wet/dry" – „The kick-off was too early/late" – „The weather was too hot/cold/dry/wet" – „Most surprisingly, the opposing team has allowed player XY to play, who could have foretold that?" and more of the funniest, meaningless excuses. There are lists of what luxury cars the national players and their wives or girlfriends are driving, and there are polls on whether it wouldn't be better if the players were sent into a coal mine to mine coal, because they were surely better off there. In chat rooms people debate (hundreds of thousands of people get their pleasure out of it) how it could be arranged that the Chinese national team took part but once in the World Cup finals. The proposal was made to convince FIFA that a place was conceded to Antarctica, next, China must somehow manage to be admitted to the Antarctic play-offs. Then, in the first leg in Antarctica, the Chinese team must achieve a draw versus the team of penguins, and then, in the return match in China, the penguins could possibly be beaten, ideally during the sweltering hot summer in southern China. There are fervent debates whether this cunning plan could be implemented ...

The Chinese TV media serve the best interest of the spectators. They present the Games and their analysis and discussions in a very knowledgeable and extremely dedicated manner, at the same time relaxed and humorous, so that in comparison, the German commentators on German games are like choir-boys. Chinese commentators are visibly competent and enjoying themselves. Spanish, Portuguese and Brazilian TV commentators commenting on Spanish, Portuguese, Brazilian goals or victories can hardly compete to the cheers of the Chinese TV commentators when commenting on games of Algeria vs. Slovenia. They are critical, committed, knowledgeable and just show their passion for football.

In the case of the 2010 World Cup, everything seems to me a little different at first. In preparing, China beats France in Réunion, France is already kicked out from the preliminary round.

The Chinese comment: ‚Sure, if even China can beat France, how should it prevail against such strong countries like Uruguay, Mexico or South Africa?'

When Italy also does not survive the preliminary round, there is national mourning, at least on television. Immediately after the decisive game that Slovakia won 3-2, CCTV 5 is endlessly reading comments that viewers have sent shortly before to a website. Everyone is complaining volubly that the World Cup was now so empty, grey and no longer exciting. Until, to roars of laughter among the panellists on the dais, the moderator reads another posting: ‚I have been working several years in Slovakia and I have to wonder how much it is mourned that they eliminated Italy. Can you not even for a minute assess the performance of the Slovaks?' The moderator puts on a play straight face and drops a few sober words of assessment, laughter increases, then more grief for Italy follows, but with a lot of humour.

As the final representative of Asia who anyway is not regarded with much affection – Japan – is as well eliminated, the mental support of the Chinese focuses preferably on Germany, more so because the young German team this time plays an entertaining brand of football. In the final that the Germans miss because of the defeat by Spain, Spain does receive the moral support of hundreds of millions of Chinese, as the Spaniards are to some extent regarded as semi-Italians, and their league is followed in China also with much interest.

One impressive feature are the 3-D-simulations that help in analysing game situations. The repetition of a game scene is stopped at a desired moment, the image is transformed into a model allowing the presenter to zoom in and out, illustrating from the perspective of the goalkeeper the position of the wall, the free kick taker or the flying ball, approaching by a shot from 25 metres distance. To me it is a mystery how they can convert the 2-D-image into such a 3-D simulation, very impressive.

This goes on all around the clock, you can switch on CCTV 5 at any time of day and night, and you are supplied with all current and less recent news, images, summaries, or even a complete game of the night before.

The quarter-final, Germany vs. Argentina, is watched by 52 million Chinese TV spectators, although it began at 10 o'clock in the evening (local time) and ended at midnight. China was the prime TV-spectators' nation of this World Cup. The same game had been watched in Germany by nearly 26 million viewers.

I do not know whether there is any other country in the world that features so many (hundreds of millions!) football fans, while both the domestic professional football as the national team earn no interest, but only spitting sarcasm. Of course, the Chinese do in fact want to have a powerful national team, too, but they have – at least at present – given up hope that ever this should come to pass. Which does not diminish their enthusiasm for football!

And then the departure of the Italians, them who this time played unmistakably bad, now even Italy's toughest hardcore fan from China cannot deny that this country as well does not have a good national team any more! How depressing, you may need to reorient yourself?

But it is not like that. No one reorients, they go on taking part in everything the World Cup has to offer. On television and the internet everything is shown, analysed, annotated, and compared what may be shown, analysed, compared and commented:

- An Australian group of fans is arriving in South Africa at the airport, shortly after, a Chinese group is following. They meet at the baggage carousel, the Chinese television is there, the Chinese ask the Australians, ‚Where are you from, what are you doing here?' The Australians truthfully reply that they wanted to support their national team, and now the Australians ask back, ‚And where are you folks from?' – ‚From China.' – ‚But China is not taking part at all!' – ‚Of course, we know that, too, but we just want to watch some football!'
- A Chinese businessman needs to travel to Japan; in the evening he wants to watch the World Cup in a pub, the TV is on, but it is a soap opera! The pub visitors are only interested in the background noise, not in the World Cup, even though Japan had not yet been eliminated at that time.
- When England is eliminated, it takes only two days and the World Cup has disappeared from the headlines there, at once, Tiger Woods with his marital problems and the resulting financial problems is more interesting.
- In the days before the semi-finals and the finals, as there are no games, CCTV 5 repeats even preliminary games in full-length; in-between there are analyses, discussions and the constantly updated gallery of the most beautiful goals and the best goalkeeper saves of the tournament. Likewise historical programmes are broadcast, old finals between Germany and the Netherlands, Germany and Brazil, and the Wembley goal. In fairness I must mention that during these days also other sports receive coverage again, such as the Tour de France and volleyball.
- On the internet, dozens of websites compile all information on all the teams, how many people are members of the supporting team (in Germany, there's a ratio players-to-carers of 1:2), the wives and girlfriends of players are presented and photographed (Xiao Zhu's – the reader recalls, perhaps, that is is the Chinese name of Schweinsteiger – girlfriend is chosen as the nicest among German players' wives), all children of all players can be found on websites, people discuss whether today's Löw or former Klinsmann are more handsome; photos of key players are enlarged, showing the eye area, so that they can be compared and analysed: ‚Messi has a glance that's full of sadness, Kaka has a bright and open look.'

And of course the fans are getting informed that most products used in South Africa during the World Cup were produced in China, including 60 million condoms in World Cup proper packaging, all of which go to South Africa, all the stadium seats, of course, almost all mobile phones that are required by the organisers, coaches, players and fans, 12 million official balls that are for a smaller part used in the games, for a much larger part sold to active fans all over the world.

Not to mention the vuvuzelas, those long horns with the piercing sound that give the TV-viewers at home the impression that several large clouds of hornets are buzzing around the microphones. They are produced in a handful of small, inconspicuous back-house plastic factories in ZheJiang and GuangDong.

One of the factories (evidently the vuvuzela manufacturing pioneer in China) reported that first, they received a few months ago an order for ten thousand items. Then the whole thing grew, however, and they received an order for three million units. They could not accept it because they were not prepared for such an extreme mass production (apart from semi-automatic injection moulding, the horns are assembled manually by workers who earn two or three thousand RMB a month), and so they took but a partial order for one million units. The remaining order portions went to a few other factories that had to adapt in an incredibly short time to this boom of orders, and they made it. Neighbouring factories produced accordingly the requested amounts of ear plugs.

The manufacturer sells the horns, probably to a first of the many intermediaries, for four RMB; as soon as the big order came, the price was "gruesomely" increased to five RMB per item, equal to about 0.60 €, after all, they wanted to have a share in the boom. In South Africa they were finally sold for more than ten times that much. I don't want to know what they cost in Germany. After all, this little company, that in normal years earned 18 million RMB, increased its sales in 2010 to 28 million (or about three million Euros), of which remains according to their own claims only 5% profit. The lion's share of the profits is thus stuck again at the intermediate trade ...

Only the referee whistles are not produced in China, but in Germany. They have to meet tough specifications, for their sound has to drown the vuvuzelas from China. Only German whistles can manage that, so the Chinese admit without envy. 'We do the vuvuzelas, you do the whistles, that's fair, isn't it?'

So the Chinese say of themselves that ultimately the World Cup relies on China, not only because they achieve the largest group of television viewers, but also because they provide by far the largest number of products you need for the World Cup. So China was actually the 33rd team in the tournament.

The Chinese New Year

"Mayor" Song – former farmer actually, now real estate entrepreneur in ShenZhen, from the village XiaShaCun – is no religious man. Essentially he does not believe in any gods, but who knows, if not maybe ... and also, no one knows what exactly is going on after death. Actually, "Mayor" Song claims that then everything will be over the way one did not exist before birth, and everything was not even black, but nothing. Like that it was after death, too.

But he does not think about that much, yet (in case that his way of nihilism was proven wrong) wants to leave a small door open, it cannot hurt.

So once a year he visits a temple to engage in the currently prevailing religious tasks. An outsider who knows after all that ShenZhen is just 30 years old will be surprised to find that there are many temples in this modern, new city. This atheist country and this newly established city are building temples? Indeed they do, and better still, there are, surprisingly, even some temples that had originated several hundred years ago. Now industrial or new residential areas have grown all around them. There are chan-Buddhist (known to the West as Zen-Buddhist), Daoist and Confucian temples, or mixtures thereof, and of utmost interest is that there are temples with Confucian orientation, even though Confucianism is not quite a religion.

But also Buddhism and Daoism (or Tao) are no religions to our understanding of the word. All of them are rather dedicated to more secular aims, to creation of harmony, ethical behaviour and enlightenment through meditation. While there are gods, these are better called ancestors or historical figures, in compliance with the Chinese people's faith which is enormously revering and respecting one's ancestors. In contrast to Islam and the Christian religions, theirs are not religions to claim sole representation and don't urge you to confess your faith. They are tolerant, open, flexible. To Chinese it is strange, altogether incomprehensible, that religion could be a reason for warfare or perpetrating terror attacks. It is just a way to organise one's life and togetherness in the family and society and to prepare for the fact that there may be an afterlife or a re-birth, until you eventually access nirvana (as far as the Buddhists claim). Why kill for that?

The Chinese religions are rather philosophies and rules, or collections of aphorisms assisting in better understanding life and regulating the cohabitation. Everyone is free to decide whether and how and what he or she believes. Thus it is understandable why the Communist Party and the Government tolerate religions and religious activities (as long as they are not directed against the state) and to build new temples.

"Mayor" Song is old, he has been thinking a lot about life and death. He does not believe in gods, but still a little altar to worship the ancestors is in his corridor, lovingly maintained by his wife and supplied daily with fresh fruit; he does not believe that the various gods of the Chinese will make a difference, but still before any large investment ('just in case!') he prayed to Cai Shen (财神), the God of Finances. He does not believe in ghosts, but respects the concerns of his wife who sees them everywhere. Most remarkable he finds that his wife will get off an elevator when stopping on a floor between and no one enters: 'Then a ghost has entered the elevator, I would not share that place with it!' But he lets her talk without a word against, smiling softly to himself, shaking his head unnoticeably. He does not believe in re-incarnation, but will not ultimately exclude anything. ('It cannot hurt.')

Since he does not quite know which back door to leave open he also is not determined on which temple to visit but changes every year. This year again, it was pure chan-Buddhism's turn, with the large HongFa Temple (弘法寺) above the botanical garden. It is the only pure chan-Buddhist temple in ShenZhen, and the most modern temple of its kind in China.

There is a varied crowd. Old and young, poor and wealthy, healthy and sick, individuals, unmarried and married couples, groups, adults with and without children – here you can meet a blend of all residents of ShenZhen. In many places memorabilia are sold, such as incense sticks and other accessories which are necessary for the prayer and the offerings.

Wang QingFang's mother is a deeply devout Buddhist, whatever that may mean. She is studying the books and teachings of chan-Buddhism, and her daughter has shown her (because that is modern) corresponding websites, set up with bookmarks on an older laptop, which she received from her daughter's husband. She buys CDs of enlightenment, meditation, and training content.

Often she visited a temple, gives offerings and prays. For her daughter shall conceive a healthy baby, no matter whether son or daughter. She is not as crazy as all those Cantonese who want only sons. Where are they supposed to come from if there are no daughters? So she prays often. Four weeks before birth, they travel together to a temple in the home-town. Wang QingFang's mother is praying, Wang QingFang herself does not, but she respects her mother. Later she will say, 'Yet it helped, you see!' For Wang QingFang has conceived a healthy boy.

Every time her mother is in ShenZhen, visiting her daughter and now also the child, she goes to the botanical garden, not for watching plants and birds, but to climb the little hill, passing through a dense rainforest, and then up the stairs to the HongFa Temple.

Today, a week before the Chinese New Year, she is back again, her daughter has taken her (and her son) there another time. Wang QingFang is walking with the baby in the stroller while her mother goes to the temple. In previous years, her daughter travelled with her husband at New Year to the respective families, back in the home-towns, but since the year before the last, it is the other way round. Her daughter and her son-in-law have rented an apartment nearby from friends who went to their respective parents, there, the parents of the son-in-law and the young couple are living. Herself and her husband are meanwhile living in the apartment of the young family, and this year they do so together with their grandson.

During the day they will meet in either apartment, beginning on New Year's eve. Now, there are still six more days to come until then, so it's time to pray for success. The gathering of the two families is not as smooth as last year when everything was new, because the maternal grandmother likes to rule the roost though she is only the mother of the mother! Unfortunately, it is so that the family of the son – and this is supported by millennia of tradition –, claims the proper rights. For that reason, the Chinese language distinguishes between the two grandmothers. In English we may describe them as paternal resp. maternal grandmothers, but both are equal "grandmothers", the Chinese write different words: 祖母 zǔmǔ – literally "ancestor-mother", is referring to the mother of the father, 外祖母 wàizǔmǔ – literally "(from) outside ancestor-mother", is a reference to the mother of the mother, she is "from outside", not belonging to the actual family. Colloquial Chinese also treats the respective grandfathers and grandmothers differently: Yeye and apo are the parents of the child's father, while waigong and waipo are those of the child's mother, here again the "外 wai" = foreign, from outside, shows up.

Therefore Wang QingFang's mother takes the right this time not only to offer and to pray for the welfare of her grandson and her daughter (and the rest of the family), but also in particular that this time there would be no tension.

She kneels on the place of prayer before the great temple, regularly swinging back and forth with the incense in the folded hands, murmuring her prayers. Now next to her somebody is kneeling down, an elderly, somewhat pot-bellied man in shabby clothes, wearing an old leather jacket and just a vest underneath, he is agitated and noisy. He is "mayor" Song but QingFang's mother does not know that. He prays aloud for his son and his family, asking for enlightenment because of the investment he is up to make. 'What kind of investments is this rude guy up to?' thinks the mother of QingFang. It is her impression that this man came just from somewhere in the hinterland and is actually a peasant, or at least he is behaving that way.

Already he has stood up again. 'He has already finished praying? How shall this work out?' the mother is asking herself. He advances to the offering table where he lays flowers and fruit and bows another time before he goes to one of the censer huts. There, he burns some paper money imitation which the ancestors can use in the afterlife. And now he is gone.

Mother Wang thinks that either these investments cannot be very serious or instead, cannot turn out well. You must not pray like that. She performs better, in recent years she has learned that by reading, internet and meditation. She promises to the responsible gods that she will restrain herself a little more in the future when criticising her husband, just that there will be no quarrels with the other family during the New Year week this time, and that the little grandson will get rid of of his feverish cold. ('I will not yell at my husband that often any more then.')

A trade like that has almost always worked so far. Her daughter has made a good degree, married a good man, found a good job, bought a good apartment and conceived a healthy, strong, young son. Ample proof that praying helps! And her offerings and return services had always been just right, it seems. So, offer harmony to receive harmony, that may do the trick this time.

Today she has also brought a tidy sum of real money that she will donate to the monks. 'This is what that would-be investor should have done, then his investment might prosper!' She remains for at least one hour on the temple grounds and performs her various exercises.

Then she meets her daughter again who is already nervously bouncing up and down at the car, waiting to go home, the grandchild, too, is somewhat ill-tempered. 'They're both so impatient!' The two ladies have to prepare the New Year celebrations. In a few days, the other half of the family will arrive.

Everywhere in China the travelling is prepared. Trains, aeroplanes and coaches are fully booked up to the last seat, trains even beyond, many people will not have a seat and are forced to stand or sit on the floor for 12, 24, 36 or 48 hours. On New Year almost all families are getting together. In 2010, about 210 million Chinese were travelling this way or that. Previously, the rule was almost without exception that the children went to their respective parents. Young couples separated for at least a few days unless they did by chance originate from the same town, like the engineering couple Chu/Sun did. Nowadays, this is treated more flexibly. Mainly in the case of ShenZhen it has become customary for the parents to visit their sons and daughters who are living and working there.

Not only is the transport occupied, but all hotels are, too. If as a business (wo)man you come to ShenZhen during the New Year week and are looking for a hotel, you will find nothing, unless you have booked months in advance. But why should you? All the companies are anyway closed and all the business partners focussed on their families anywhere else in China.

Most companies close during the New Year week. In the weeks before (a few are late and catch up after New Year) a New Year dinner is held, roughly equivalent to our company Christmas dinners. However, with one big difference: Usually, people do not just eat and drink (or bowl), but there is a programme. A programme committee has prepared everything, the different departments of the companies have been appointed to tasks or voluntarily assumed some.

There are song and dance shows, cabaret, karaoke contests, riddle solving in exuberant mood. The highlight is always the lottery. The grand prize being valuable electronic toys or even a red envelope containing a few thousand RMB, the firms have got donations from suppliers and other business partners and bought from that money and some of their own budget more or less valuable gifts, everyone gets at least a little something. You go from table to table, toasting as long as you can walk or stand upright. Not very late in the evening, suddenly everything is coming to an end; once the program is over, some indefatigable fellows may go once more around toasting each other, but the tables all of a sudden fall empty, within ten minutes the entire room is deserted.

Because the economy is anyway for a week in standstill, many foreigners dwelling and working in China make it their habit to travel this week themselves, but not within China. That's impossible. Thailand, Australia or Japan are the destinations of choice.

ShenZhen itself looks these days even more colourful than usual, because of the bright red flags and the lanterns that are suspended from all major roads at intervals of 50 to 100 metres, because of the New Year's jewellery dangling from almost any door or gate or window, but also because of the countless tangerine trees framing the doors and gates of residential areas or shops, hotels or corporate lobbies (a tradition that is practised in southern China only).

The Chinese New Year is the second new moon after the winter solstice, approximately between 21 January and 21 February of our calendar. The oddest hustle takes place on New Year's accessories markets. Especially on the day before New Year's eve, and at New Year's eve itself – so to speak, on 12-30 and 12-31 of the Chinese lunar year, the market is overcrowded, you are walked, you are pushed, and if you are not careful to leave your feet steadfast on the ground it may happen that you are carried for some metres!

New Year is not true without New Year odds and ends, quite analogous to our Christmas trees and accompanying Christmas decorations. Here, everything is bright red and not gold and silver like during our Christmas season; all the wise sayings and good wishes are printed or painted in black or gold on red background. The animal of the new year will be sold in all possible variations – the various years of the Chinese sexagenary cycle are symbolised by twelve different animals, such as tiger, mouse (or rat), rabbit, snake, pig, and others. The odds and ends are hung on doors, windows and walls, inside and out, and laid out on tables.

On each market you can have your own sayings written down on long narrow "wallpaper" (also most of the time red) in beautifully painted characters, either vertically or horizontally, on request.

In addition, there is everything else: snacks, sweets, fish for the aquarium at home, birds for the living room cages and flowers everywhere. The New Year markets are events full of colour, expectation, joy, they are life at its most colourful.

During the New Year's week, the roads at least as crowded as usual, but people are more relaxed. Now the families are strolling about, either grandma and grandpa have come to visit the young parents with the grandchild, or it is the parents who are working elsewhere but have come to visit their own parents in turn who are living in ShenZhen and raising the child.

The restaurants and parks are packed, except for the actual New Year's Eve. Then everyone is at home and takes part in a long, together extensively prepared, feast which drags on for hours, interrupted by MaJiang, card games and television (there are cult programmes re-run every year that day, similar to the "Dinner for One" sketch that has caught on in Germany, Scandinavia, and Australia). On the first day of the new year people are out, though, on the streets, in parks, shops and malls and restaurants, visiting museums and exhibitions, and cinema, they have long enough been perched on each other.

For a whole week, even before the New Year's Day, especially in the New Year's night, and also more than a week later, there is popping in every nook and cranny. Chinese love fireworks. In contrast to western pounding, the Chinese kindle their New Year firecrackers not at midnight of New Year's Eve, but whenever they like.

Thus it can happen quite possibly that on a Wednesday after New Year you are sitting at 11 o'clock in the late evening on your balcony, warmly dressed because in February the outside temperature is ten degrees centigrade. You may have a glass of red wine in hand, looking at the hustle and bustle of traffic on the street below. What you don't see is what is just now being prepared beneath the balcony, down on the street.

Suddenly, without any announcement, a crash will detonate just underneath you that would be banned in Germany because of the decibels released by the explosion (say you're happy if you were still sitting on the balcony and not lying in bed and dozing off, for that would have been a very nasty awakening). A tenth of a second later, a rocket passes by from below, unfolding a colourful rain of stars precisely at the altitude of your private balcony, but fortunately 30 metres off, and then the private fireworks, free for the passive observer on the balcony, is really get going and will calm down again maybe 15 minutes later.

And that you may experience for a whole week. Of course not always just below or in front of your private balcony.

On the evening of the first day of the new year, the pounding is most intense. Then you may roam the streets of your "village" in ShenZhen and watch all the families and gatherings of friends and neighbours having prepared larger or lesser fireworks and eager to set them into action. Particularly eager – Chinese not being different from Germans – are children and men. Women carry the baby or comfort the little ones where something has failed or if they burnt themselves. Big sisters or neighbourhood children assist the little brothers or fellows from the neighbourhood (big brothers do not help because they have to pop themselves). Most amusing is the observation of small children playing with fire during the day and the greater tries to care of the younger and helps setting fire but is as well rather scared in doing so.

Two weeks later, full moon rises, the Lantern Festival is coming up. Originally (and certainly in some areas even today), lanterns are made and displayed, in ShenZhen you may observe one metre wide hot-air balloons with internal flames that are launched. During the day, in some places people hang riddles on ropes (once at the hanging lanterns), hundreds of people make a kick out of solving them.

In theory, the Lantern Festival is the completion of the New Year celebrations, work at the job resumes already one week before, but on the evening of the Lantern Festival, if the weather is fair under the full moon, you may watch the hot-air balloons sailing through the air, and the final fireworks.

The family of "mayor" Song meets only the day before New Year, to the banquet, and on New Year itself. The son, chief doctor at the hospital in ShenZhen, is living there, too, after all, and the hospital does not close. But the families of programmer Wang and his wife QingFang will stay together for a week. The prayers of Mother Wang have largely been fulfilled, New Years passed in harmony. The weekend before the Lantern Festival, on Saturday, Wang Qing-Fang's father is taken to the train station, on Sunday, the in-laws follow. Slowly normal life returns.

» Furnace at the temple.

» Many people have lit candles and hope to gain support "from above".

» Prayers and offerings.

» In the temple there are statues of various gods or immortal beings.

» At the New Year market these artist produces large-scale calligraphy.

» In the evening, the market is completely immersed in deep red light.

» While the markets are buzzing with life, people rest on the public road,

» or have an extended tea break outside the shop, the tangerine tree belongs with the New Year season.

» Meanwhile, there's haggling going on in the market,

» and shoving.

» Even beggars are hoping to be a part of the business.

» Florists recommending their products.

» Transportation service people offer to bring home the purchased plants and other goods.

» The girls help the younger child (brother? Boy next door?) to ignite the blast.

» Another girl is sketched in a marketplace.

» This older girl helps igniting, but keeps behind the smaller girl, so, if the explosion is too severe it will not be her who suffers the most harm ...

185

» After the New Year celebrations at home you go to the museum, watch at ancient works of art (this is an important – obviously male – individual in a tailor-cut sarcophagus of gold).

» The boys are more interested in this new "book", a kind of glass representing a thick book, if you wipe with your hand across the page, the display will scroll to the next pages, back and forth as desired. The boys do not read, they browse and find it great.

» At least as appealing is this model of the city of ShenZhen below the glass plate, now you can locate your own residential area and the school and the apartment of friends,

» if necessary, by looking very close.

» Riddles are hung during the Lantern Festival.

» Phone a friend, obviously.

LaoWei does not only play football

The reader might think the book has nearly completely described life as LaoWei in China by telling of observations made during the private and weekend time, but it is not so. 80 % of the time in China are dictated by job requirements. For LaoWei, a normal working day begins in China between 6 and 8 o'clock in the morning and often ends after midnight. There is no intention, though, to set up a kind of diary of LaoWei's life and work in China, but merely to retell some observations of and considerations about China. For this, the business life is less suitable, and for the reader rather a bore, although for LaoWei as a chemist enormously exciting. But of course, many interesting things about China can be learnt from working life, too.

Almost every day there are one or more meetings with customers or business partners, rarely, perhaps once or twice a month there is a "day at the office," taking place either in the home in ShenZhen or in the office of the company. Even more rare, there is a day off, and if that is so, then only on Chinese public holidays, and even then I am not really off but working in advance and catching up.

For much is left lying unattended, due to lots of driving or travelling by car, bus, train or aircraft to customers in GuangDong, ShangHai and JiangSu, or BeiJing, TianJin, ChongQing and elsewhere, and despite the constant use of the laptops, which is all the time – even in the car, bus, train, plane – on LaoWei's thighs to work on e-mails, read or generate reports, lectures and presentations, scientific articles and patent applications.

This is then processed on weekends and occasional holidays. There has not been any time for tourist travel within China for the past more than five years. On a few occasions I've used a morning or afternoon to see something other than airports, train stations, hotels, conference rooms and production facilities: beautiful gardens in SuZhou (苏州), two old water towns near SuZhou and KunShan (昆山) (towns that provide only narrow lanes, no roads for cars, but channels), once, of course, the Great Wall, some temples in different cities, the Forbidden City and TianTan (天坛) Temple ("The Temple of Heaven," a very impressive wooden structure) in BeiJing, the Technology Museum in ShangHai, zoos in GuangZhou (广州) and ShangHai (once to see a live panda), the new park on the Yangtze River in NanTong, very appealing is as well the "Bai Yun Shan," (白云山) the Mountain of the White Cloud in GuangZhou, with a large free-flight aviary full of birds. Again, these were at best half-days in the context of a multi-day business trip.

I am not travelling as a tourist within China, not even on the weekend. Weekend football games on Saturdays and Sundays are my very important balance for body and mind, allowing at the same time to casually be part of the life of ordinary people in China and make some observations, some of which are reflected in this book. I prefer to spend the weekends that way.

But in the professional life, you cannot avoid to make some observations, too, which on the one hand are new or different from those in Western countries (where you do not make uniform observations, either, but ever may meet a surprise), on the other hand, unlike those to be found in various books about China, most commonly in guides for managers and entrepreneurs in China.

There are, coarsely said, three ways to do business in China with Chinese companies, listed here by – according to experts and consultants – increasing degree of difficulty:

Most simple case (relatively simple case, of course, this way of doing business is not easy, either, but always full of unforeseen complications): To buy products in China and export them to Germany, for example, or to have the producer or its agents export them to Germany and sell them at home.
 More difficult: To produce either by a joint venture or a special, 100% owned subsidiary in China, exporting mainly to the (western) foreign countries and to a lesser extent (increased difficulty) also in China.
 Most difficult case: To produce abroad, in our case in Germany, and import and sell to China.

I was often asked, especially by well-meaning "experts", why I had chosen just the most complicated way to find. I confess I have not chosen at all, it has just happened, I had no choice.

Since I left the University as a chemist, at the age of 25 years, I am researching on a new chemical technology that (I) developed into a novel nanotechnology – along with many employees during three decades. I filed several dozen patents and published numerous scientific articles describing the principles and applications of this new technology. In parallel, the medium-sized company where I led and drove forward the research and development (it was my second job after leaving the university) produced raw materials for the plastics industry. When I was 33, I took over as manager and soon after bought a quarter of the shares.

In the mid-90s I spun off the former research division as a subsidiary, sold the business and all the assets of the plastic raw material producing parent company and focused at a new location on the perfection of the new nanotechnology. This we wanted to sell, especially in the electronics industry.

The suitable special markets were at that time still for about 60 % in Europe and the U.S., and along with Korea, Japan and Taiwan, this made about 90 % of our target markets. That changed abruptly in 2001, our customers or potential customers migrated massively to China, there entirely new companies emerged, the market was turned upside down as if struck by typhoons.

If we were determined to weather this typhoon without having learnt how to swim properly, we had to intervene in China. In Korea and to some extent in Japan, we were able to perform remarkable breakthroughs, but the action was more and more in China.

That's how it started.

Today I have to tell that the decision to go to China and to focus there has been right, as well as the decision to move for two-thirds of my time to China and take matters there in hand while monitoring research and development mostly from a distance, and once every four or five weeks in person.

I do not like to make "general" statements in this book, but there are two which I would like to try now. The first: Just about everything that my former colleague sales director, my sales manager and my two distributors have told me about the road to success in China was not true. The other: Many of the rules which can be found in guidebooks for businessmen in China, either are of no use or incomplete, not always, not everywhere (or only rarely) true and sometimes even totally incorrect.

Conversely, though, I would like to warn against generalising my observations and conclusions, especially those made in this chapter on business and professional occurrences. Each individual will be exposed in his or her environment to a different situation, and even if there are similar situations – everyone has to respond in a way best fitting him- or herself, the opposite, employees, customers, suppliers and partners. Ready-made rules do not help, everyone must analyse for themselves, think about and decide how to move forward.

Anyway I'm not a fan of standard schemes, I prefer test several options at once, even conflicting ones, varying them if necessary at full speed. That's part of my scientific and research-based approach, I do not do it in the market any differently. (And football is just so: The one has lost who plays by standard rules, knowing only one variety and responding at new situations with old stuff.)

Against the wishes of almost everybody I have therefore deliberately set up three distribution channels in China (virtually trying out which route was the most successful one, or perhaps we even needed all three of them?): a trading company registered in HongKong for customers who are largely controlled from there or invested from HongKong or Western funds, a Taiwanese trading company for mainland China customers, headquartered in Taiwan; and with both distributors I've insisted that we sell directly as well, once we have identified the potential customers ourselves, but I promised that we would not go snatching off their customers.

Also, I've made sure that, as long as it comes to technical things, I (and later our engineers) may visit the customers at any time alone, without distributor manager, without notice, so as to talk to them directly in any way, without mediation by their staff. Pricing and logistical matters, I would not negotiate as a supplier to the customers. All technical aspects, I would always report, but vice versa expect complete reports.

So I have reduced the dependency on the distributors and earned us a stronger position in the confusing Chinese market. But that was not the key to our success, only a formal boundary condition. And we were successful, though only after some very painfully difficult years. We could get our way with our new technology, have put out numerous competitors from small and large companies from abroad and from inland China and, in most cases, only compete with one single global player.

With all the major users of our processes and almost all the medium ones, either our competitor or we ourselves are present with one or more process lines, in some we are both present and run the competition on the spot.

One thing is critical to our success against the (initially) many and big competitors, and it is crucial for sharing today this (important) special market with the only remaining competitor in the field, although the company of our competitor is disproportionately larger:

CONFIDENCE.

This sounds perfectly normal, and it is. In most cases worldwide (sustainable) transactions are made only if the parties rely on each other. Confidence must be established between the companies, between the supplier and the customer, but above all between the people involved. The top managers should learn to know each other, as the sellers and buyers, technicians and technical management.

The customer – that is, the top and the middle management, but also engineers and technicians who are directly operating the systems and our chemical processes – must develop the confidence that the delivered processes are stable and reliable, and meeting the requirements demanded by the customer's customer.

A large company, already established, will make it easier: their sellers and after-sales servicemen may just claim: 'Listen, mate, we're supplying already all over the world, we're delivering to you already processes X, Y and Z, your U.S.-based customer, Intel, has already released our process, too, therefore you can really RELY on that all is well.'

We couldn't say that in the early days. Our breakthrough in Korea was a milestone, but which Chinese customer is impressed by the fact that the Korean company O, P or Q has already installed the process? None.

There, in Korea, and now here, in China, I had the advantage, though, that I am both chief inventor, chief engineer and chief manager. I can argue and decide binding contracts both in technical and in business matters. This has helped us enormously in China, but was also not yet sufficient.

Now you can read everywhere that "the" Chinese culture should be taken into account – but which one? From no book about China (at least from any that I know of) you may learn that in the Chinese private companies there are working mainland, HongKong and Taiwan Chinese, that each of them have a different cultural background, and how the differences in cultural mixtures that can be casually found in any company are to be considered. I believe that the authors of these various books have seen a lot in China and gathered all kinds of valuable experience, but they may have gained no experience in technical (and high-tech) marketing and sales to Chinese companies in China.

This is a completely different matter than to establish a joint venture with a Chinese company under supervision, control and guidance of the provincial authorities, something quite different, too, from selling consumer goods in China. Selling engineering goods, processes, special chemicals, new technologies is all around the world different from promoting BMWs, Luis Vuitton consumer goods or French wines for sale to the individual consumer. No easier, no harder, just completely different. And for sure, it is completely different from being in China as a journalist for a German newspaper.

Here in China an additional problem occurs which is comparable with the marketing and sales in Europe: there are as many cultures, there is not "the" unified Chinese culture any more than there is "the" European culture. Italians think and act differently than Bavarians, Northern Germans, Frenchmen (whether southern or Breton), Poles or Norwegians.

China is larger than (Western) Europe and at least equally diverse. And Chinese companies have employees and managers from all corners of China, North, South, East, West, Central. And there are many different norths and souths and centres. Moreover, there is a huge difference in whether companies are financed by investors from HongKong or from Taiwan or Japan or Europe or the U.S. Or by mainland Chinese. And if from HongKong, have they recently moved in from the mainland or have they always been HongKong Chinese, or have they lived for ten years even in Canada? (Many HongKong Chinese "fled" to Canada as it became clear that China would get back the city-state, but when they realised that China kept his word and the reforms of Deng Xiao-Ping became visibly effective, they returned en masse and are now more or less successful businessmen in HongKong and throughout China.) All this widely influences attitudes, but in what way? And like with business everywhere else in the world, it does matter a lot whether the customer is a private company, perhaps with a founder and investor actively at the head of the company, or a branch plant, a subsidiary of a corporation or a differently structured big company.

How do you want to follow pre-set rules? Neither did I know any, nor did I intend to follow them. I argued with – hopefully – common sense and relied on arguments, expertise, conviction and confidence building.

Many books claim a lot about how you have to go eating and (much) drinking with your Chinese business partners, and that you have to visit karaoke bars (which are called KTV here). During those more than five years that I am writing about here, I have been not once in a KTV, let alone with a customer. (My football friends wanted to invite me once, but for some reason I was prevented that night. I've not regretted it yet.)

Of course we went to eat with customers and other business partners, this is normal and nothing extraordinary, neither in the West nor in China. Unusual, perhaps, is the notion that we were never in a particularly extravagant restaurant. We were merely "eating together", sometimes in a larger restaurant near the company that we visited, full of ordinary people from the neighbourhood, sometimes in a small "restaurant" just around the corner, on small plastic chairs, in the throng of passers-by and workers from the opposite side of the street.

It does not matter – I think neither in China nor in Germany, Europe and the U.S. – what standard the restaurant or eating place subscribes to or how much to spend, but how to communicate with people. Eating together is a wonderful foundation for informal connections and communication creating confidence. This is true for Italy and for China as for France alike, while in Germany or USA I am rather under the impression that eating was an annoying formality meant to impress the guest rather than to communicate intensively.

And maybe the standard lunch, wherever it is, with various employees and managers of many Chinese customers is an even more important foundation, because unconsciously many things are noticed ('What does he like or refuse, what is he talking about? Whom does he accept, whom doesn't he? What does he know about China, what doesn't he?'), and consciously many things are getting asked: 'In what way does your process differ from that of the competitor? How long will you be here? Where are you otherwise? What do you do on weekends? What – playing football, not golf? And you don't go shopping in HongKong?'

All this helps to create a model of the other. 'Is he reliable? Is he familiar with the technology he wants to sell us?'

Ultimately, I believe, without having it planned that way, that the crucial aspects were my unrestricted availability ('Can we meet tomorrow, maybe tomorrow afternoon?' – 'I'm sorry, at that time I have scheduled another appointment, but the day after tomorrow I can shift a forenoon appointment to the afternoon, is that OK?' – 'Yes, that's fine, see you the day after tomorrow!') and the fact that I am always "staying on the ball".

"Staying on the ball" means to accept phone calls at once, never to look for pretexts, never to "talk away" any problems but always to investigate by analysis, to suggest resolving the issue only based on detailed analysis, to write any major report or important e-mail both in English and Chinese; not delaying even unpleasant appointments, and always being personally available when required.

Finally, the customers notice that I'm almost always present, my statements and those of my staff are reliable, the measures we propose are sound, the analysis reports are world class.

For Chinese customers it is a completely different matter whether they may speak with someone from overseas who is dropping in during a one-week visit to China (and, if at all, maybe will show up again in a year or two) or with someone who is actually living in China, one who is able to tell of the weekend and the Chinese language lessons, is coming when needed and performing with professional competency. Even today, I notice that some new manager working for an old customer may react startled when looking into a Westerner's face if my visit with a technician was not specially announced before. Foreigners are such a rare sight that it is always a spectacular affair (and one to be avoided where possible and where not, to be shoved across the desk to another manager). Only after learning that I have for years before been coming and going at this customer's office and realising that this is neither my first nor my last visit, this new manager will get warmer.

In the past I was told, Chinese are unreliable with regard to keeping appointment. Both my sales director and my sales manager told me that more than half of the appointments had not taken place because of late cancellations: 'Such insolence, with such customers we don't want to have business!'

Yes, it is true: even today, sometimes more than half of my own already agreed-upon appointments are "cancelled" – but not for dropping them but for moving them! And if "we" were not available for more than a few days, where should the appointment be rescheduled to? For me it is not a problem, we always find a new date, I put about dates as a tiler may lie tiles in a complicated pattern, until everything fits.

The Chinese are not doing otherwise, there are no differences between the different cultural backgrounds, whether mainland, HongKong, or Taiwan Chinese: their attitude is similar in this respect: If the appointment is important and of help for the customer, it takes place, if useless, it is not agreed in advance at all; if an important agreed appointment is cancelled, then in order to move it to a different date, because something else intervened.

And that is precisely the only thing that distinguishes them from customers in the West: In the local market and for each customer, not only for our suppliers but everywhere, an extreme stress is prevailing, exceeding extreme pressure. Our customers first have to serve their customers: If suddenly a manager of that customer from ShangHai, HongKong, the U.S. or Germany shows up (scheduled for Monday, but because of another appointment moved to Wednesday, exactly to that Wednesday when my appointment was scheduled), then the supplier from Germany will be moved, not cancelled. If the German has no time then, that's his problem. But I do have time, I am the tiler jigsawing my tiles.

I quickly learned that a market growth of 20 % per year cannot be managed with rigid planning, and our Chinese customers have to be extremely flexible, so do I.

Often this may deteriorate to unhealthy stress, but this has to be dealt with. You must even learn to like it. Those who fail are lost and will not be successful. There is no meeting during which there is not all the time buzzing, ringing or playing some participant's phone, the call is usually answered. And regularly, the very person is called who has just asked a question, and the call arrives just as I answer. It is very difficult to keep calm then, but I have to, and after the phone call I continue right where I left, but repeat a few sentences from before.

With time, our customers are getting aware that I am "always" or almost always, present and available, even late in the evening and at night I can discuss a problem; I am flexible enough to return the next day or the next week if the problem was not solved. They understand that my technical statements are reliable, as are our processes, as long as our predefined parameters are met, that the recommendations by me and our technicians, both German and Chinese, are helpful and to the mark. They notice that by and by I learn to speak some Chinese, and they gradually develop

CONFIDENCE.

This confidence is not a fugitive, greasy confidence acquired on common passes through pubs or brothels or even by bribery, it is real, stable, gained with technical and personal reliability of the kind that the Chinese are accustomed to and demanding from each other, whether mainland, HongKong or Taiwan.

A key element of that confidence is the recognition: 'This German has stamina, he cannot be shaken off, not put off.' The Chinese have a term for it: 吃苦耐劳 chī kǔ nài láo (the accents indicate the emphasis on the syllables), meaning: 'eat (something) bitter and withstand hard work'. That's what I can do.

The Chinese have thousands, if not tens of thousands, of proverbs to all situations. Two of them very clearly characterise their relationship to the development of confidence: 路遥知马力 and 日久见人心;; in phonetics, they are written as: lú yáo zhī mǎ lì, which is almost literally, '(Only) after a long haul you will know the strength of the horse' and the second is: rì jiǔ jiàn rén xīn, '(Only) with time you get to know a man's heart'. This caution to develop confidence only after a long period is part of Chinese culture.

Based on my experience, I also disagree about the "cronyism" that is regarded as a characteristic of China, often referred to in books and articles. I believe that China (at least where I can tell that) is not primarily operated on what we describe as "cronyism". That would be: The relative, neighbour, friend who is closest to me is preferred, regardless of performance. (I don't deny that this does exist in China, and I do not know to how much extent. And no doubt there is a large amount of corruption in China, just: We are not involved in this "market".)

I can only describe what I perceive: From our environment we shall select those for a business, a job position, supply or partnership who are reliable, those to which we have CONFIDENCE. These are not the closest cronies but those friends and acquaintances, or their friends and acquaintances, who are competent to the task, and on which you can absolutely rely.

So we found a system manufacturer in ShenZhen whose Chinese name is already promised reliability, but a name can promise anything, can't it? This small company, whose factory accidentally set up within walking distance of SunLi's apartment, has developed into our construction partner in China.

We started with small jobs, repairs, minor adaptations. And gradually, we realized: They can do more, we hired them as system builders for us and our customers. This unassuming company, located in an older industrial area in the middle of NanShan, provides excellent work, especially if we have tough questions or new ideas. For years we have had confidence in each other and were never let down. The head of the company (or his right hand) and I very rarely meet in a "hot pot" restaurant halfway between the factory and SunLi's apartment. Without words (or in crude Chinese) we go splendidly well with each other, but SunLi is the better communicator, she maintains contact, she develops a personal relationship with the system engineers and coordinates bid solicitation, project management and payment. The result is a mutual full confidence.

How did we find this unassuming and yet so powerful company? We have asked around and finally found an indirect acquaintance who was very pleased with a machine manufacturer and gave us his recommendation. We have relied with full confidence on the confidence that the acquaintance had already developed. From the outside, one could be tried again to call this "cronyism." But there are no cronies relayed through recommendations here, but business partners who have developed confidence in each other. Confidence of the client is in that the machine builder provides a solid quality, complies with the dates and after installation of the systems provides a reliable and fast service (repairs, spare parts). Confidence of the machine manufacturer is in that the customer pays, even if in most urgent cases only a verbal offer is made, followed by a telephone agreement on the technical design and the price and a verbal order – even then everything has to operate smoothly, and it does. This is the mechanism by which the large scope of the Chinese economy outside the sphere of big business and state enterprises is maintained.

The same way we selected our tax adviser and auditor in NanTong. Having already developed confidence in the people whom we have indirectly found through my friend, the painter and professor YeDan, who had proven to be so helpful and absolutely reliable, we asked them also to make recommendations for a tax adviser. He should pass all our tax returns, prepare and check the financial statements, pay salaries and file wage tax and social security.

YangMei and her boss recommended the office HuaDa (华达), a consultant with no more than a dozen employees, in size just right. But are they the right ones? I talk to the boss who speaks a tolerable but not particularly well English, SunLi discusses with him in Chinese, referring to me at times. His enterprise advises primarily some Japanese companies here in NanTong, he shows me the references.

All of this makes a good impression, we discuss the details, including an annual payment for their services (fair and not excessive, not cheap, but not overpriced, either). Some details are concerning the daily routine operations. To file taxes and transfer all funds, for example (both to the employees and to the tax office and suppliers), they need the company stamp. If I do not want to hand it over – which they would understand – they would send each procedure by express to ShenZhen, I would sign and stamp down, send back, and then the procedure can be performed at the bank.

I wage everything back and forth, finally I come to believe that if I want to work efficiently with this office, I have to show them confidence, and I may, because this office has guarantors – YangMei, her boss and, indirectly, my friend YeDan. I say, 'No, that's too complicated, I will leave the stamp here, we give you an account authority today, but each transaction must be authorized by me by e-mail.' – 'Agreed.'

My confidence was not abused once. On the contrary. These tax professionals have helped us more than once in difficult situations. And these people in some ways have become our friends. We do not meet often, but heartily, and SunLi phones at least once a week with the boss or the person in charge. At that opportunity, also personal subjects are exchanged (husband, girlfriend, wife, child, parent, problems, buying a car, etc.).

Like in Germany, the largest share of the gross national product in China is also generated by individual entrepreneurs, small and medium enterprises. In this sphere, mutual CONFIDENCE is the lubricant.

There are certainly many, probably too many things in China driven better or in the first place by bribery as the lubricant, even among medium-sized enterprises. I have never used this lubricant. Wherever I realised that this lubricating oil was essential and not the technical and price performance, I have retired, aware and openly. With technology and quality I can compete, but not with corruption, and I will not.

On the contrary, I believe that the financial corruption is at the long run devastating any business, for everyone will distrust each other, everyone is vulnerable to blackmail. This is not sustainable, even in China. It is the opposite of confidence.

The middle production management of one customer, ChangGuang, evidently wanted to be bribed, and for that reason we had to endure for months that all contracts were awarded for even higher costs and a higher effort to elsewhere, for months we had no revenue. The background was clear: The production manager wanted to blackmail us to give them bonuses. I did not allow myself to be blackmailed, though, but stayed tough – we would not pay bribes.

Finally I decided to address the ChangGuang top management, although SunLi disagreed. She feared that open words would be counterproductive, but I said: 'What do we have to lose, now already we don't have any business any more!' So we went. Of course, I did not tell the head of the company, 'Your production managers want to be bribed.' Instead, I asked if he knew that their production line running with our process chemistry had been shut down for months, and therefore all products were further processed on external contracts, though that could be done internally a lot cheaper (we knew the external price and the internally calculated direct costs).

He did not know it. He summoned his production managers into his office and questioned them. They claimed that our quality was not sufficient and this or that customer had complained. I made clear that this was not the case, and I called for an objective comparison test. When this was done under our supervision, it was clear that our quality was much better.

A short time later, the process line with our processing chemistry was put back into operation. In the following time it became clear that our quality was much more solid and better, currently we even are in the process of replacing the competitive chemistry in the external facility, that was preferred by the production managers, by our chemistry. The resistance against getting drawn into the bribery system is paying off. The top management is only from Taiwan, the middle management is composed largely of mainland Chinese. It was a sleight of hand which has been successful. ChangGuang develops ever and better and could soon become our second largest customer.

The widespread active and passive bribery is a terrible disease in China. I know some business people who participate actively or passively, and

I know they are not too happy with it but do not know how to get out. We have discussed this issue many times in my Sunday football team. We all have to agree: It's sick and a serious weakness of the Chinese economy and politics.

During the second year of my work in China I get from our customer service technician in East China for the umpteenth time in the middle of the night a call: 'Our process line in ShuXin (曙鑫) has just been shut down again, I can bear it no more!' With this big customer, who is today (unknowingly) competing with ChangGuang for 2nd and 3rd place in our customer ranking, features every few weeks a sudden drop in the quality of the final product, as if by magic, then the facility is stopped. Our technician there, ChuLuo, is exhausted, he will be leaving us soon, he cannot stand the stress any longer.

Analyses reveal that there are spontaneous glitches of one parameter. It is mysterious why and how this would happen, and why so sudden and so irregularly? Any time then we need to fill thousands of litres of fresh chemicals into the process line, at tremendous cost, not only because of the materials, but also because we often need to quickly obtain supplies by air from Germany to ShangHai. This is particularly expensive because it is "hazmat", hazardous material. In the night suddenly a realisation matures in my brain: This must be sabotage. Someone fills a certain harmful chemical into our tanks, thereby flipping the process.

I'm starting to calculate and slap on my brow: Why did I not think of that before? It is obvious that by the process itself, this parameter can never get out of hand, let alone so quickly! During the night I write my thoughts and calculations in an e-mail, the next day I let my team in Germany recalculate and run experiments. The result is evident, my nocturnal presumption is confirmed. The deviation can only have been caused from the outside.

As with ChangGuang the company is controlled from Taiwan and run largely by Taiwanese in eastern China, and as well, the middle management consists almost entirely of mainlanders. In both cases, our distributor was of the opinion that trade could only flow through his company, this customer hat to be handled "with utmost care", me, being German, could not do that, and even with them as dealers it was less than certain whether we would gain those customers. I did not give in to that, in either cases I assumed the direct sale without intermediaries. In both cases, we are confronted with massive extortion, here, at ShuXin, even with sabotage!? This shows me what the distributor had in mind when claiming that "this customer had to be treated with utmost care!"

Once again all of the consultants tell me: 'By no means mention the suspected sabotage frankly, this contradicts the way how to approach such problems in China, and – you can lose everything there!' And once again I answer, 'What else do we have to lose? We cannot every few weeks fly thousands of litres of chemicals to ShuXin for free, relaunch the process line and stare at the next event to occur! If this should go on, we will anyway have to cut the business relationship!' In any case we had to make a decision, either we would pull back from ShuXin, or I would grasp the thistle of ShuXin.

And that was what I did. I talked to the responsible production director. He has worked many years in the U.S., we can discuss in English. He was beside himself with rage. We screamed at each other (in English). I told him clearly and openly. 'If these events are not going to stop, we cannot provide any more chemicals.' I laid open all our calculations, explained why it could not be anything but sabotage (just never calling it "sabotage" for which there also is a Chinese word, but "event"), he became quieter and quieter, pensive and more pensive, the more I revealed to him the analytical data and my calculations.

In this first decisive and open discussion we agreed that we would monitor the process line for four weeks, 24 hours around the clock. And all parameters were to be analysed at regular intervals. We hired two guards (employees of a company we are friends with), to whom I inculcated: Not even to the bathroom you are allowed during the shift! The process line must NEVER, not one minute, be left alone!

This month, nothing happens. When we remove the guards, it is silent at first. Suddenly an "event" – in rage I call the production director, asking for an immediate meeting, rejecting replacement for the facility is safely installed, this is now my tool for blackmailing. ShuXin's customers will sooner or later exceed pressure, "sooner or later" meaning within 24 or 36 hours.

I take a flight to the customer at once. During the meeting next day we agree on a further phase of one month of continuous monitoring. I insist also on extracting each day a sample from the process line. Once again for four weeks nothing happens. We have collected more than 30 samples. Two weeks later another event – now I'm sure. I tell our engineer, "Take a sample, we will analyse that, but we do not replace the chemical, ShuXin will have to stew in its own juice.'

Three days later, I receive the written analysis: An additional substance has surfaced after the "event", a substance that is not included in our chemistry. At once I know where this stuff comes from: from a process line of our competitors in the same building, just 100 metres off. This is the final proof that I present a few days later to the production director.

All of his excuses and attempts to explain I can wipe off. There is no doubt about it: Someone throws waste from the competitor's process line into our system. I can even calculate how much: there are between 5 and 10 kilograms, so not as small an amount as could be carried hidden in a handkerchief, because the various tanks in our facility hold 1,200 litres of chemicals each! All alternative theories of how this stuff can get into our system I can refute, they would be even more embarrassing for ShuXin than admitting that there was a saboteur.

I leave no doubt that if this pollution gets into the process line due to weaknesses in the internal system, we need to immediately cancel any supply of chemicals. If the contamination is the result of sabotage ("events") in the plant, it winds up to the same effect, unless the sabotage will stop.

The process line has been stopped. Customers jostle: 'Where are the products?' I remain freezing cold-blooded and ask to speak to the supreme boss. At last we meet. He is a young open-minded manager, the son of the majority shareholder, he is fluent in English. He knows the market and the technology inside out.

From the very beginning we go well with each other. I ask him outright: 'Do you want to have saboteurs in your company? If the saboteur is not stopped, we can give you no more chemicals, but I will tell you this: It was the competitor that has caused this, do you want to have such a supplier?' I'm as brutally straightforward as possible, violating all the rules of communication with Chinese people, SunLi is silent, pale and speechless with horror. But during those months in which we are having this discussion, I have always left my opposite the chance to save face. I always accepted the proposals of the production director (as long as they were targeted), even if they included a further delay of two months. And now in discussion with the boss I do not insist that he will admit I was right, but I will give him the opportunity to show that he is acting honourably and ethically.

The boss replies: 'Yes, I can't tolerate any saboteurs in my company. We'll install a video camera. Please send fresh chemicals. If during the video surveillance no "events" should happen, I'll pay back every replacement that was so far invested by you.' An exclusively oral agreement was made, without any document, I have not even confirmed by e-mail, but we have used an ancient (German?) handshake.

This is what happened, even if it took an additional year to settle everything, lighten things up and enforce the payments. Finally we could even make an educated guess about which ShuXin employee carried out the sabotage on behalf of the competitors, I leaked a little, the employee was transferred. All our expenditures were refunded, the total amounted to a sum equal to one complete annual turnover we have with ShuXin!

That has tied the confidence between us most deeply, because of my firm stand, me and the whole company were met with enormous respect, the boss, the production director and many other top managers have become good friends of mine, not friends in the sense that we are playing golf together or go to KTV (neither are my hobbies), but in the sense that we are very honestly (and criticisingly!) interacting with each other and have full confidence in each other on business issues.

Bribery and corruption are the sheer opposite of genuine confidence. They are the basis of cronyism, which holds only as long as money flows. Both sides are also vulnerable to blackmail. Confidence is built over a long period of time, starting with small steps that involve small risks, until the confidence is perfect.

One example of "full confidence" is most remarkably the (self-organising and probably illegal) system of betting in China. Here you do not go into a betting shop, deposit and get a betting ticket issued. No, here you call a friend who is a betting agent. He calls the organiser of the bets (or perhaps another intermediate friend). Football World Cup and European Football Championships, but also Champions League games are events challenging some (or many?) Chinese to bet. The Chinese passion for gambling and betting is legendary.

Before the start of the game, HuXie calls his friend, the agent, betting, for example, 'thousand RMB on Chile to win', if that will come to pass, he will get back 1600 RMB, thus make a profit of 600. In case of a draw, he will get 500 refunded (i. e. lose 500), if Honduras wins, he has lost everything. But he can still bet more and does so: '500 RMB on Chile to win by at least two goals.' – Do you want to bet as well when the goals will score? All of them in the second half, or at least one in the first, at least one in the second half? '– No, this HuXie considers for now too risky, especially since there are three games this evening, and there are still many days, many games to bet on.

How does the betting agent get his money, if HuXie has lost, how does HuXie get his money if his bet has won? It's simple: After the World Cup both will set up a balance sheet, both have taken notes, and the difference in one direction or another will be settled in cash at the next opportunity when they meet again. Neither will ever think of not paying, no matter how much it is.

HuXie's friend the betting agent is betting himself, too. In the summer fairytale World Cup 2006 in Germany, he won more than 20,000 RMB. In the subsequent European Championship, he lost almost as much …

I often wonder why, why I cannot or not as pronounced observe many of the things that I could read in China guidebooks.

Of course, "saving face" and "giving face" (the latter being your active part in helping somebody to save his face) is playing an important role in my business and personal environment, but somehow I have come to believe that it really is not all that different than, say, in my own case, I also wish all the time to save my face, not to be exposed, and it is difficult to admit a mistake in public. Honestly, I never realised why Chinese should have more right to protect their face than I or other westerners.

Of course, Confucianism is determining the culture here in China – but the quest for harmony is hardly noticeable in the rough everyday business. "Suppliers" are not treated in China in a different way than in any other country: in case of doubt they are the doormats or mangy dogs that can be beaten with sticks or kicked with boots. Whenever our Chinese customers have any problem, they always try first to unload it on us. This often takes place with by no means friendly methods, that can be applied very rudely and even be connected with screaming and trickery.

German and American companies do the same, but I'm tempted to say, Chinese people are world champion in that respect, and when comparing the three different areas of origin (mainland China, Taiwan, HongKong) the Taiwanese lead my secret ranking of rudeness unchallenged, followed by mainland Chinese (those from the north and east score higher than those from the south and west), while the HongKong Chinese occupy the third and internally last place – meaning in reverse: The HongKong Chinese whom I met in business are still most pronouncedly interested in harmony, Taiwanese least (this is of course a non-objective perception, and the exception proves the rule).

One thing however has also become clear: The more I got to know certain managers, the more often we met, the better the Chinese learned to know me in turn, the less unfair practices have been applied on me. My conclusion is: In the beginning I was not part of the network, I was one of many foreigners who would briefly breeze in, drop important-sounding phrases, only never to be seen again.

With such a foreigner, especially as a supplier, you will not develop confidence. You can scream at him or put him unfairly under pressure at times. You cannot test the horse on the short track properly, and it probably would not hold out on the longer track.

But to the extent they more and more realise that I am a regular here and reliable, the voice will become more moderate. I am gradually accepted, because I "eat the bitter stuff, and withstand hard work", and because I am competent in technology, because my predictions and analyses are correct, this German horse shows surprising endurance on the long track.

As a foreigner, you will not be taken serious if you appear only rarely, this way you cannot become part of the network. How will you be recognised by the Chinese as equal partners if you, the foreigner, show up for a visit once a year or every other year?

Or even if some managers move for a year or two to China with their family but rent an accommodation in a residential area that is mostly or even exclusively inhabited by foreigners? If even the furniture they bring from home by ship, to eventually live as they did at home and to vanish again after two years? And if many foreigners, as I am noticing again and again, in the evenings and on weekends only stay among themselves, Italians with other Italians, Americans with other Americans? How do you suppose to get to know China and Chinese people this way, how shall confidence develop either way?

Perhaps they will also have Chinese acquaintances, but no real friends, they will not be included in any network.

Chinese are networked together in a way I have experienced in no other country. They have saved hundreds of phone numbers in their mobile phones and are linked with dozens of people on MSN and Skype, and with dozens of others at the same time via QQ (the Chinese MSN or Skype). I use only one, Skype, Chinese use three different channels. Often simultaneously.

They also have "KaiXin" (开心网, the "Facebook" of the Chinese), chat rooms, blogs and everything else the modern Chinese needs to live. Each individual is participant of a number of different networks that may overlap, but do not need to. In the networks are found school friends from the middle and high school years, fellow students, current and former colleagues in the profession, staff of customers, suppliers, business partners, as long as people have come closer over time.

Chatting is casual. You need not answer if addressed, but only if you happen to have time and inclination (and aren't at the phone right now). It is different when you get asked a serious question, then the one who was asked will respond in any case. This can be done with a concise 'I'll have to think about it,' or, 'I don't know, I cannot help here', or, 'I don't know about that myself, but I know someone who knows, I will ask, he will help you.'

Thus, within minutes during the day, but especially in the evening, a chain reaction is started which produces a useful answer.

At a Korean customer I once had been presented a problem: a curious phenomenon (associated with a potentially very large, multi-million impact damage) that came up in a large meeting without any preparation, and I could not define it. Of course we were accused that our process had caused the problem, even though it was entirely unclear what was actually happening. While still at the meeting, I sent the image files via Skype from Korea to China, to SunLi. She asked a former colleague from the time of their first job. He was technically closer to the subject, but not familiar with this strange phenomenon, either.

He knew someone who was, but alas, working for one of our competitors who is not our biggest nor our strongest competitor, but just in Korea makes us some trouble – not a good precondition from our perspective, after all, the competitor can only be delighted if we have problems in Korea.

The meeting in Korea was interrupted for a ninety minutes lunch-break, also because I asked for some time to consider. Shortly before the end of the break, I got response from China: The friend of SunLi's former colleague had a perfect explanation for the phenomenon, I even got some internet links to sites discussing similar symptoms and explanations how the damage may be caused. Nothing of this had anything remotely to do with the performance of our process.

Armed with these competent arguments and files that I got out of our Chinese network in no time and with the aid of a competitor's valuable assistance I joined the second part of the meeting, in which about 20 people took part including top management, as well as the customer of our customer. I blocked the first attack against us for now, impressing the circle with speed and competency so that our customer's client (a huge international corporation) was delighted, but a damning light cast on our customer.

At the end I got samples of the defective products and was discharged on the condition to submit of a report on the examination of the parts within latest three days.

Under normal circumstances we would make such studies in our laboratories in Germany, because at least at that time we did not have our own laboratories in China. What was there left to do? The network knew: When I arrived late at the airport in ShenZhen, a messenger was waiting for me who brought the parts within the same night to another friend of SunLi's former colleague, he immediately set out, outside of the working hours, to examine in the lab of the company for which he was working as a laboratory manager.

Late at night he sent the findings to us, we sent them to the helpful expert of our competitor. He gave us more very useful explanations for the now much clearer examination results, which kept well on the originally chosen line of argument. On the afternoon of the same day, i. e. about 24 hours after the meeting in Korea, I had prepared a full report, including data, facts and background, and sent it to Korea.

At the same time I asked SunLi to make sure in what way ever that our volunteers from the network of her former colleagues would receive my gratitude, at least in the form of a dinner that she should arrange for with her colleague and his friends. This was appointed a few days later, I was invited and able to notice: the network is alive.

The event in Korea illustrates which problems and time constraints we have to cope with in Asia. The affairs at ChangGuang, ShuXin and in Korea are certainly extreme examples, but many other less dramatic events together will produce as many worries. About once a week we have to solve a technical problem: the customer's product, made with our process, does not meet the specifications – trace the cause; the process itself is on the edge or outside of our specifications – trace the cause, remedy it; an existing or a new customer wants to get a certain sample for testing, but either we just have no staff available for all are busy, or the process line in which we can manufacture samples is occupied with other tasks, but the customer will need the sample RIGHT NOW – find a solution. Everything must be done in breakneck speed, other than in Europe or the USA, and our German team has to comply with the Chinese pace, too.

One example of the incredible pace is, in my view, the construction and extension of the rail network for high-speed trains. Mid-2010 the line ShangHai-NanJing was put into service, after only a little more than two years of construction. 120 trains per day are now running on this track, some of them at intervals of five minutes only, transferring more than 100,000 passengers daily. Occasionally I am also among them, for now I can reach customers outside of ShangHai without extended car rides. The trains run at up to 350 km/h, for a ticket fee that is only slightly higher than it was fifteen years ago on the much longer and much slower track that SunLi took to BeiJing. Even First Class, you pay for the overall distance the equivalent of just under 30 €, and in a little more than an hour you will have passed along 300 kilometres. In contrast to the First Class in German ICE trains, which is used mainly by business people, it is here full of young people, couples who are moving with or without children, students, grandparents with grandchildren, just "ordinary folk".

Of course, in relative terms, i. e. per capita, China still is far behind Europe and the U.S. with regard to the development of the rail network. But the growth is rapid. China focuses on high-speed lines, i. e. on tracks which allow an average speed of at least 200 km/h. Today, China features more than 7,000 km of high-speed tracks, enjoying the longest rail network of this kind, the only tracks in the world that match a speed of at least 350 km/h; in two years, in 2012, the high-speed network of at least 250 km/h will extend along 13,000 km, making it longer than any other high-speed networks in the world added up. By 2020, there will be 50,000 km.

China is developing dramatically fast, and in all areas, including in our market, and we have to accommodate with that. And in our market, we can keep up, as we have learnt a tremendous lot.

When passing review of my now more than five years in China I may tell that in the first two years, we were almost exclusively dealing with emergency rescue operations, often having to extinguish several fires at once (figurative "fires", that is, when the situation at some customer had become really "hot"). In the third year we began to actively pursue marketing and could become more aggressive, in the last two years we have been increasingly successful in dealing with our closest competitor. We are recognised, known and respected as a stable, innovative, competent and scientifically leading supplier.

From business in China and other parts of Asia I have learnt a lot, not only how to perfectly eat with chopsticks (which I had previously known) or the more relaxed handling of appointments. I am no longer irritated by not knowing on Friday afternoon which appointments will take place next week, experience having shown that all too soon the daily schedule fills in itself, even during the weekend.

Most difficult to understand in my opinion (and I must confess: I have not understood it even now, over and over again I bounce into dead ends or against walls) is the way Chinese people will discuss and approach problems (these Chinese whom I met, that is, certainly not all Chinese). And I would like to preface that often I encounter similar problems with Germans, other Europeans and especially US-Americans, but particularly emphatically with the Chinese people (with Japanese it is again different, but discussing this will not come in here now).

Part of my problem is probably that I am pursuing a scientific way of thinking and an approach that is based on Western thinking and German university education in chemistry, at least I think this is so. In simple terms: I would like to solve a problem or to answer a question by drafting a number of alternate hypotheses, confirming or refuting them by appropriate experiments or analysis, or discussing and designing them with others. Simplified again, my hypotheses are usually structured like this:

'Either A or B or C, or A in combination with either B or C' – where A, B and C are different from each other. In this abstract example, at least B and C are so different that they cannot occur together while A can occur or "apply" with both either B or C.

The first problem which I barge into is a worldwide feature: Unless they have enjoyed a scientific education like myself, my discussion partners, whether German, European, American, Japanese or Chinese, will not understand how I may claim so many different things: 'Either there's A or B or C, why do you complicate that much? It's quite obvious, and we see that clearly: It's B and nothing else!' They do not understand that these are games of mind, hypotheses helping us to execute the proper tests without getting entangled in a thicket of observations, facts and opinions. Many people conclude from mere appearances (often mislead, alas) on what might happen on the nanoscopic or even the molecular level. And what they have concluded on before we made any real analysis is, unfortunately, for them often enough already equal to the final official results, and it will be hard to detract them (if at all) from that course by hard-hitting facts of analysis and by experiments. So far this is no more difficult in China than anywhere else in the world.

In China, however, matters are complicated by the notorious 阴 and 阳, yīn and yáng, representing opposing principles (concisely translated as: "dark, cloudy, threatening" and "sunny, bright"). They are interconnected, interdependent and mutually conditioning each other. This principle is very deeply rooted in Chinese philosophy and probably, at least unconsciously, in any reasonably educated Chinese: opposites are not mutually exclusive, but interdependent. They are part of a greater whole, just as we indeed believe that there can be no magnetic north without magnetic south (even if latest fundamental research in physics seems to indicate that at the most profound level of temperature isolated magnetic monopoles may appear, but we will pass over this for simplicity's sake). Without the interaction of yin and yang, there can be no development.

Thus, the female is considered Yin, the male as Yang, and we all know that nothing would go on without the two combined. "The average Chinese person" (if I may say so) will try consciously or subconsciously to interpret any kind of phenomena as effects of the contrast between two alternatives AND THEIR COHABITATION (!).

I cannot and will not discuss this in detail, I am not a philosopher, but a chemist and observer (and photographer), but we must consider this at least superficially, if we are to understand at least to some extent the Chinese way of thinking and discussing. When we say as in the above abstract example, 'B is different from C, both cannot occur together, especially not in context with A', then the majority of Chinese people will not understand at all what I'm talking about, for Yin and Yang occur jointly all the time, though not being the same thing, yet depend on each other!?

In several discussions with Chinese people who are aware of these principles, the following example has emerged to describe the differing typical patterns of thinking: We Westerners believe either the chicken or the egg must have come first – What came first? chicken or egg, this is our clearly manifest question; but the Chinese will wonder that maybe both have somehow been at the same time, maybe not necessarily as separated from each other.

What we perceive as either black or white may for a Chinese be absolutely, without inner conflicts of conscience, be both white and black or, for the sake of convenience, grey. And already we are into the principle of harmony which permeates everything somehow.

In a technical discussions we may hardly claim that 'both 30 °C and 70° C or, as a compromise, 50 °C are all right' should pose a valid solution to a problem. And my Chinese counterparts are ready very fast to accurately ask: 'What else then, 67 °C or 70 °C?'. Thus, the imaginary worlds are sometimes very difficult to bring into agreement with each other.

In addition, costs and interests play a role. This often results in that even if everyone has realized that 'B cannot simultaneously be true with C', at the end of the discussion when it comes to the matter of costs, everything is rolled up again and called into question.

But in this Chinese are again not so different from Germans or Americans: Where interests are concerned, and especially costs, facts or what I take as facts are often not that convincing any longer.

Other lessons were much easier to learn. I quickly learnt how to pay the bill at restaurants in China: You must argue with the others at the table about who is paying, finally give in generously and let someone else pay. If you want to pay for all or it is your turn to pay, anyway, you either must assert yourself or pay in secret at the cash back left when visiting the toilet, for it is not permissible under any circumstances always to have the others paying! It must be compensated in the medium term! And never anyone pays separately, where appropriate, all will combine their share to full money bills.

The restaurant owners will have many a laugh if a group of Germans or Americans wants to pay the bill: The poor waitress who does not understand any word of English, nor English with a hard German accent, is suddenly faced with a computing task – she is supposed to split the total amount (for four guests, say, altogether 152 RMB, or about 18 Euro) among four people, but not to equal shares but according to consumption: one guy drank no beer, another had two bottles, so in the end one will pay the equivalent of 6.53 €, the second guy, 3.37 €, the two others will generously share the rest, although they ate different amounts, this is fun.

But there are still some major issues I see absolutely no point in, in China, in Chinese business life and when eating:

How do the Chinese, especially the business people, manage that 50 % will already fall asleep on the plane when closing the doors at the snout of the gate, the remaining 49% of the passengers, though, latest at take-off, while I cannot close any eye during the whole flight, why that? The same thing on the bus, on the bumpy highways: out of 60 passengers, 59 are asleep, just not me!

Who is eating all the duck meat that you do *not* get to eat in the restaurant when ordering "Peking Duck"? With delight you eat the skin, removed from the body with veritable martial arts tactics, while the waiter disappears with what is in Western view the essential part of the duck! Does the kitchen staff take all the ducks home to eat them selflessly and mobilising all capacity to suffer, because the meat is so much less valuable than the skin? (Even the Chinese could not answer me this.)

Another unanswered question: What to do with 50 "moon cakes" (月饼) presented to you during the Moon Festival at the 15th day of the 8th lunar month, usually some time in September, Greg.? I may perhaps eat one of these tasty, yet caloric thingies of 5 cm across and 3 cm in height but feeling like 2 kg of weight. This will mean a whole breakfast or dinner. But what shall I do about 50 of them?

Even more difficult: What do you do with 20 "zong zi" (粽子), which is a glutinous rice with different ingredients, wrapped in bamboo leaves to a pyramidal shape and heated either in the microwave – that I do not have – or in hot water – which I am perfect in –; it tastes great, but replaces two meals, not just one, as in the case of the moon cake. This speciality is given to you, and maybe one or two loads are eaten as well, at the Dragon Boat Festival, Duan Wu Jie (端午节), which takes place on the 5th day of the 5th lunar month, which is in June by our reckoning. According to legend, such pyramidal leaf-wrapped lumps of rice were thrown into the lake in which a poet was drowned, according to the narrator either because the poet will then not starve or because the fish will have something else to eat and do not devour the corpse of the poet.

Allegedly the Chinese pass on any moon cakes received by others, about zong zi, my investigations provided no reliable results.

Without question, the work in the Chinese industrial market is extremely stressful. Whenever I am spending two weeks in Germany, I perceive the work there as a kind of holiday ("only" twelve hours a day, much less on weekends, almost no travelling). But I always try to like the situation. What alternative do I have? Forever to mutter, complain, despair? No, even from the most stressful situations I will gain something because at least I can learn something. And if the problem is solved, I may consider it to be a success for us and for me.

I am able to perceive the journeys, lunches and dinners with customers as a broadening of my horizon which gives me great pleasure.

Sometimes, if rarely, very surprising and beautiful things happen at work. One morning I'm sitting at my desk in my apartment, scheduled to leave the house by 11 o'clock and to drive to the airport because I have to take a flight to ShangHai. I am working on a complicated report, a thunderstorm is raging outside, black clouds drift by, wind is howling.

After one hour the storm has passed. Occasionally I turn left in thought, looking out of my large window which is providing me with a clear view of the Bay of ShenZhen and an island opposite that belongs to HongKong. Over HongKong the clouds tear apart.

I continue to work, having to concentrate very much, because I have to present twisted analysis results both correctly and understandably to laymen. Suddenly I notice in the left corner of my eye that something has changed. I turn to the left:

There I am looking at a tornado tube! Right at the edge of the black cloud that is hovering over my apartment and ShenZhen, there, where the sky has cleared up over HongKong, off-coast an uninhabited streak of land, there is a small tornado!

At once I rush into the next room where I keep my camera, out to the balcony and aim the lens, thinking this will be over quickly, quickly take some pictures!

But no, the show has just begun! One tornado tube after another comes and goes, sometimes two or three tubes are visible at the same time, to the right a new one is developing, in the middle another tube is in action, left, a hose passes away. Overall, I count six such vortices of, I guess, up to thirty metres in diameter. They move very slowly. We would refer to them as "landspouts" or "waterspouts"; water is dispersed on the surface of the sea and sucked upwards; you do not want to be in the middle.

Most ships and boats keep a respectful distance. But one boat is approaching the last and strongest tornado tube, that is, the tornado has turned toward the boat. It circles around the hose on the opposite side and is finally seen again – unharmed.

The whole event lasts for twenty minutes, I have taken 83 photos.

While I continue to work, I download the photos to another laptop which I usually use to edit photos, because this is time consuming and extremely memory-intensive. This way, meanwhile, I can work on my actual laptop. After I saved the images and converted them from the raw data into the "digital negative", it comes to my mind that not that many people will have seen this, and not everyone who saw it will have had a professional camera with a 400 mm-telephoto lens at his disposal! (The tornadoes were about two kilometres away from my balcony.)

So I quickly write an e-mail to a newspaper in HongKong, asking whether they are interested in such images. But now I have to start driving to the airport.

On the way, I'm already getting e-mail reply from the "South China Morning Post" – they want to publish the images if they are of good enough quality, whether I could send them for approval? I compile a quick little selection, enclose them in a PDF document and send them from the car to HongKong.

In the airport I learn that the take-off will be late, as always in recent times. At least we may soon get on the plane, but I am afraid we will be sitting on the plane and wait for hours. It turns out like that. This is annoying. But today I am saved by the "South China Morning Post", for the photo editor in charge is calling – they want to print four of my photos and have decided which ones to take. We negotiate the price, these will be the first images I ever sold. Within the next few minutes I will get a contract, and after signature I will be asked to send the images in sufficient resolution as JPGs. And be quick, please, because they want to publish the images tomorrow, it is already late afternoon as we have been sitting on the plane for two hours, being three hours late.

Now I hope (not telling anyone on the plane!) that we will sit around yet for at least another hour, for my mobile internet access is fast (3G), but not as fast as a Wi-Fi in Germany. I save the images in a size of about 5 MB per file.

Soon I get the contract, I sign by hand, digitally, on my tablet laptop, and return the contract. Out of the plane which is still standing there I am sending now one image at a time, call the editor and confirm: 'All uploaded.' The flight attendant announces in unintelligible Chinese that we will depart now, being 4 ½ hours late, terrible, but this time to my advantage.

This is fun! Images sold commercially for the first time, the fee allows me to go eating properly about 30 times; not exciting if converted into Euros, but not a bad deal in purchasing power! Business partners from HongKong whose attention I directed to my "prank" (to make sure they buy me a few copies), tell me later in the evening that the news had told about it, saying, 'Fishermen reported on tornadoes in the Bay of ShenZhen. There are no photos of the event.' Well, wait until the South China Morning Post will be published tomorrow!

The next day I find in other news websites that I was actually the only one who has documented this event in professional quality. Otherwise, there are only relatively poor images made with cell phone cameras and one very shaky video. According to statistics by the governmental weather observation station "Hong Kong Observatory", within the last 50 years waterspouts had occurred once every other year on average, but not six in a day. The Observatory too is interested in my images, because they are documenting the entire progress. A German website dedicated to natural phenomena has a focus on "tornadoes" and has also asked for taking up my photos.

Perhaps this is the beginning of a new career as a professional photographer, once I will have enough of a life with business and chemistry?

» The tornado tubes before the uninhabited island which belongs to HongKong.

Appendix

What happened "after the deadline"?

After completion and printing of the first edition, life in China has not stopped even in the context of LaoWei. Some readers will certainly like to know how the prominent characters of this book were doing further.

SunLi's son and his maternal grandparents come to ShenZhen and move into the new apartment. There they live together with the young parents. At a little more than one and a half years, HaoKang is almost dry. He understands everything you tell him, even complicated matters (he even understands LaoWei's hesitant Chinese), but doesn't yet speak more than a few words.

Wang LanBo's son lives with his grandmother while his parents are separated from him and work in ShenZhen.

"Mayor" Song begins to renovate one of his houses. His "spring chickens" take over the sale of the apartments. First, however, the current rental income is lacking (all tenants having been terminated), money from the sale of condominiums cannot be expected until the end of the conversion work. The financing of the extensive and therefore expensive remodelling can be managed without banks. He has about half of the necessary money on his own accounts, the other half "lets" his son, the head physician of the central hospital. He doesn't want to get it repaid.

One of the pretty grand-daughters is pregnant, LaoLao will soon be great-grandmother.

The friends of programmer Wang who emigrated to Australia are unhappy. They can't cope with the Australian way of life. The woman is regretting particularly that she is now for the first time in her partnership financially dependent from her husband, and as a housewife she does not feel challenged enough and also has difficulty with learning English. She would like to go back with her daughter to China, but her husband is hesitating.

Finally, many months after the World Cup in football, there is again a major sporting event: the Asian Games. They have been held in GuangZhou. Again the Chinese are offering an opening show which is stunning, imaginative and exciting. My football friends comment, 'After this show no country in Asia will like to host the next Asian Games again, for how do they want to surpass that?' CCTV 5 is broadcasting as usual 24 hours a day, the other stations as well are occupied with sports. An interview with, if I understood correctly, a deaf athlete from Macao struck me: she seems to be reading from lip, writes with 10 fingers at a prodigious rate her answers on a keyboard, the text appears on a display in the studio; the discussion is of course slower than usual, she sometimes deletes a half or a whole sentence, starts again, but they take all the time which is necessary for this interview.

On a business trip to GuangZhou during the Asian Games, we wind up with a police control. Our driver was for almost eight hours "arrested", because he had quite large knifes in his car, in case that he must defend himself in dark streets. He finally gets off it with a fine.

Also in this year, in 2011, there will be no boredom for a few weeks: the Universiade will be held in ShenZhen, across the city the countdown is running. At the weekends I am riding four times along the construction site of the central stadium, the complex is on the way to my pitches. Then China has really been allowed to host many international major sporting events. Only that within in the foreseeable future there will be no football World Cup in China.

HaoKang and many other small children, but much more so the larger ones, can observe on TV how "Chang'e 2", China's recent lunar probe, is launched to the moon.

For HaoKang, the rocket doesn't fly to the Man in the Moon, as my grandson would call it, but to the Woman in the Moon. Chang'e is the goddess of the moon who according to Chinese myth soared to the moon as against professional advice she took an overdose of a medication that would make her immortal. Other Chinese (and old Aztec) positions perceive on the moon not a woman (Chang'e), but a rabbit or a hare.

The launch is effected on National Day, 1 October 2010, the 61st Anniversary of the founding of the Peoples' Republic of China. For the first time a probe was successfully launched straight to the moon, without acquiring an extra boost from a few previous orbits around the Earth. The probe was guided into an orbit around the moon, taking it down to 15 km above the lunar surface, so as to transmit high-resolution images to Earth. No doubt, China is capable of highest technological achievements, and certainly as well to provide decent safety pins that would not twist. See considerations of safety pins and other quality issues in a section of the next chapter.

Conflicting findings in books on China

Of course I've read books about China, like probably everyone else did who plans to work or frequently to travel to China on business. Only in the course of time I noticed that some statements in some books do not coincide with my observations. These are usually not very significant things, but sometimes they are characterising views of others, and it's at least entertaining to see what other authors have observed, and perhaps find out why they perceived that differently. Here I will mention a few such examples:

Soup, rice

To the surprise of the respective author, there was in China no rice available in the restaurants and the soup was served at the end of the meal rather than at the beginning, like we Germans are used to.

I cannot confirm either. There is rice available in any restaurant, but you have to ask each time. In most cases, the rice is eaten at the end of the meal, because you do not want to fill the stomach before all the real delicacies, but take only so much rice as you like to top with, at the end. However, this is handled very individually: Many Chinese people eat rice as an aside like Germans would eat potatoes, and some take much rice, others little or none. And of course, many (but not all) restaurants also have rice dishes on the menu ("fried rice with seafood," for example).

The "soup observation" that I read repeatedly, is interesting by itself and reveals that these writers were living in North China (BeiJing): There, soup will be eaten after the meal, 'because you wouldn't want to pump up your stomach with liquid stuff before you begin with proper eating'. In South China, soup will be eaten as a first serve (if you order it, that's not compulsory).

Chinese characters

'To avoid confusion, Chinese people often communicate by writing the characters in their hands.'

Not for once I have observed that. I think this is simply a statement that the authors have copied from some previous writer on China. In *Japan*, this is not unusual, but in China definitely it's not the case. I have asked many Chinese people, whether they are doing this or have done so before, the universal answer was denial and surprise.

What Chinese people are doing, especially on the phone, is to specify a mentioned syllable (say, "wu") with a common compound word in which this syllable is also found, especially when passing on a personal name or a street name. For this we have to keep two things in mind: first, that when writing "wu" in phonetic spelling, this syllable may occur in any of four different pitches (wū constant, wú rising, wǔ lowering and rising again, wù lowering), but even within each of these categories there are many syllables which are pronounced the same way; altogether there are at least 190 characters which are pronounced "wu", about evenly spread between the four pitches. Second, that contrary to widely held beliefs, Chinese words or phrases are often composed of two syllables, i. e. two characters. This establishes the formation of words.

The context thus tells a Chinese which "wu" is referred to, as the syllable will occur most often in a compound with other syllables, thus forming the actual words and terms. A crude approximation in the English language may perhaps illustrate my intention: the term "television" is composed of Greek *tele*, "remote, far", and Latin *visio*, "I see". Thus, when taken literally, these words will suggest "I see afar", but the compound word refers to something entirely different, namely the viewing of programmes in an electrical device that is also called a TV-set. Many Chinese terms are composed the same way, in case of TV: 电视, dìan shì, "elektrisch sehen".

Thus, if specifying a street or company name on the phone that does contain the syllable "wu", there is no immediate context. However, the speaker might say, 'dòng wù de wù' = 'This "wu" in the word for "animal"' (dong wu = "animate object"), using a common word where this syllable occurs; which is similar to our habit of spelling a name and adding, 'No, it's not "k", it's "c", as in "Charlie".'

Books

'Books are read from back to front and from top to bottom.'

That had been so once and is still the case in Japan, but no longer in China. All new books are "normally" printed, and people do no longer write as before from top to bottom, but just like us from left to right.

Craftsmen

'Chinese do everything only half fit, never perfect, Chinese craftsmen always think that somehow it will just about fit.'

I thought French, Italian and Spanish craftsmen were described like that. Or maybe someone was complaining about a number of German craftsmen, as we can find that in Germany too, and quite often so. My observation is this: According to the craftsman, depending on the character and on the way of dealing with the service provider, you will get either a perfect, fast and very cheap labour, or you won't. It is just as in Germany. If you hire any craftsman, perhaps the cheapest one or one who has no references, or if you treat the craftsman in a patronising manner, you may be served German-style – from the Service Wasteland, as the Germans say – bad, condescending and arrogant.

To me it has not happened yet in China.

China, the Shangri-La of Servicing/rude servicing

'China is a Shangri-La of Servicing.' But, 'Why is the servicing so rude?'

Both statements are right. In the first place, China is a veritable Shangri-La of Servicing. The stores are always open. In most cities and in many districts there are small shops that are either open till midnight or even continuously for 24 hours (analogous to the British convenience stores).

In restaurants and shops not only I have noticed, and many Chinese have confirmed that impression, that there is a stark difference between northern and southern China, with ShangHai belonging rather with North China, although is geographically a part of southern China, to be precise, of (South-)East China.

In southern China, except for individual cases, the waiters – as well as the craftsmen – are usually very friendly, helpful, accommodating, come back later and ask if everything is OK or whether you want another beer. They want to sell, and they know: They can do that best if the guest is satisfied, will order sufficiently today and in the future will come back again.

In northern China, apart again from more or less numerous exceptions, you will be served more gruff and unfriendly or even not at all, this trend expanding to ShangHai, and being most prominent in BeiJing where indeed most of the authors of books on China have lived, often in foreigner's districts. Chinese say that in BeiJing you have to file for being served, and such an application may be rejected or approved. In BeiJing you will be surprised when the service comes along voluntarily, sometimes you need patience in frequently and intensively waving or calling. Germans are familiar with this attitude (I use to claim that waiters get basic training sessions in how to avoid eye contact with guests; such courses are available for prospective waiters in BeiJing too, I guess).

Diligence

'The Chinese are busy as bees.'

This is a common and most of the time certainly not false statement. But you should not believe that this is the case everywhere, and would apply to all Chinese. Especially in large companies, especially in companies of western background (i. e. branches of U.S. or European companies) you can certainly find a lot of very lazy staff, and I've seen this quite often.

(Southern) Chinese claim that Southern Chinese are the most industrious, especially in GuangDong (Canton), the further you get to the north, the more sedate (to avoid saying "lazy") were the Chinese people.

I had to fire some staff, too (or had to wave clear messages that preferably they sought another job and quitted on their own) who thought that in a German company, you might even in China work comfortably or sometimes for many days not at all.

And if the managers – often, alas, Western

managers – indicate by their own behaviour that you can get away with a more relaxed posture yet climb up the career and salary scale while working till 17 o'clock meant an unbearable demand when beginning "already" at 9:30 – then many Chinese will also take this stance.

In this context I would like to repeat that there are Chinese companies that employ neither "overseas Chinese" (i. e. those who have several years studied or worked abroad), nor those who have worked in Chinese branch plants or subsidiaries of Western companies, 'for we cannot teach them any more how to work because they are spoiled.'

(Un)timeliness

'Chinese are never on time.'

Yes and no, this is again a generalising statement of the same kind as to claim that Germans were always on time. Indeed it is not the case. If you would like to describe the degree of the (average) timeliness in a ranking, you might do as follows, as perceived from my viewing point: Japanese > Swiss > Germans > English > Americans > Chinese > French > ...> Italians > Spaniards.

My football playing friends are largely on time, the games start on time. My business partners are all usually very punctual, of course there are delays, when a meeting before for some reason takes longer.

Trains are about as (un)punctual as in Germany, the timeliness of the Japanese train system being unmatched. Flights are about as unpunctual as in the U.S., but the European air transport also tries to achieve this standard. In 2010, both airports of ShangHai have been world-record holders of unpunctuality, probably due to the world exhibition.

Chinese tally marks

Europeans and Northern Americans use tally marks arranged in blocks of five, for example, if a lorry is unloaded and you want to know how many bags of flour have arrived. 卌

'The Chinese use for that the character 五, "wu" = five'

I don't doubt that this little item has been observed by the respective author correctly with someone. But the letter 五 for "five" has only 4 strokes and is written as follows: 一 丅 兀 五 (characters not only have a clearly defined number of strokes, but also the order of strokes follows clear rules). There may still be Chinese who are counting flour or tea bags by such blocks of five. My research showed, however, that actually the character "zheng" (正, meaning "correct, proper") is used for such purposes, and you write it like this: 一 丅 下 止 正..

Driving schools

'In China, practical driving lessons are held only on separate places, not in the real urban traffic.'

That may be the case in BeiJing, perhaps as well in ShangHai, but it is not so in ShenZhen. Although the first lessons are given on side streets or large parking lots, and the reverse parking is practised there as well, in ShenZhen the driving school cars take part in normal traffic, this being reason for impatient overtaking and honking.

Jogging, walking, fitness

'Chinese people do not believe in running for reasons of physical exercise, to walk and to subscribe to fitness, they want to relax in peaceful walking. Chinese people do not want to access some destinations much exhausted, they prefer to stroll.'

I do not doubt that there is this sort of Chinese people, and for lack of knowledge of representative studies I cannot argue whether the above statement is at least depicting the rule that allows exceptions. Perhaps the rule is again mostly applicable to BeiJing and ShangHai, but in no case may the sentence be absolutely true, at least not in ShenZhen.

If I jog, I meet mostly Chinese people (the proportion of jogging foreigners is much higher than that of foreigners among the population, perhaps at 5 % where I live, whereas far less than 0.5 % of the residents are foreigners), not only joggers, but also fast walkers of all ages (I'm far from being the oldest).

Most obvious this is on the Big Southern Mountain, "da Nan Shan", in the sub-district of SheKou where I live. The hilltop can be accessed from two sides, it seems to be around 350 m high and in parts quite steep. The climb is achieved on a path that consists entirely of stairs. When I didn't play football on Saturdays yet but (in addition to Sundays) on Wednesdays, I often assailed this slope in Saturday mornings or, if I enjoyed one of my all too rare days "off", during the week as well. Now I am doing it only about once a year.

No matter when I'm there, no matter how hot it is – there are hundreds of people on the go. No matter how early I start to climb – I will always meet other "mountain climbers". They go alone, in groups or families; often Grandma and Grandpa come along and remain behind with the grandchildren half-way or quarter-way to the top, while the young parents go on till the "summit". Foreigners are represented at less than 0.5 %.

Many take a normal speed, some and not too few walk at maximum pace and run down again at a trot; quite a lot wear a jogger's dress. I guess that at the weekend, tens of thousands have been on the hill, I know from conversations with fellow "climbers" that they meet regularly at least once a week, including rainy days, to assail this rise, and even the slowest walker has no opportunity for contemplation here, but stamina is required (and strengthened).

Until his physician advised him against, because of knee problems, our driver Fang ShiFu was climbing for exercise almost every day on the hill, and during the course of three years he has thus lost 15 kg in weight, which he is very proud of.

City life: anonymity

'In China, you can observe an increasing anonymity in cities and pervasive individualization of life.'

It may be, but I cannot judge, that this is again true for BeiJing. One reason could be that many residential areas in BeiJing are residential only, so that restaurants and shops cannot be accessed walking. For ShenZhen with its many "villages", this claim is in my opinion not true. Not only that life on the streets is anything but anonymous, but also people know each other: I know more people in ShenZhen, and more people know me, as at my primary residence in Germany.

Even in the settlements ("gardens"), at least in those I know, and I do know several of them, no one needs to remain anonymous. Those who want to meet people from the neighbourhood visit the small parks in the settlements, sit on a bench or walk around and address other people. Of course, children and dogs are the best tools for making contacts, both I do not have either in China, dogs I don't have even in Germany, and my children have already grown up, so that I use football (at the weekend) and the laptop (in the restaurant), but also my bike provides for making contact, such as to craftsman Wang.

Those who do not want to do that, may visit many dance events on Saturday and Sunday evenings, outside on the squares and in the parks, or the gymnastics club, tennis squares, pools or anywhere else where hundreds of people may gather and the whole village meet. The residential areas in ShenZhen do not favour any case of possible anonymity, and when considering those many groups of people who meet and do something together, I do not believe it. At least not in ShenZhen.

Barber shops

'Hairdressers are open until well after midnight, but why are only men their clients? Caution – there will be offered different services.'

In other words, in BeiJing the barber shops seem to be brothels. I cannot confirm that nor deny from ShenZhen, not having visited by far all the hairdressers in the city. I know of no brothels, only of three or four hairdressing shops.

They are, however, not to be qualified as craft, but as decorative art. Everything is arts: the washing, the cutting. First of all, the local hairdresser turned out to be "three-class society": With regard to hairdressers, the classless society of communism is obviously not what they subscribe to. Class A (the lowest) is for reception, sweeping and the cash – no artistic activity, there may be women/girls or men/boys; class B assumes a part of artistic craft with hair washing and scalp massage, by girls or boys; class C covers the real artists, the hairdressers – only (preferably young) men.

We begin with washing: you will lie down, your head rests on a cushion, and underneath is the water basin. If you have weathered several nights working half of the time, you must be prepared to falling asleep. The washing is not restricted to wetting, shampoo on, rinse, done – not at all! After applying the shampoo it will be rubbed in with rhythmic head massage and rinsed after endlessly relaxing minutes. Then again a serve of shampoo with the same intensity, according to the performer's progress in training, with some artistic quality.

Those who think that this had been the head massage of which they heard before, will have to think again: Now we get into the real stuff, including shoulders, arms, and hands.

Next you are asked whether you would like to have your ears cleaned – go for it! It is done with extreme caution (not too deep!) and care.

Follow me to the artist. The real hairdresser is using comb and scissors like other artists would their brushes, chisels or carving knifes. The artist is ready to listen to customer's suggestions, as long as the customer does not interfere with his artistic licence. The haircut is almost never completed. Before the blow-drying here and here and everywhere another tiny hair still has to go, a slight unevenness ought to be corrected, here something is protruding. Even more so after the blow-drying, how many faults will still show up then!

After that, you are washed again, not quite as thorough as before, for there is only half a grasp of hair left, and then blow-dried again. And again, here and there and everywhere tiny faults are discovered that must be addressed urgently.

Only then can you go and pay, according to which shop you are in, three to five Euros per hour and a half for the arts ...

'Safety pins that bend, and the pedals of my bike dropped off'

A local newspaper of the German district in which I live published an article about a couple in a neighbouring town who had returned to Germany after spending several years as lecturers in China. The article mentioned an occasion at which the couple wanted to report in public about their experience. Among other things, it was stated:

> Experts agree that the Middle Kingdom's economic growth will make it rise to a major power. Already, the struggle for resources has become harder. "We can compete only by quality on the global market," said Horst Santjer. Here, Germany is still ahead. "I have bought safety pins that bend even when piercing the fabric," says Martha Santjer. On his bike the seat post bent and pedals dropped off, her husband added: "This way the craftsmen get their work, due to the frequent repairs."

The full German-language article can be found here:
 http://www.shz.de/nachrichten/lokales/stormarner-tageblatt/artikeldetails/article//der-lange-weg-zur-demokratie.html

I replied to the article with a Letter to the Editor, which was unfortunately not published, not even in excerpts. I will get to that here:

> Letter to the Editor, concerning "The long road to democracy" (23 September 2010), Stormarner Tageblatt
> Ladies and Gentlemen,
>
> having lived and worked for over five years in China (and going on), I read your article with interest. Unfortunately I cannot participate in the forthcoming lecture, as I will be that time in China. I would have liked to participate in discussions there, because I think that at least what was discussed in the article is not quite fair to China and the Chinese people.
>
> Every day I meet rather normal and average Chinese, having found many friends there (mostly in sports) and got acquaintances. Within those more than 5 years I have learnt a lot about life in China and thus especially have become more cautious in my judgements.
>
> Surely we can have an engaged discussion about how and to what extent the common practice in China is not what we call freedom and democracy in Germany. But are we really in the position to make proposals which are adequate to their situation, on how the Chinese should organise and govern their country and their society better?
>
> Information and debate is available in China in a much wider scale and more freely than pretended by Western media. The official newspapers and news are only a (surprisingly small) section of the Chinese media reality. In addition, in blogs and all sorts of news and social networking web sites (KaiXin, virtually the Facebook of China) there are free, open and critical discussions kept in a manner which we do not know about here (in Germany).
>
> It is certainly true that the "big politics" are receiving less criticism (for Chinese are consistently too loyal to their country to do so, and the "big politics" are of much less interest to the Chinese as they are to us). Yes, there are many plans for

road and building construction executed without asking any of the citizens – but is that different from Germany? I know plenty of examples for how citizens' initiatives forced major road constructions to be diverted, in one case such that a mangrove forest in ShenZhen (southern China) could be preserved and turned into a National Park. Originally, the highway was intended to be led straight along the coast, which would have meant doomsday for the mangroves.

Matters such as illuminated by the examples of the safety pin and the bent seat post I interpret rather differently. It is simply and effectively not the rule that poor quality was produced. You can buy goods of poor quality, no doubt, but that we can also do in Germany if we are reluctant to pay a fair price. If you want to spend in China only the equivalent of 10 € for a bicycle, you cannot expect any quality. I have been driving for 5 years now a very high quality bicycle which never has bent anywhere, taking it to ride altogether at least 60 km per weekend (to the sports pitch and back), and I paid only 150 € for it.

A country which is already featuring a railway network of over 7,000 km of high speed trains (average speed being more than 200 km/h, not: top speed, the fastest trains achieve currently up to 380 km/h), within two years they will have 13,000 km, i. e. more than the entire rest of the world added up – such a country has no problems in making strong enough safety pins and seat posts. You have to buy only the right quality.

All too often, and also in your article, I observe that Germans put towards China a kind of pitying smile, meaning that 'they are not yet as advanced as we are' (and do relieve themselves still in the middle of the road). We are deceiving ourselves! China and the Chinese are much farther and faster and more flexible and more modern than we would have liked them to be.

Too bad that I cannot attend the discussion meeting.

Sincerely, Dr. Bernhard Wessling

A few months after this local media event, a far more important message was released by the international media: China now has the most powerful supercomputer in the world ("TianHe-1A", 天河, Milky Way 1A); moreover, among the list of the 500 largest supercomputers in the world, China is represented 41 times, twice among the top 10, with TianHe being first; the United States got 275 computers on the list, France, Japan and Germany each rank with 26, Russia with 11. This achievement is particularly remarkable since until the early 90s of the last century China had to import any computers, and all major computers could be used only with foreign assistance.

Just weeks later, China announced a new world record: the train, mark CHR380A, that will soon connect BeiJing with ShangHai, has achieved the speed of 486.1 km/h, holding thus the world record for not specifically modified high-speed trains. The previous record was held by a train of the same design, serving the rail ShangHai - HangZhou (which I have taken several times already): 416.6 km/h.

I really have no doubt that you can buy in China proper safety pins (although I have not checked), and that you can get high-quality bikes, I know from personal experience.

'Privacy'

'There is no privacy in China, there is not even a word for it.'

Yes, there is some truth to it, if you look at my experiences in hospitals, for example. Another mark of this is the open curiosity of distant acquaintances, such as an operator in the store who may ask you, 'When will your baby arrive?'

But no, there is a word for something like "privacy" – 隐私, "yin si", personal secrets. I cannot confirm whether it really means something similar to our definition of the term. I can confirm however that the Chinese do desire to protect and define their privacy. For sure there is a trend among the modern educated young residents of ShenZhen to protect their privacy at least in parts. It is difficult to assess for myself whether this is a new phenomenon or something completely normal which always has been.

My football-playing friend, Wang LanBo, was considerable hesitant on the day (more precisely: evening) I suggested to him in the middle of the week to bring along this evening some of the photos I had taken during the football game at the weekend. I felt after a while on the phone (he did not say it directly) that he would feel uncomfortable if I would visit him at his home. As I said then that I was going to eat anyway in this or that restaurant and that he might come there after work if it was easier for him than receiving me at home, then it was all right, he agreed immediately. A little later, we met at the restaurant.

Friends

'In China, you are quickly called "peng you" (朋友, friend), but that has no meaning.'

Well, that's the same thing in the U.S., for example. Our German word "freund" may have a similar connotation in France ("ami"), for a "friend" means for us someone to whom we feel closer connected than to "acquaintances". In the U.S. you can quickly be the "friend" of someone who will not even remember you a few weeks later, neither calling nor answering your emails.

This is no different in China where superficial acquaintances are concerned. Here, "peng you" is used in a similar generous manner as in the U.S., "friend". But the closer you get to know people, the more such a superficial acquaintance will turn into a genuine friendship. This takes time, recall 日久见人心 – rì jiǔ jiàn xīn, with time (only) you get to know a man's heart.

Ultimately, "peng you" may become "xiong di" (兄弟) – brothers. If you are told, 'You are my brother,' then you know: You have gained a real friend.

Foreigners in China: seven different stereotypes

Mark Turner, an editor for "echinacities.com", begins his article like this: 'Everyone knows that stereotyping is a dangerous game to play and that it can hurt feelings and stir heated debates. Having said that, stereotyping is sometimes great fun, especially if it's only intended as a light-hearted joke.' He then describes seven types of foreigners you will find in China (his text provoked Homeric laughter for me, the following is only a summary):

- The "hu tong" Sinophiles (hu tong are districts mainly in BeiJing, consisting of small narrow streets with a long-time established neighbourhood), these sinophilic (i. e.: China-loving) foreigners work part time as a journalist or in creative work and consider

BeiJing to be the true China (rather than ShangHai)
- The international school teacher is the cream of the crop in China's education system, working in China because at a comparable salary he is faring significantly better than at home, dwelling in an 'expat enclave';
- The expat packager; reason for being in China: 'I don't know; my company sent me here.' He has developed a love/hate relationship with China and lives in an expat enclave characterized by vast complexes of western style villas;
- The aspiring screen writer, he enters into a temporary contract at a school and has the rest of the day for creative activities;
- The journeyman professional specialist English teacher (who had practised in his home country a different career, such as an engineer) is highly respected as a teacher and can be found wherever there are teaching jobs for 250 RMB per hour;
- The international language students are flocking to live in five bedroom apartments and have problems in the morning to appear in time for the class because they have to drink cheap beer till four o'clock in the night;
- The ageing world traveller who wanted to travel for a while in China, then stayed a bit longer still and then a little longer still, when asked why they are in China he replies: 'I don't know man, I just kind of found myself here.... Awesome eh?'

The full article can be found at http://www.echinacities.com/expat-corner/expat-stereotyping-7-different-types-of-foreigners-in.html